SIMON PETER
in Scripture and Memory

SIMON PETER
in Scripture and Memory

The New Testament Apostle
in the Early Church

Markus Bockmuehl

Baker Academic
a division of Baker Publishing Group
Grand Rapids, Michigan

© 2012 by Markus Bockmuehl

Published by Baker Academic
a division of Baker Publishing Group
P.O. Box 6287, Grand Rapids, MI 49516–6287
www.bakeracademic.com

Printed in the United States of America

Library of Congress Cataloging-in-Publication Data
Bockmuehl, Markus N. A.
    Simon Peter in Scripture and memory : the New Testament apostle in the early church / Markus Bockmuehl.
        p.   cm.
    Includes bibliographical references and index.
    ISBN 978-0-8010-4864-7 (pbk.)
    1. Peter, the Apostle, Saint. 2. Apostles—Biography. I. Title.
BS2515.B635 2012
225.9′2—dc23   2012024098

Unless otherwise indicated, Scripture quotations are from the New Revised Standard Version of the Bible, Anglicized Edition (with occasional alternatives based on the author's preferred translation), copyright © 1989 by the Division of Christian Education of the National Council of the Churches of Christ in the United States of America. Used by permission. All rights reserved.

Scripture quotations labeled ESV are from The Holy Bible, English Standard Version® (ESV®), Anglicized Edition, copyright © 2001 by Crossway, a publishing ministry of Good News Publishers.

Scripture quotations labeled NIV are from the Holy Bible, New International Version®, NIV®, Anglicized Edition. Copyright © 1973, 1978, 1984 by Biblica, Inc. All rights reserved worldwide.

Unless otherwise indicated, all quotations from Eusebius's *Ecclesiastical History* are adapted from the Loeb Classical Library edition (trans. K. Lake and J. E. L. Oulton).

The internet addresses in this book are accurate at the time of publication. They are provided as a resource. Baker Publishing Group does not endorse them or vouch for their content or permanence.

In keeping with biblical principles of creation stewardship, Baker Publishing Group advocates the responsible use of our natural resources. As a member of the Green Press Initiative, our company uses recycled paper when possible. The text paper of this book is composed in part of post-consumer waste.

12   13   14   15   16   17   18   7   6   5   4   3   2   1

green
press
INITIATIVE

Contents

Abbreviations

GENERAL

//	parallel	LXX	Septuagint, Greek translation of the Old Testament
ca.	*circa*, around	MS(S)	manuscript(s)
cf.	*confer*, compare	NB	*nota bene*, note carefully
chap(s).	chapter(s)	NT	New Testament
Ep.	*Epistles* (various authors)	OT	Old Testament
esp.	especially	pars.	Synoptic parallels
ET	English Translation	Q	Gospels sayings source
frag.	fragment	v(v).	verse(s)
Hist.	*Histories* (various authors)	*v.l.*	*varia lectio*, variant reading
lit.	literally		

OLD TESTAMENT

Gen.	Genesis	1–2 Sam.	1–2 Samuel
Exod.	Exodus	1–2 Kings	1–2 Kings
Lev.	Leviticus	1–2 Chron.	1–2 Chronicles
Num.	Numbers	Ezra	Ezra
Deut.	Deuteronomy	Neh.	Nehemiah
Josh.	Joshua	Esth.	Esther
Judg.	Judges	Job	Job
Ruth	Ruth	Ps(s).	Psalm(s)

Prov.	Proverbs	Amos	Amos
Eccles.	Ecclesiastes	Obad.	Obadiah
Song	Song of Songs	Jon.	Jonah
Isa.	Isaiah	Mic.	Micah
Jer.	Jeremiah	Nah.	Nahum
Lam.	Lamentations	Hab.	Habakkuk
Ezek.	Ezekiel	Zeph.	Zephaniah
Dan.	Daniel	Hag.	Haggai
Hosea	Hosea	Zech.	Zechariah
Joel	Joel	Mal.	Malachi

New Testament

Matt.	Matthew	1–2 Thess.	1–2 Thessalonians
Mark	Mark	1–2 Tim.	1–2 Timothy
Luke	Luke	Titus	Titus
John	John	Philem.	Philemon
Acts	Acts	Heb.	Hebrews
Rom.	Romans	James	James
1–2 Cor.	1–2 Corinthians	1–2 Pet.	1–2 Peter
Gal.	Galatians	1–3 John	1–3 John
Eph.	Ephesians	Jude	Jude
Phil.	Philippians	Rev.	Revelation
Col.	Colossians		

Old Testament Apocrypha

1–4 Macc.	1–4 Maccabees	Sir.	Sirach

Old Testament Pseudepigrapha

Ascen. Isa.	Ascension of Isaiah	Par. Jer.	Paraleipomena Jeremiou
2–4 Bar.	2–4 Baruch	T. Levi	Testament of Levi
1–3 En.	1–3 Enoch	T. Sol.	Testament of Solomon
Odes Sol.	Odes of Solomon	T. Zeb.	Testament of Zebulun

Qumran/Dead Sea Scrolls

CD	*Damascus Document*	4QOrd[a]	*Court of the Twelve*
1QH	*Thanksgiving Hymn*	11QtgJob	*Targum of Job*
1QM	*War Scroll*		
1QSa	*Rule of the Congregation (Appendix a to 1QS)*		

Rabbinic Literature

b.	Babylonian Talmud	*Qidd.*	*Qiddušin*
Ber.	*Berakot*	*Šabb.*	*Šabbat*
Giṭ.	*Giṭṭin*	*y.*	Jerusalem/Palestinian Talmud
Pesiq. Rab Kah.	Pesiqta de Rab Kahana	*Yebam.*	*Yebamot*

Apostolic Fathers

1 Clem.	*1 Clement*	Ign. *Rom.*	Ignatius, *To the Romans*
Did.	*Didache*	Ign. *Smyrn.*	Ignatius, *To the Smyrnaeans*
Herm. Vis.	*Shepherd of Hermas, Vision(s)*	Ign. *Tars.*	Ignatius, *To the Tarsians*
Ign. *Eph.*	Ignatius, *To the Ephesians*	Ign. *Trall.*	Ignatius, *To the Trallians*
Ign. *Magn.*	Ignatius, *To the Magnesians*	*Mart. Pol.*	*Martyrdom of Polycarp*
Ign. *Phld.*	Ignatius, *To the Philadelphians*	Pol. *Phil.*	Polycarp, *To the Philippians*
Ign. *Pol.*	Ignatius, *To Polycarp*		

New Testament Apocrypha

Apoc. Pet.	*Apocalypse of Peter*	*Ps.-Clem. Hom.*	*Pseudo-Clementine Homilies*
Apos. Con.	*Apostolic Constitutions*	*Ps.-Clem. Rec.*	*Pseudo-Clementine Recognitions*
Gos. Thom.	*Gospel of Thomas*		
Ps.-Clem. EP	*Pseudo-Clementine Epistula Petri*		

Greek and Latin Authors

Ambrose of Milan

Exp. Luc.   *Expositio evangelii*
                 secundum Lucam

Augustine

Conf.   *Confessions*

Grat. Chr.   *De gratia Christi et de*
                 peccato originali

Clement of Alexandria

Strom.   *Stromateis*

Cyprian

Unit. eccl.   *De catholicae ecclesiae*
                 unitate

Cyril of Jerusalem

Procat.   *Procatechesis*

Epiphanius

Pan.   *Panarion*

Eusebius

Eccl. Hist.   *Ecclesiastical History*

Gregory of Nazianzus

Or.   *Orations*

Hippolytus

Haer.   *Refutatio omnium*
                 haeresium

Horace

Sat.   *Satires*

Irenaeus

Haer.   *Adversus haereses*

Jerome

Pelag.   *Against the Pelagians*

Vir. ill.   *De viris illustribus*

John Chrysostom

Hom. Act.   *Homiliae in Acta*
                 apostolorum

Hom. Jo.   *Homiliae in Joannem*

Hom. Matt.   *Homiliae in Matthaeum*

John Malalas

Chron.   *Chronographia*

Josephus

Ant.   *Jewish Antiquities*

J.W.   *Jewish War*

Justin Martyr

1 Apol.   *First Apology*

2 Apol.   *Second Apology*

Dial.   *Dialogue with Trypho*

Origen

Cels.   *Contra Celsum*

Comm. Jo.   *Commentary on John*

Comm.   *Commentary on*
  Matt.   *Matthew*

Hom. Num.   *Homilies on Numbers*

Pausanias

Descr.   *Description of Greece*

Pliny the Elder

Nat. Hist.   *Natural History*

Ptolemy

Geogr.   *Geography*

Sozomen

Hist. eccl.   *Historia ecclesiastica*

Tacitus

Ann.   *Annales*

Tertullian

Marc.   *Adversus Marcionem*

Praescr.   *De praescriptione haereticorum*

Pud.   *De pudicitia*

Scorp.   *Scorpiace*

Theophilus of Antioch

Autol.   *Ad Autolycum*

MODERN EDITIONS AND TRANSLATIONS

ANF   *The Ante-Nicene Fathers*. Edited by Alexander Roberts and James Donaldson. 10 vols. New York, 1885–96

FGH   *Die Fragmente der griechischen Historiker*. Edited by F. Jacoby. Leiden, 1954–64

NPNF   *The Nicene and Post-Nicene Fathers*. Edited by P. Schaff and H. Wace. 2nd series. 28 vols. New York, 1886–1900

PG   Patrologiae cursus completus: Series graeca. Edited by J.-P. Migne. 162 vols. Paris, 1857–86

Introduction

Who was Saint Peter? For several centuries the neglected stepchild of critical (overwhelmingly Protestant) biblical scholarship, Simon Peter has for the last two decades enjoyed a remarkable literary renaissance. A growing number of studies by both Protestants and Catholics have pointed the way to a less polarized, more constructively engaged understanding of Peter's role in the first generation of the Jesus movement. In a sense, the impulse set by Oscar Cullmann over half a century ago has borne impressive fruit, even if after considerable delay.[1] At the time, it was highly controversial for a Protestant scholar to argue for the essential historicity of Matt. 16:17–19 and on that basis for Jesus's commissioning of Peter (though not any successors!) as a pivotal figure for early Christianity, as "the rock, the foundation for all churches of all times" (Cullmann 1953, 238). Now it is almost unremarkable to suggest that the new focus on Peter helps correct several centuries of neglect and distortion, as Martin Hengel notes that "the historical and theological importance of the fisherman from Bethsaida has been generally underestimated within both evangelical and Catholic exegetical circles" (Hengel 2010, ix).

The present book is the second of two that have arisen out of over a decade of work on the apostle Peter; the first one, *The Remembered Peter*, saw the light of day in 2010 (Bockmuehl 2010a).[2] But the project on which I thought I was embarking in 1999 was certainly very different from the one that I here bring to a conclusion. What I had conceived of originally as an integral, single work, perhaps

1. Cullmann 1952 (ET, Cullmann 1953); cf. the 2nd English edition, Cullmann 1962, most recently reissued as Cullmann 2011.
2. One or two responses to *The Remembered Peter* have helped to clarify certain points for the present volume, while reviewers impatient with a lack of overarching conclusions ("historical" and otherwise) in that more technical earlier volume may find a few more of those here. Despite some inevitable disagreements on matters of interpretative detail, I have been particularly grateful for the attentively probing and appreciative critique offered by John G. Cook (2011).

even a *magnum opus*, slowly became a volume of specialized studies that would need a follow-up, which is the present work. In this book, I draw extensively on the research of the first volume but synthesize it in less technical form, providing a narrative of exegetical engagement with the NT Peter and his reception in the second century. Some of what I originally set out to produce was overtaken in due course by the increasing interest in Simon Peter. A "new Cullmann" is certainly not as necessary today as it may still have seemed in the late 1990s.

It is my hope that the two volumes may prove complementary, with the present one serviceable especially to students at graduate or senior undergraduate levels, and perhaps to their teachers and pastors. Intended as an orientation for a wider audience than was the previous volume, this book will more often serve as a discussion starter on particular questions than as a definitive answer. Readers looking for more detail may wish to consult not only that earlier volume but also the companion website that I hope may prove useful for the study of both books.[3]

Much of what appears here has benefited significantly from student-level road testing in various academic and ecclesial settings. It would be impossible to mention all to whom I owe a debt of gratitude, but among these settings have been summer schools of the vacation term in biblical studies at St. Anne's College (Oxford, 2004) and Regent College (Vancouver, Canada, 2008), as well as a series of plenary lectures at the 2010 Australasian Christian Conference for the Academy and the Church in Brisbane. Others include the College of St. George at Windsor Castle; Westerly Road Church in Princeton, New Jersey; St. Andrew's Church in Histon; and St. Nicholas' Church in Cuddington. The needs and interests, vital pointers, and questions of these supportive audiences have contributed considerably to both the form and substance of the present work. In addition, I am most grateful for institutional support through a British Academy Research Readership, sabbatical terms granted by the Universities of Cambridge and Oxford, and two memorable periods of residence at Princeton's wonderfully hospitable Center of Theological Inquiry (2000 and 2005). In the final stages, the completion of this work was also aided by two small research grants from Keble College and Oxford University's John Fell Fund, which made possible the help of my doctoral students Benjamin Edsall and Nicholas Moore, to whom (along with my colleague David Lincicum) I am most grateful for vital editorial assistance and numerous suggestions for improvement.

Given the genesis of this book, I have sought to avoid foreign-language references in the text and to keep footnoted documentation economic rather than exhaustive. Fellow scholars seeking more technical discussion or fuller documentation may often find *The Remembered Peter* a useful initial point of reference.

Methodologically, I see the important but elusive NT figure of Peter as a kind of test case for both the potential promise and the limits of an approach that seeks to attend more carefully to the way Christianity's originating figures left a

---

3. http://simonpeter.bodleian.ox.ac.uk.

footprint in living memory. A few years ago, I attempted to analyze and assess the late modern crisis and potential futures of NT study, suggesting that, at a time of fragmenting conversations and evaporating confidence in previously mainstream biblical criticism, there could be genuine merit in seeking a renewed common conversation around themes of the texts' implied readers and readings, as well as on their early effective history (Bockmuehl 2006).

In the end, whether the proof extols the pudding is a question on which readers will judge for themselves. Attention to implied readings and footprints in memory may not yield enhanced confidence about historical-critical methods and their assured results, but it does, I believe, encourage an understanding that history's Simon Peter, like history's Jesus of Nazareth, is from the start always already embedded in communal memory and interpretation of one kind or another. This apostle, in other words, is always *somebody's* Peter, whether friend or opponent—rather than a neutrally or objectively recoverable figure. And from the earliest days, that somebody turns out to be, above all, the ecclesial community in all its remarkable diversity of practice, belief, and understanding.

A profile of Peter has often served as a symbolic linchpin for biblical scholarship, especially in the Protestant Academy of the last two centuries. The question of Peter's opposition to Paul, iconically conceived in some early Christian (as well as early historical-critical) reflection, was more directly addressed in my first volume on this topic (Bockmuehl 2010a, 94–113, cf. 61–70). Readers of either volume will note the extent to which the nineteenth-century German scholar F. C. Baur's critical legacy continues to loom large in many key debating points regarding the nature of early Christianity: conflict versus consensus, legalism versus the "law-free" gospel, Jewish Christian particularism (of a supposedly narrow and introspective type) versus Pauline progressive Christian universalism, Protestantism versus Catholicism as the true heir of the apostolic gospel, and so forth. "Paulinism," Baur once wrote, "made the principle of Christian universalism an integral element of the general Christian consciousness," thereby permanently securing for itself and for the church the progressivist "power to step forward again and again with all its original keenness and decision, whenever hierarchical Catholicism should again overgrow evangelical Christianity, and offend the original Christian consciousness in its most vital element" (Baur 1878, 1:113).[4]

The course I plot here does differ in important ways from that classical portrait of the Protestant Paul, however formative it was and perhaps remains in some quarters. Readers will, I trust, find here no ham-fisted attack on the ghost of Baur's radical hyper-Paulinism as it is supposedly found in contemporary biblical or philosophical scholarship. Nor will this be a piece of countervailing apologetic in the service of "conservative" agendas—whether biblicist, Roman Catholic, or any other sort. Instead, I wish to suggest that nineteenth-century polarities such as progress-through-conflict or structure-versus-freedom may give

---

4. I owe this reference to David Lincicum.

way to more nuanced accounts of unity and diversity in our understanding of the emergence of Christianity. Once one considers that point, the otherwise nebulous figure of Simon Peter assumes an unexpectedly vital role close to the epicenter of Christian origins. Precisely in its bewildering diversity, early Christian memory of Peter, in my view, underscores the strength of insight in James Dunn's intuition that "*Peter was probably in fact and effect the bridge-man* (pontifex maximus!) *who did more than any other to hold together the diversity of first-century Christianity*" (Dunn 2002, 577 [italics original]; 1977, 385–86). My reading of Peter similarly links Petrine *fact* and *effect*, though it additionally allows itself to entertain the thought that the latter sometimes offers useful historical guidance in understanding the former.

PART 1

Peter in Canon and Memory

1

Simon Peter . . .
in Living Memory?

I t is one of the inscrutable ironies of Christianity's humble beginnings that we
know so little about Jesus of Nazareth's leading disciple—the one identified
in the Gospel of Matthew as the "rock" on whom Jesus would build his
church, listed in later Christian tradition as Rome's first bishop, and one of its
two apostolic martyrs at the hands of Emperor Nero. But who was this man, and
what happened to him?

Any conventional quest for a "historical Peter" runs into the ground rather
swiftly. There are of course a variety of relevant early Christian sources, both from
the first century and from the second; a basic inventory is not in principle difficult
to compile.[1] Yet they remain remarkably vague or silent about many of the things
we would like to know about this apostle's origin, character, missionary career,
and death. Why would these sources show such a lack of interest in the fate of
such a prominent apostle? This can only leave the modern reader frustrated and
mystified. The historical Peter himself left virtually nothing in writing, and even
less of archaeological interest—whether in his native Galilee, in Jerusalem or
Caesarea, in Antioch or Corinth. Only Rome may be a partial exception, though
here too we soon find reasons aplenty to ask probing questions.

1. See http://simonpeter.bodleian.ox.ac.uk.

Among the numerous extant writings in his name, there are of course two short and remarkably different letters of uncertain date and origin in the NT. Beyond that, we have a bewildering range of apocryphal sources, styled as written by or about him, dating from the second through (at least) the sixth century.

The authenticity of these documents remains contested among scholars of diverse critical presuppositions. On perusing the scholarly secondary literature, it seems hard to dispel the impression that the vast majority of leading specialists on both sides of the Atlantic now regard neither of the NT's two Petrine letters as coming from Peter's own pen. As for the Gospel of Mark, almost universally accepted as the earliest of the canonical Gospels, it too is widely held to have no demonstrable or even plausible link with Simon Peter—despite persistent claims to the contrary in antiquity. For the past century, a steady stream of scholars have continued to deny the possibility that Peter himself had any historical link with Rome at all.[2]

Some consider Peter's relative obscurity in the early sources as an accurate reflection of a historical figure of only marginal importance for the formation of earliest Christianity. After all, the NT seems to suggest that the apostle Paul had far greater reach as a traveling missionary, let alone as the author of at least a number of authentically transmitted letters.

These are certainly significant and worthwhile cautions. Nevertheless, to underrate Peter's significance has the effect of rendering key historical quandaries about the origins of Christianity more or less unanswerable. Where were the continuities of either personality or ideological substance that allowed the Jesus movement to survive the death of its founder and early dispersal of its leadership from its heartland in Galilee and Jerusalem? Christianity, of course, did fragment and scatter, but without losing its asserted or perceived cohesion. A century after Pentecost, the widely scattered Christian communities were highly diverse in belief and practice, a fact that is also reflected in the increasing acceptance around this time of not one but four authoritative Gospel accounts. Given the history of radical disruption, opposition, and change, one may marvel that Christianity survived this long at all. But one of the features that most consistently characterizes and grounds that phenomenon is the recourse to Simon Peter, rather more than to Paul, as an anchor figure or key reference point for the literature and traditions of virtually all these diverse groups—including, for example, all four canonical and several noncanonical Gospels.

In this connection, as well, it is surely significant that Peter is, after Jesus, the most frequently mentioned individual both in the Gospels and in the NT as a whole.

2. Scholars in this category include Deschner 1986; Drews and Zindler 1997; Erbes 1901; Goulder 2004; Guignebert 1909; Heussi 1936 and 1955; Lapham 2003; Robinson 1945; Smaltz 1952; Zwierlein 2009. Contrast most recently Barnes (2010, 6–9, 40, and passim), who accepts Peter's execution in Rome by being burned alive rather than by crucifixion and thinks his body was probably not recovered. Paul was, in Barnes's view, executed in Spain. The state of the question is ably surveyed by Dassmann 2011.

As even Paul affirms, Peter is the first of the Twelve to witness the resurrection and a paradigmatic "pillar" apostle.[3] Peter appears in the Gospels without fail as the spokesman of the apostles and as the first named in every list of disciples. Acts makes him the first preacher of the gospel to both Jews and gentiles. This is the case even though his image clearly differs in subtle but significant ways between the Gospels: Mark sees and hears Jesus through Peter's eyes and ears; for Matthew, Peter is the messianic congregation's bedrock and gatekeeper; for Luke, the pioneering convert, evangelist, and strengthener of believers; for John, the spokesman and shepherd of Jesus's flock. Though at times brutally candid about Peter's flaws, the NT authors depict no other individual whose personal or ecclesiological stature approaches that of Simon Peter. If one takes the cumulative effect of these insights seriously, it seems difficult to avoid the conclusion that in key respects Peter's role evokes the apostolic leader *par excellence*.[4] Even where this profile is associated with positions of controversy or dispute, a good many of the great historical and theological puzzles of Christian origins remain unintelligible without an adequate understanding of Simon Peter in his relationships with both the Jewish and the gentile missions. Especially in Protestant NT scholarship, Peter has long been, as Martin Hengel liked to put it, quite simply the *underestimated* disciple.[5] For anyone seeking to understand why the church continued to develop and grow beyond the lifetime of its founder, it is worth noting the early Christian affirmation that Jesus entrusted his message and memory not to the whim of anonymous tradition but to named apostolic witnesses who went on to encourage his flock—and to take his gospel to the world. For almost all early Christian writers of whatever persuasion, the first and chief among these witnesses is Simon Peter.

Why History Is Always More Than Archaeology

But can we really say anything historically meaningful about Peter if we have no significant written sources extant from his lifetime? All we receive from the first century is a small handful of contested references in Paul's letters, the four Gospels,

---

3. Whether Peter is either historically or even biblically the first witness of the resurrection remains contested (contrast, e.g., Brock 2003 with Kessler 1998). For Matthew, the first witness is Mary Magdalene along with another Mary (Matt. 28:9); for Mark, it is uncertain (Peter and the disciples are implied in Mark 16:7, Mary Magdalene only in the longer ending at 16:9); for Luke, it is Cleopas and another disciple (Luke 24:13–35); for John, it is Mary Magdalene (John 20:14); for Paul, it is Peter (1 Cor. 15:5). For Paul's view of Peter as a paradigm, pillar, and foundation, see, e.g., 1 Cor. 9:5; Gal. 2:9; cf. Eph. 2:20.

4. Cf. similarly Hengel 2010, 28–36, who warns against prioritizing the diverse "images" of Peter in individual NT books over against the remarkable internal consistencies ranging from Matthew and Mark, 1 Corinthians and Galatians, to 1 Peter and second-century Petrine apocrypha.

5. So the English title of Hengel 2006 (ET, Hengel 2010).

a truncated account in Acts that ends on something of a whimper (12:17–18; 15:6–11, 14), and a couple of very different "Petrine" NT letters that strike many as inauthentic. If we limit our quest to history reconstructed from NT evidence alone, we will be rather like the bewildered prison guards of Acts 12:18, left to wonder "what became of Peter"—and unable to account for his unlikely escape from obscurity to prominence.

To think about how we might address this problem, consider for a moment what it is we are looking for when we study any person—especially a dead person. The Greek historian Herodotus famously attributes to the Athenian lawmaker Solon the view that one should call no man happy until he dies (*Hist.* 1.32). But while that appears in Herodotus as advice for a philosophy of the good life, there is also a sense in which it is true for historiography: the dead are the only people we can have any confidence of knowing in the round, better than through snapshots of a moving target. In the case of someone still alive, our knowledge is only ever partial, and unless we have a long personal history with them, we rarely get more than a freeze-frame. Did contemporaries ever know the "real" historical Caesar or Caligula, Cromwell or Churchill? But there is the rub of our problem: even if you could take a video camera back to the lifetime of a historical figure, you might discover additional facts, but it is far from clear that you would gain the measure of the real person.

For much of its history, modern biblical scholarship conceived of its work in largely archaeological terms, shoveling away the mounds of piety, dogma, and ritual to discover, concealed somewhere underneath, the "real thing," the pristine first-century facts. To get at the truth we need the earliest sources, and the earliest layers of the earliest sources; the later our material, the more corrupted it is. This was the classic conception of OT and NT study at the beginning of the twentieth century: the real Bible lies buried beneath the strata of centuries of tradition and interpretation, and it is historical criticism's task to recover it.[6] But for all the well-intentioned concern for dispassionate objectivity, it also began to dawn on thoughtful scholars during the last century that the more we keep deconstructing our sources, the taller our speculations become—and the more we are in danger of finding in them mainly ourselves and our view of the world. Most famously, this discovery was originally the upshot of the nineteenth century's so-called Quest of the Historical Jesus, which Albert Schweitzer found wanting because the Jesus it uncovered was nothing but a liberal Protestant drawn in its own image[7]—wholly moralizing rather than thoroughly and irretrievably eschatological (Schweitzer 2000).

More recently, scholars have shown a willingness to recognize that the so-called New and Third Quests for the historical Jesus have been in many ways equally

---

6. So, e.g., Briggs 1899, 531, discussed in Kugel 2007, 42–45; similarly Jowett 1861, on which see Bockmuehl 2009, 130–31.

7. Cf. the famous characterization of that quest as resembling Narcissus of Greek mythology, mesmerized by "a Liberal Protestant face, seen at the bottom of a deep well" (Tyrrell 1909, 44).

elusive, with an ever-broadening range of contradictory Jesuses. Paula Fredriksen (2000, xiii–xiv), among others, has commented on the bewildering fact that

> in recent scholarship, Jesus has been imagined and presented as a type of first-century shaman figure; as a Cynic-sort of wandering wise man; as a visionary radical and social reformer preaching egalitarian ethics to the destitute; as a Galilean regionalist alienated from the elitism of Judean religious conventions (like Temple and Torah); as a champion of national liberation and, on the contrary, as its opponent and critic— on and on. All these figures are presented with rigorous academic argument and methodology; all are defended with appeals to the ancient data. Debate continues at a roiling pitch, and consensus—even on issues so basic as what constitutes evidence and how to construe it—seems a distant hope.

Reactions to these insights about the elusiveness of early Christian history have been diffuse, perplexing, and contradictory. In response, some would merrily redouble their efforts to construe NT scholarship as "the task of removing from an original painting the work of later hands"—as one recently deceased, influential Oxford don liked to put it, apparently without a hint of irony or self-doubt.[8] To others, not unreasonably, this seems a desperate case of whistling in the dark. At the other end of the spectrum, some of a more postmodern inclination have advocated giving up any pretense that we can or should prioritize primary over secondary literature, of ancient sources over their past or present interpreters. Some would now say that historiography, and the historians *themselves*, can be the only proper subject of the study of history. In the end, we are told, history is nothing but texts about texts, and we should desist from misguided and dangerous delusions about "truth."

These are significant and sobering admonitions. The leading American scholar Dale Allison, for his part, has been prompted by what he calls "the enduring discord of the experts" to articulate the provocative suggestion that since history remains irretrievably outside our grasp, our irreconcilable reconstructions must inevitably exist in an uneasy coincidence of opposites with the affirmations of faith (Allison 2009, 8–14). Yet if this is so for Jesus, how much more must it be the case for far more tenuously attested figures like Simon Peter?

But in the experienced world of love and suffering, we do not have the luxury of disregarding questions of truth and justice, regardless of our political or religious posture. As the historians of twentieth-century totalitarianism have amply shown, the past cannot simply be reduced to a set of conflicting vested opinions about the past. Historians may of course offer diverse accounts, but they cannot collapse these into the past itself. All history that matters—of genocide, for instance, or of liberation from oppression—is necessarily perspectival, offering a point of view, a way of stringing together and only thus of beginning to

---

8. Cited with apparent approval in Anonymous 2009, an obituary of the don, J. C. Fenton, that includes the equally quaint advice that Fenton's 1963 Penguin paperback remains, half a century later, the best (non-specialist) introduction to Matthew.

make sense of the mass of brute facts. On the other hand, such history is never merely "discourse" or "narrative."[9] Cutting-edge critics of the late twentieth century frequently generated readings of texts understood primarily as the construal of subtexts, suspicions, and subversions—and especially of discourses of power. Too frequently, however, this potentially fine-tuned archaeological tool was wildly misappropriated, and so, ironically, some scholars (sometimes the very same critics) moved from overconfidence in their stratigraphy of the past to the opposite extreme of bulldozing their archaeological tell in the name of ideological advocacy of one kind or another. Needless to say, understanding of the past was, in such exercises, not aided but crushed and brutalized. Workable historical optics require of us both criticism and self-criticism. Without this, we degrade the past achievements and sufferings of real individuals in favor of what our successors will soon enough expose as ideologically ephemeral, unself-critical twitterings.

Understanding What Happened from What Happened Next

But is there any alternative? Is it not painfully obvious now that all historical knowledge is inevitably relative and perspectival, that both sources and interpreters are necessarily shaped by their own cultural and personal agendas, and that therefore an important part of all interpretation must be to *deconstruct* our sources for their ideological and power interests? We should not deny the force of that question. And yet the Western philosophical and Judeo-Christian theological traditions are at one in affirming the overarching importance of truth and of a world in space and time that is, in important respects, both ordered and intelligible. This in turn supports the conviction that the quest to understand the past, though inescapably difficult and fraught, is neither pointless nor impossible.

One idea that has become enormously influential in recent years is the value of studying the *impact* and *aftermath* of historical persons, texts, and events, either for their own sake or, somewhat less commonly, as a potential clue to the original meanings. This is sometimes called "effective history" or, using the German term, *Wirkungsgeschichte* (history of effects), typically associated with the philosopher Hans-Georg Gadamer (e.g., Gadamer 2004, 299–306). It is a way of recognizing the perspectival nature of historical events and our knowledge of them, in part by acknowledging the causes and effects that link events and texts to their aftermath (and ultimately to us).

In NT scholarship, a pioneer in this recently burgeoning field is the Swiss scholar Ulrich Luz, as seen especially in his great commentary on Matthew (Luz 2001–7). He has compiled a marvelous wealth of evidence illustrating the subsequent textual, artistic, and cultural effects of the text; but perhaps the most

9. A point well underscored by Evans 1997, 103–28, esp. 109, 124; also 239.

important achievement is his reflection on the nature of reception history and what it can contribute to biblical interpretation. Many other scholars have followed in recent years.

Luz memorably compares the biblical interpreter and historian to an environmental scientist analyzing the water of a great river while seated in a small boat that is itself carried and driven along by that same river.[10] This analogy, I believe, captures something important about the context of historical scholarship today.[11] More specifically, it also adumbrates the fact that the NT authors and actors themselves were part of a living process of memory and tradition, about which we might fairly expect to gain valuable understanding by sampling the river a little way—a generation or two—*downstream* of the founding events.

To be sure, that image is not without epistemological and theological weaknesses, on which I have commented more fully elsewhere (Bockmuehl 2006). It is, on the one hand, quite vulnerable to the challenge of a radical relativization: can such analysis really tell us *anything* worth knowing? Theology, on the other hand, poses the rather different epistemological challenge that this particular river may well scrutinize the scientist much more effectively than could ever be the case vice versa (cf. Heb. 4:12). Edwyn Hoskyns rightly warned that interpreting the Bible is a bit like the scientist staring down a microscope only to find, rather alarmingly, that instead of the lifeless piece of tissue he expected, there is God peering back at him and declaring him to be a sinner (quoted in Barrett 1995, 57)!

That testing of the river is, to be sure, an untidy exercise. We should not expect assured results or unambiguous eyewitness evidence, let alone proof of the historical reliability of the Gospels. The contributory streams of tradition, testimony, or memory, like those of rivers, cannot be dissected or picked apart. Memory's DNA has no Y chromosome that permits reliable tracking through the generations. And it is certainly right to be cautious about a sort of evidential positivism when dealing with claims of memory or of eyewitness testimony.

But neither is serious historical study of the early church helped by inherited critical prejudice that rules out of bounds the very questions of memory and reception. Polluting the source does have an appreciable effect downstream; yet conversely, the salmon that enter the sea were indeed spawned at the river's headwaters. These processes remain in principle open to careful investigation. Similarly, a series of recent studies has offered excellent historical grounds for supposing that both collective and *personal* memory played an important role in early Christian narrative and traditioning processes.[12] Even if the historical conclusions drawn may have been optimistic at times,[13] research in the field of memory and "eyewitness" testimony is rightly drawing attention away from the sorts of anonymous

10. Luz 1985–2002, 1:79 [ET p. 96]. See also Luz 1994, 23–38, and the earlier study in Luz 1985.

11. See my further remarks in Bockmuehl 2006, 163–67.

12. See, e.g., Bauckham 2006; 2007; Byrskog 2000; Dunn 2003b (also McKnight and Mournet 2010); a number of cognate questions were also previously discussed by Schröter 1997.

13. A criticism sometimes raised by reviewers of Bauckham; note also Allison 2010.

or indeed freely inventive processes once imagined by form critics. Instead, we are being alerted to the remarkably persistent interest, through a wide range of early Christian literature, in the Jesus tradition's concrete connections to the memory, indeed the eyewitness testimony, of specific and often named apostolic individuals.[14]

What encourages our attempt to attend to such association of living memory with particular individuals is that the first and second centuries do offer plentiful evidence of the early Christians *themselves* employing and appealing to such categories—not least when discussing specific apostolic figures. We shall discuss some of that evidence later in this chapter.

To understand history in the round, then, we will do well to attend to the historical aftermath, enhancing our understanding of what happened in the light of what happened next. A key part of that aftermath, perhaps the most crucial part, is that which takes place while there are still people alive who claim a firsthand memory either of the events and people concerned or of those who personally knew them.

There is an irony in the fact that we may not properly know who someone is until they are dead, and at that point we may benefit enormously from the memory of those—quite possibly friend and foe alike—who did know that person. As we shall see, it is during this liminal and patchily documented period that Christians of diverse stripes still quite explicitly appealed to certain key figures who embodied a "living memory" of the apostolic era. The survival of such memory, or at least of apparently uncontested claims to such memory, can be shown in rare but specific pivotal cases to extend up to a century and a half beyond the apostolic generation.

Contemporary observers often turn out to be pretty poor witnesses to the history of their own times. What they perceive as successes may well turn out in retrospect to be little short of disastrous; people they damned as failures can end up celebrated for far-sighted courage and wisdom—and vice versa. It may seem a platitudinous truism to say that only the past can be known as history; and yet the same in important respects applies to people: we learn to understand a person really only from the end rather than from the beginning or the middle. For readers familiar with the events of World War II, the changing fortunes of events like the 1938 Munich conference and of leaders like Chamberlain and Churchill constitute a salutary reminder never to mistake the verdict of journalism for the understanding of history.

In seeking to understand key players in the drama of Christian origins, therefore, we may not always be best served if we imagine contemporary written sources to be the best points of access. The quality of historical insight is not always proportionate to proximity of our sources to the events and persons they describe. Although a privilege when we can get them, the voices of ancient contemporaries are no less myopic about their own times than we are about ours: proximity typically precludes perspective.

---

14. See Dunn 2003a; 2003b; 2005a; 2005b; also the critical engagement with Dunn's work in Bockmuehl 2010b.

Conversely, the experienced and remembered effects of a person's words and actions are often as valuable a clue to their meaning as a knowledge of the original causes and circumstances. At the same time, it must be right to limit the extent to which we travel down the road of consequences, or we will lose sight completely of the original story.

In the case of early Christianity, that remembered aftermath invites access for a limited period to a number of identifiable individuals and communities who could—and did—relate memories of people and events of the apostolic generation. Not only did they claim this themselves, but their younger contemporaries affirmed it, and even their enemies apparently did not contest it. To give such living memory a cautious, critical welcome may help us make sense of the way the apostle Peter's ambiguous historical origins generated such an astonishingly important footprint in subsequent Christian history.

The importance of memory in the second century for the early Christians' own understanding of the apostolic tradition is strikingly voiced by Clement of Alexandria, who speaks of the gospel not as a story but as a true account passed on and guarded in memory (in Eusebius, *Eccl. Hist.* 3.23.5). To be sure, this hardly counts as a straightforward assertion, let alone as evidence for controlled transmission of eyewitness memory. We do well to read such statements both critically and *dialectically*: all memory is, at least to some extent, a reflection on itself and on its own ideological commitments.

Certainly this is true for Petrine memory, which scholarship has long since shown to be notoriously complex and often contradictory (see, e.g., Grappe 1995). On the other hand, scholars of oral history and social memory have also uncovered countervailing evidence that memory tied to particular objects, landmarks, or individuals may retain a certain sticky or persistent quality that is a function of its attachment to specific instances of what the French scholar Pierre Nora has more generally dubbed "landmarks of memory [*lieux de mémoire*]" (1984; ET, 1996). There is no question that memory, even of the eyewitness sort, is remarkably malleable and subject to distortion when it comes to the witness's own experiences and encounters. But on the other hand, where it is tied to momentous or life-changing objects, persons, or places, these can become "pegs" for the memory of events and persons,[15] especially when these pegs concern aspects of formative importance to an emerging consensus position. People may have exceptionally vivid and detailed memories of the day they met the queen or the pope, of what they were doing when President Kennedy was killed, or when they first heard of the attack on the World Trade Center on September 11, 2001. At the same time, such individual memories also typically come to be calibrated in relation to an emerging communal consensus—either reactively or, more often, in convergence with it.

15. See esp. van Houts 1999, 93–120.

Memory of this sort is of course highly episodic, lumpy, and often somewhat formulaic—characteristics to which even eyewitnesses are hardly immune. And it can often be generative of meaning, rather than merely retentive.[16] Nevertheless, in many cases, the formation of consensus around a social memory is a contested and haphazard process, which occurs over the period of a generation or two after the death of an important figure, a period when what is remembered of an event or a life remains open, to some extent, to re-evaluation, correction, confirmation, and, of course, harmonization. In this book, we will see clear cases of this phenomenon applied to the memory of apostolic figures like Simon Peter. This certainly requires us to beware of exaggerating the historical value of memory; but on the other hand, we should not be misled into the opposite error of underrating memory's importance just because it is contested and tenuous. A student of mine once suggested to me that there remains even today an intriguing and complex connection between phenomena like the 1960s Bob Dylan "of history" and his iconically remembered cultural persona "of faith": each is in its own way deeply historical, contradictory, and conflicted—and yet each also remains in important ways intangible and unintelligible without the other.[17]

One obvious objection to this way of reading the texts is to regard such theorized concern for memory as the importation of an anachronistic modern affectation to the context of late antiquity. It is most intriguing, however, that Christians in the second century do care passionately about their living and organically rooted link to the apostolic persons and events at the origin of their faith. What is more, this passion for a living connection is attested by no means only among traditionalist or sectarian groups but across the whole theological spectrum. The proto-Orthodox concern to derive the authority of Mark the evangelist from his service to Peter is echoed in living memory as late as Irenaeus of Lyons, who claimed in his youth to have heard Polycarp, one of the last to have been an eyewitness and personal acquaintance of the apostles. Conversely, however, even the Valentinian Gnostics claimed that their master, Valentinus, had been instructed by Theudas, a hearer disciple of Paul, while the followers of Basilides traced his pedigree through Basilides's teacher, Glaucias, who was said, like Mark, to have been Peter's expositor (*hermeneutēs*).[18]

While Greco-Roman sources are not unaware of this issue of memory, explicit appeal to it is made among Jewish and Christian accounts of the lives of great

---

16. Cf. also Allison 2010, 2 (in relation to Jesus, memory is "reconstructive as well as reproductive").

17. I am grateful to my student James Harland for this point, amply illustrated in reviews like Ferguson 2009.

18. Clement of Alexandria, *Strom.* 7.17. Winrich Löhr (1996, 26–29) has shown that Clement's knowledge of Basilides, a fellow Alexandrian of an earlier generation, is generally trustworthy. This particular tradition too is historically at least conceivable, although Hippolytus's report of an alternative claim that Basilides received secret dominical revelations from Matthias (Hippolytus, *Haer.* 7.20.1) seems rather less so. For a useful recent assessment of the complex problem of Hippolytus's identity, see Volp 2009.

teachers and their pupils, including on the Christian side singular figures like Peter, Paul, James, and John, as well as the wider family of Jesus and their descendants.[19] For obvious reasons, such figures were highly plausible "landmarks of memory" in Nora's more wide-ranging sense of "place."[20] So also, Richard Bauckham has shown that the gospel traditions are by no means anonymous collections of the sort once imagined by twentieth-century form criticism, or even, arguably, in the construal of early Christian "memory" favored by more recent writers like James Dunn and his students.[21]

Remembrance of the person and the work of Jesus was an explicit imperative at the heart of even the earliest Christian act of worship: "do this in memory of me" (Luke 22:19; 1 Cor. 11:24–25). In the Gospel of John, apostolic remembrance of the Lord is said to be the work of the "reminding" Paraclete (John 14:26). The disciples' faith in Jesus draws on memory of him (2:17, 22; 12:16; 15:20; 16:4). Above all, perhaps, the Fourth Gospel repeatedly calls to mind the Beloved Disciple as the one whose eyewitness testimony guarantees the truth of the narrative (19:35; 21:24; cf. 1 John 1:1–4).

So the memory of Jesus is clearly an important topic for the NT. But the recollection of the apostles, too, soon becomes a topic of explicit reflection. Especially in later NT books, readers are frequently urged to call to mind the apostles, initially in their absence but also, and increasingly, after their death. As a matter of fact, the claims of living apostolic memory continued, surprisingly, for many decades—an observation that runs against ingrained assumptions of much conventional historical-critical scholarship of early Christianity. As we will see in the next chapter (see "2 Peter" under "The Petrine Letters"), a particularly striking example of this concern occurs in 2 Peter, composed perhaps not long after the year AD 100.

Three additional brief illustrations may help give definition and color to this idea of a living memory of the apostolic generation. First, Papias (ca. AD 60–130) was a bishop of Hierapolis in Asia Minor whose lifetime overlapped with that of Polycarp. Although best known for his influential but much-debated comments about the origins of the Gospels, in the same context he expresses a specific preference for living oral apostolic tradition over merely written sources like the Gospels. Interpretations of his position have sometimes assumed either a vote for uncontrolled proliferation of oral tradition or else a crudely apologetic desire to

19. See, e.g., Bauckham 1990; Lambers-Petry 2003, with reference to Julius Africanus, Hegesippus, and others.

20. Cf. further Mendels 2004, who would include Eusebius as a "site of memory" in Nora's extended sense. Note also Eliav 2004 in relation to the tradition of the tomb of James and, *mutatis mutandis*, Valdez del Alamo and Pendergast 2000 on the medieval function of tombs as fixing communal memory.

21. I have developed this query about the otherwise excellent work of Dunn (2003b; 2005b) in Bockmuehl 2010b. Cf. also Mournet 2005.

press the Gospels' apostolic authority. Recent scholarship, however, has tended to confirm that Papias is in fact mildly *critical* of the canonical inscripturation of the Gospels: while doubtless acceptable and authoritative, they are nevertheless written texts at one remove from the living apostolic voice that is still present in his own exposition of the gospel, as one who stands in direct contact with the apostolic generation.

This claim of a living connection with Christianity's founding voices is what primarily concerns us here. In his famous statement of this position, Papias clearly underlines the importance of that personal memory of the apostles in understanding the Christian tradition:

> And I shall not hesitate to append to the interpretations all that I ever learnt well from the presbyters and remember well, for of their truth I am confident. . . . If ever anyone came who had followed the presbyters, I used to inquire into the words of the presbyters, what Andrew or Peter or Philip or Thomas or James or John or Matthew, or any other of the Lord's disciples, had said [*eipen*], and what Aristion and the presbyter John, the Lord's disciples, are saying [*legousin*]. For I did not suppose that information from books would help me so much as that which comes from a living and surviving voice. (Eusebius, *Eccl. Hist.* 3.39.3–4)

I am concerned here not so much about establishing historical facticity but rather about the explicit mention of Simon Peter in connection with an indigenous tradition from Asia Minor affirming a living chain of apostolic memory. Papias's somewhat naïve and uncritical affirmation of this "living voice" over against written documents was, in due course, relativized by the need for a finite and written canon. What matters here, though, is that Papias represents an important point of reference for the role of living memory and its appropriation in the second century.

A generation later, Justin Martyr (ca. AD 100–160) on numerous occasions refers to the Gospels as "memoirs" of the apostles, both in the two apologies addressing pagans and in his *Dialogue with Trypho*, set in Ephesus as early as 135.[22] It is unclear how much personal memory that phrase implies for these sources. It may also echo a biographical commonplace well known, for example, ever since Xenophon (ca. 430–355 BC) published his "Reminiscences" (*Apomnēmoneumata*) of Socrates: those earlier "memoirs" are cast in the form of conversations whose function is to be "convincing," even where, at times, they may not be strictly "authentic" (cf. Tuplin 1996, 1630).[23] Nevertheless, Justin's conception of these memoirs does seem, like Xenophon's, to imply more than a stereotyped convention of reverence for a great sage. For Justin, the Gospels in some sense reflect genuine apostolic recollections of Jesus derived from the testimony of eyewitnesses and

---

22. Examples include *Dial.* 100.4; 101.3; 102.5; 103.6, 8; 104.1; 105.1, 5, 6; 106.1, 3h, 4; 107.1; cf. *1 Apol.* 33.5; 66.3; 67.3. For a recent discussion of Justin's notion of memoirs, see Luhumbu Shodu 2008, 59–107.

23. According to Eusebius (*Eccl. Hist.* 2.23.3), Hegesippus, another second-century Christian writer, similarly titled his five-volume church history "Memoirs" (*Hypomnēmata*).

their disciples. Even more to the point for a scenario set in the mid-130s, in his *Dialogue with Trypho* Justin identifies Mark's Gospel in particular as representing specifically the memoirs of Peter (*Dial.* 106.3)—a point we shall discuss more fully in due course. My point here is the modest one of Justin's concern for memoirs, not for any particular claim of historicity.[24]

We turn, finally, to Irenaeus of Lyons (ca. AD 130–200), who recalls his childhood memories at the feet of his teacher, Polycarp, in Smyrna. He writes as follows to his estranged friend Florinus, a formerly "catholic" priest who has become a Valentinian:

> I remember the events of those days more clearly than those which happened recently, since what we learn as children grows up with the soul and becomes one with it. As a result, I can speak even of the place in which the blessed Polycarp sat and disputed, how he came in and went out, the character of his life, his physical appearance, the discourses he gave to the people, how he used to report his conversations with John and with the others who had seen the Lord, how he remembered their words and what he had heard from them about the Lord, and about their miracles and their teaching, and how Polycarp had received them from the eyewitnesses of the Word of Life, and reported everything in agreement with the Scriptures. By the mercy of God given to me, even then I listened eagerly to these things, and made notes of them not on paper but in my heart; and by the grace of God I always truly meditate on them. So I can bear witness before God that if that blessed and apostolic presbyter had heard anything of this kind [i.e., the Valentinian teaching] he would have cried out, and shut his ears, and said according to his custom, "O good God, for what a time have you preserved me that I should endure this?" He would have fled from the very place where he was sitting or standing, when he heard such words. (Eusebius, *Eccl. Hist.* 5.20.7)

As in his better-known treatise against the heretics, Irenaeus here insists on a harmony of Scripture and its interpretation that is in keeping with a tradition inherited from the apostles. Far from a euphemistic label for the imposition of an ecclesiastical construct, that tradition genuinely represents, for Irenaeus, a quite specific chain of personal memory reaching back to the apostles. Nor is this simply a device of apologetic convenience. Writing in another context, Irenaeus notes in passing that Clement of Rome's personal connection with the apostles, which Irenaeus believed to be factual, lends *gravitas* to his interpretation of their writings (*Haer.* 3.3.3): "He was one who saw the apostles themselves and conferred with them, and who still had their proclamation ringing in his ears and their tradition before his eyes." Peter is not mentioned by name, but the principle is clear.

We can only speculate how Irenaeus's friend might have responded, given the Valentinians' remarkably progressive-sounding conviction that the apostles were

---

24. Curiously, despite his appeal to apostolic memory, Justin makes more expansive claims about Simon Magus's activities in Rome than about Simon Peter's.

children of a very different time and culture whose moral and doctrinal views required reinterpretation and reconfiguration in the light of superior contemporary knowledge and experience.[25] On the other hand, it is interesting that some followers of Basilides cited Glaucias's connection with Peter, while students of Valentinus believed their master to be the student of Paul's disciple Theudas. This suggests their concession of the merit and significance of an apostolic chain of tradition, at least (though perhaps not only) for polemical reasons.[26]

Conclusion: The Remembered Apostle

Our introductory chapter has been concerned with the problem of how we might understand Simon Peter in the face of his seeming historical elusiveness. We have seen that early Christians of diverse convictions continued for over a century to show a much greater concern for living personal memory of the apostolic generation than would traditionally be allowed in a reconstruction of early Christian history along standard critical canons. This concern can be shown not only to have existed but also to have become the subject of specific appeals in negotiating disputed interpretations of the Christian gospel.

We may safely conclude that the early church recognized well into the second century a select group of what we might call sub-apostolic bearers of memory, who were widely regarded as—and in some cases perhaps were in fact—living links between the leaders of the apostolic generation and the churches that followed them. Second-century assertions of this sort exist for a number of apostolic and sub-apostolic figures, including Simon Peter and his students, both in circles that came to be identified as orthodox and among those that were eventually known as Gnostic or heretical.

It is worth acknowledging here that such early Christian stress on individual and collective memory may appear to some readers suspect and naïve when interpreted from a hermeneutic of suspicion, trained as we are to attend to contemporary cultural concerns about power and vested interests. Such are, of course, important critical caveats. Yet we must recognize too that even these very concerns of ours cannot exist without the context of living personal and communal memory to sustain them.

Absent such a store of sustaining common memory, our political and theological agendas collapse into absurdity—as, for example, David Keck (1996) has

---

25. They "[maintained] that the apostles preached the gospel still somewhat under the influence of Jewish opinions, but that they themselves are purer [in doctrine], and more intelligent, than the apostles" (Irenaeus, *Haer.* 3.12.12 [*ANF* 1:309]; cf. 1.13.6 on the disciples of Marcus Magus; also 3.5.1–2). Irenaeus famously mocks such Valentinian *aggiornamento* as resembling one who takes apart a mosaic image of the emperor in order to reassemble it in the likeness of a dog (*Haer.* 1.8.1).

26. On this point, see Pearson 2005, 4, citing Löhr 1996.

movingly illustrated in relation to Alzheimer's, "the theological disease."[27] This consideration also warns against identifying memory too closely with the self, as much of Western thought has tended to do.[28] A hint at the theological key to memory may lie in Clement of Rome's assurance that the faithful are irreducibly "engraved upon God's memory" (*1 Clem.* 45.8). This suggests that the one who "will wipe away every tear from their eyes" (Rev. 7:17; 21:4) is not thwarted by an impediment like Alzheimer's disease: in Christ, its victims retain their home, their memory, and their hope of heaven. For Christian as for Jewish faith, the gift of memory resides in the communion of those whom God remembers.

For a limited period, then, we may expect that the second-century images of Peter will have remained susceptible and also vulnerable to precisely such an appeal to the living memory of founding figures and events—for all their bewildering diversity and ideological diffusion. That fact, if we can corroborate it below, will serve to illustrate early Christianity's astonishingly diverse, yet interestingly constrained, variations on the Peter of Christian memory.

Why, finally, should any of this matter, or what is it intended to contribute? Here it may help to articulate a point that readers of my previous work will perhaps already suspect. At one level, this work offers simply a fresh perspective on Peter. In a fuller sense, however, my aim is to present an accessible test case of the twin principles of attending to the text's implied readers and early effective history, which in *Seeing the Word* (Bockmuehl 2006) I proposed as possible ways to rekindle a common conversation about the object of the NT in an otherwise intensely balkanized discipline. Whether this proves a productive way forward will be for others to judge, but it is my hope that the present work may be an aid to such reflection.

27. In Keck 1996, see esp. chap. 3 (pp. 75–96): *liturgy* is "the central vehicle of our faithful remembering of God" (p. 96).

28. Cf. Augustine: "Great is the power of memory, an awe-inspiring mystery, my God, a power of profound and infinite multiplicity. . . . So great is the power of memory, so great is the force of life in a human being whose life is mortal" (*Conf.* 10.17.26 [ET, Chadwick 1998]; cf. 10.8.15). (NB: for Augustine, memory is significant not simply for the human "self" but also as a vestige of the Trinity.)

2

The New Testament Peter:
An Overview

In the overall outline of this book, it makes sense to turn now to a brief survey of the most significant NT evidence for Peter. This will only be an initial surface reading to profile a narrative inventory of the earliest evidence, much of which we will then examine in greater detail from the perspective of living memory. Given the particular focus of this book—attempting to find clues to the range of Petrine memory in the early reception history—readers will undoubtedly want to turn to other studies for a fuller account of the NT evidence. There are numerous recent survey treatments that may be consulted with benefit.[1]

It is probably not the case that the NT constitutes the earliest extant evidence at our disposal in *every* instance. This is, one could argue, a somewhat different situation than pertains for the Jesus tradition. In the latter case, there conceivably (if still debatably) may have been one or more written sources earlier than the canonical books (such as the sayings source Q or, some would say, an early source of the *Gospel of Thomas*). Yet none of these survive.

In the case of Peter, however, even a relatively conservative scholar like Martin Hengel would date several relevant documents prior to the latest book of the NT. On Hengel's account, these earlier sources include the letters of Ignatius and *1 Clement* (Hengel 2010, 135–37), both of which he dates before 2 Peter. In the

---

1. See, e.g., Blaine 2007; Brown et al. 2002; Cassidy 2007; Feldmeier 1985; Grant 1994; Perkins 2000; Wiarda 2000. For fuller bibliographical coverage, see Bockmuehl 2010a.

same time bracket as 2 Peter (in his view AD 120–140), Hengel dates Papias of Hierapolis, the proto-Gnostic teachers Basilides and Valentinus, and the Roman historian Phlegon of Tralles (a little-known but intriguing figure, to whom we will return below). We might add to these names a number of other, less explicit sources, including the *Kerygmata Petrou* (*Preaching of Peter*), the *Gospel of Thomas*, and possibly even the *Gospel of Peter* and the *Apocalypse of Peter*. Justin's *Dialogue with Trypho* is set in the 130s, although it may have been edited later. The Roman historians Tacitus and Suetonius, although they make no explicit mention of Peter, may also be relevant to the period before 140, as we will see. We do not need to be detained by dating questions here, since proposed dates are invariably rather tenuous and debated. What does remain the case is that, with the partial exception of 2 Peter, it was indeed the NT evidence that played the most important role in attesting, shaping, and underwriting what survived of the living memory of Simon Peter in the second and third generation after the apostles—the period up to AD 200. And that is why it makes sense to attend to this canonical inventory separately, at the beginning of our study of Petrine reception.

Generally speaking, the NT evidence is concentrated in the Gospels and Acts, in two of Paul's letters (Galatians and 1 Corinthians), and then in the two canonical epistles named after Peter.

Peter in the Gospels

We begin with a synthetic picture of Peter in the Gospels, noting major emphases peculiar to each Gospel but also attempting to offer something of a coherent narrative.

Before plunging in, it is right to observe that there are reasons both for and against the approach here adopted. Certainly individual study of each Gospel's distinctive presentation of Peter is important for NT criticism. Several good studies of this sort are available in recent Petrine textbooks (including, e.g., Cassidy 2007; Perkins 2000; and Wiarda 2000). It is also true, of course, that a synthetic account will tend to conflate Gospel accounts composed, even on a mainstream spectrum of critical views, over a period of at least thirty years, a crucial time window representing the transition from the apostolic generation to a time when the only living link to the eyewitnesses will have been their disciples.

For present introductory purposes, nevertheless, there are benefits to adopting a synthetic account attentive to distinctive characteristics. The footprint of the earliest Petrine reception almost never distinguishes between the Gospels. This is not to deny that distinctively Markan or Lukan themes, for example, do surface from time to time. The overall early patristic profile of Peter, however, tends to be mainly a *conflation* of NT themes; Matthean and Johannine emphases generally predominate, with Lukan and occasional Markan features present, and one or two apocryphal motifs blended in (especially in relation to Peter's passion). This is entirely as we would expect, given the preponderance of Matthew and John in the early manuscript tradition. Ancient Christian individual or collective memory, whether pertaining to the NT or to other "places of memory," like the role of Mark or the martyrdom in Rome, tends not to capitalize on the differences between one account and another. Although commentaries on individual Gospels do emerge from the second century onward,[2] this does not appear to detract from the frequently (and perhaps typically) "diatessaronic" picture of Jesus and the apostles.[3]

That said, the subsequent chapters on the "Eastern" and "Western" Peter will return for a second look at some individual Gospel features. For now, my Gospel synthesis will, for convenience, be structured under the headings of Peter's background, his call, his function as representative, and his role in the Passion Narrative. We will then turn to survey Acts and the Epistles.

Peter's Background

First, who is Peter and where does he come from? Uniquely in the NT, Peter is known by four distinct names: Simon, Peter/Petros, Cephas, and Bar Yona. Each of these names bears its own significance that would repay exploring more fully (see Bockmuehl 2010a, 135–57).

In brief, Peter was evidently given the OT patriarch's name Simon (*Šimĕʿón*) at birth. This is unremarkable in itself. Although the name Simon had apparently fallen out of use for many centuries with the demise of its namesake tribe of Simeon, it came into prominence again in the Maccabean period, and it may still have carried overtones of national renewal. Acts applies both the Greek (Simon) and Hebrew (Simeon) forms of the name to Peter (e.g., 11:13; 15:14), perhaps because he himself did (cf. subsequently 2 Pet. 1:1, as in Fitzmyer 1981–85, 112–13). At the same time, the Gospels are consistent in their preference for the *Greek* names Simon and Peter, just as Paul virtually always uses the Aramaic name, Cephas (the only exception is Gal. 2:7–8). While some scholars have seriously tried to argue for the existence of two different people, one called Simon and another called Cephas, most would agree that the balance of the evidence unambiguously identifies Simon Peter with Cephas.

We cannot go into the complex issues surrounding the epithet "Peter," which in the Synoptics appears only in its Greek form (contrast John 1:42). The name "Cephas" seems to date back to an early stage of Peter's association with Jesus,[4] since some of Jesus's other disciples bore comparable Aramaic epithets.[5] In the

---

2. See, e.g., the brief account in Bockmuehl 2005.

3. The *Diatessaron* was a widely influential second-century Gospel harmony usually attributed to Tatian (ca. AD 120–185).

4. So Mark 3:16; John 1:42; Matt. 16:18 (cf. Matt. 10:2) has been taken to assume a later, more specific setting, which in its present form does have overtones of post-Easter concerns.

5. Note, above all, the "sons of thunder" James and John (Mark 3:17); perhaps also Thomas *Didymos* (John 11:16; 20:24), although the latter does not appear to be an Aramaic name.

Gospels, Jesus virtually never uses Peter as a proper name (only at Luke 22:34). The name *Petros* (Peter) is, in two of the Gospels, said to be a surname given by Jesus (Mark 3:16; Luke 6:14), and that is also how Justin Martyr, for example, understands it. At the same time, other exegetical and historical reasons suggest that the situation may be a little more complex. *Petros* (attested, if rare, in other first-century sources) may have been a pre-existing Greek nickname that Simon carried from his youth, adopted perhaps in the more Hellenized environment of his native Bethsaida Julias, where his brother Andreas and their friend Philippos were also known exclusively by their Greek names. If this is true, as I have shown more fully elsewhere (Bockmuehl 2010a, 148–56), then Peter receives from Jesus only the interpreted, Aramaic epithet Cephas (*Kêpā'*, "rock, crag, cliff"),[6] which was not a known Aramaic or Hebrew name in the first century.[7] In the Aramaic-speaking churches of Palestine, Peter came to be known by the distinctive name of Cephas, which served as a kind of dominical title of honor. This would explain why all four Gospels use *Petros* freely of Peter, even before the naming episode, and why, by contrast, it is the Aramaic derivative Cephas that is almost exclusively used in Paul. (John 1:42 appears to make explicit that the name given is specifically Cephas, rather than Peter, even though that is the only time in the Gospel that the Aramaic is used: "You are Simon the son of John/Jona[?]. You shall be called Cephas.")

Matthew 16 also introduces another undeniably Aramaic element in the form of Peter's patronym, "Bar Yonah" (Matt. 16:17). Peter was evidently the son of someone called Yonah, a rare name that appears to have had currency distinctively in Galilee and Syria (and may or may not be related to the biblical prophet Jonah, who was also said to be from Galilee; 2 Kings 14:25). Although the patronym is used in Matthew and John, the rendition "son of John" is found in the Fourth Gospel's early manuscript tradition. That evangelist evidently regards the peculiar Galilean Yonah as a contraction of the familiar name Yoḥanan, which is more typically abbreviated as Yoḥai (John 1:42; 21:15–17; cf. Matt. 16:17).

As for Peter's background, we are led to assume his Galilean origin in all four Gospels, but only the Fourth Gospel (1:44) informs us that he was a native of Bethsaida, a village at the northern shore of Lake Tiberias. Bethsaida was not far from his later home of Capernaum, but it was east of the Jordan; therefore, it was not technically in Galilee but in the Herodian tetrarchy of Trachonitis, which was ruled during Jesus's ministry by Philip rather than Antipas (who administered Galilee and Perea). We know that very shortly after the ministry of Jesus, Philip

---

6. Fitzmyer (1981–85) shows that it means primarily the latter at Qumran. Rabbinic evidence also uses the plural in connection with gemstones.

7. The Israeli scholar Tal Ilan (2002; 2008) has adduced appreciable literary and inscriptional evidence for Jewish use of the name *Petros*, but *Kêpā'* is never attested as a proper name in antiquity (with the possible exception, as Joseph Fitzmyer [1998] has argued, of a single figure at Elephantine in Upper Egypt in the sixth century BC). Fuller discussion appears in Bockmuehl 2010a, 135–57.

elevated Bethsaida from a village (a *kōmē*, as Mark still calls it in 8:23) to the status of a city, a Hellenistic *polis* (as Luke 9:10 and John 1:44 anachronistically update it). The NT's silence about Bethsaida is little short of deafening, and we will return at the end of this book to the question of its formative importance for Peter.

In the Gospels, we hear that Peter was a fisherman, and (for Mark and Matthew at least) he appears to have practiced his profession in much the same way as that seen in photographs of local Arabs at the beginning of the twentieth century: deploying circular cast-nets from shallow waters near the lake's northern shore and the mouth of the Jordan.[8]

Aside from that passing reference to his place of birth (John 1:44), the NT tells us nothing about Peter's background, childhood, or youth. During the ministry of Jesus, Peter resides exclusively in Capernaum. He must have moved there a considerable time before meeting Jesus, for reasons we will consider in the final chapter of this book.

Peter's Call to Discipleship

In all four Gospels, Peter is called to follow Jesus away from his job as a fisherman, although the precise circumstances of how this happens are narrated in three surprisingly different versions.

In Mark and Matthew, Jesus happens upon Peter and his brother Andrew standing in the shallow waters of the lake while fishing with cast-nets (Mark 1:16//Matt. 4:18). One is led to wonder whether, unlike the household of Zebedee (Mark 1:20–21) or the Lukan Peter (Luke 5:3), they are too poor to own a boat. (Later patristic texts occasionally stress the theme of Peter's poverty in his youth, though it is not immediately obvious whether this idea originates here.)[9] Jesus summons them to become "fishers of people," an allusion to Jeremiah's prophetic vision of divine fishers or hunters sent out to gather Israel back to the Land in the last days (Jer. 16:15–16)—a notion that has interesting echoes with the Matthean Jesus's concern to seek out the lost sheep of the house of Israel (Matt. 10:6; 15:24).[10] Peter and Andrew drop everything and follow Jesus, only to be joined shortly afterward by James and John, who leave their father's boat and nets (Mark 1:15–20; Matt. 4:18–22).

8. Compare Mark 1:16 ("in the sea") with Matt. 4:18 ("into the sea").

9. E.g., John Chrysostom, *Hom. Jo.* 2 on John 1:1, though he makes the same claim, less plausibly, for the sons of Zebedee on the grounds that they had to mend their nets (*Hom. Matt.* 14.3) and even for fishermen in general (*Hom. Jo.* 2 on John 1:1). Peter's childhood poverty also surfaces in *Ps.-Clem. Hom.* 12.6.

10. A prophetic connection of this phrase is seen in the church fathers too: see, e.g., Augustine, *Harmony of the Gospels* 2.17.41; Jerome, *Ep.* 71; Athanasius, *Ep.* 49.8. Ephraem (*Hymn* 3) writes: "Out of the stream from which the fishers came up, He was baptized and came up Who encloses all things in his net; out of the stream whose fish Simon took, out of it the Fisher of men came up, and took him" (adapted from *NPNF* 13:230).

Jesus soon becomes a familiar guest at Peter's home in Capernaum, a point amplified in the tradition of the Jewish Christian *Gospel of the Ebionites*, where Jesus gives his report of this encounter in Peter's house (frag. 2). In an unusual domestic vignette, Mark shows Jesus at Simon's house, healing Simon's mother-in-law of a fever (Mark 1:28–31). This domestic episode, unparalleled for anyone else among the Twelve, is a key indication of the significance of Peter's family in early Christian tradition, as Martin Hengel has recently demonstrated.[11] This is despite the mobility of the story's narrative sequence within the gospel tradition. In Matthew, for instance, it does not appear until several chapters later, following the Sermon on the Mount (8:14–17), while in Luke it *precedes* the call of Peter (Luke 4:38–39).

Luke's vocation story differs even more strikingly. It takes its cue from Mark's account of Jesus teaching from a boat while the crowd listens on the beach (Mark 4:1//Matt. 13:2); but here, in Luke 5, the boat apparently belongs to Simon. Andrew does not feature in the story; in fact, aside from the two lists of the Twelve (Luke 6:14; Acts 1:13), Luke never mentions Andrew either in the Gospel or in Acts. Instead, in this Gospel Simon Peter is called to be Jesus's disciple and a fisher of people as a result of the miraculous catch of fish from that boat, in which James and John also are involved.

This Lukan call narrative is so notably different from Mark and Matthew that many commentators have considered the question of whether it may be influenced by the *Johannine* narrative of Peter's miraculous catch after the resurrection (John 21). That story too involves Jesus, Peter, a miraculous catch of fish, and a special apostolic commissioning. This is not, of course, a necessary conclusion, but it could offer one possible explanation. One of the debated issues here is whether we are dealing with *one* story transmitted in different traditions or with two different ones; scholars continue to be divided on this question.

Another odd feature of Luke's account is that the call narrative occurs not before but *after* Jesus enters Simon's house and heals his mother-in-law (4:38–39). In that earlier story, Simon appears without introduction, as if readers should already know him. Could it be that Luke's reordering of the narrative intends to stress rather more clearly than Mark that Peter really did leave "everything" (5:11), in keeping with the characteristic Lukan interest in issues of wealth and poverty? To retain Mark's domestic scene involving Peter's house just a few verses *after* Luke's call narrative might well have seemed counterproductive. And if the call episode of Mark 1 struck Luke as a relatively informal and less decisive encounter, his more dramatic story of Peter's call as a result of the miraculous catch of fish would have enabled him to underscore this central point. Matthew deals with the problem, if that is what it is, by moving the visit to Peter's house several chapters down into his first miracle complex after the Sermon on the Mount (8:14–17).

11. Hengel 2010, 103–34; cf., somewhat differently, Bauckham 1990 on the family of Jesus.

In the Fourth Gospel, far from being marginal or absent, as in Luke, *Andrew* is the one who first introduces Peter to Jesus as the Messiah (1:35–42), having apparently been a disciple of John the Baptist. Andrew follows Jesus first and is, in a sense, the first to confess Jesus as Messiah; it is Andrew who brings Peter to Jesus with the words "We have found the Messiah" (1:41).

Peter as Confidant and Representative

Not long after Peter's call, all four Gospels identify Peter as appointed to be one of the Twelve—indeed, in some sense, as their leader. In all the NT lists of the Twelve, Peter is named first (and separated from Andrew).

To appreciate the Synoptic profile of Peter, it is an interesting exercise to consider where the Synoptic evangelists' "narrative camera" goes and what it sees. Doing that for Peter shows that he is present on all the occasions when only a small inner circle of disciples is gathered, including episodes like the raising of Jairus's daughter (Mark 5:37//Luke 8:51), the transfiguration (Mark 9:2–10//Matt. 17:1–8//Luke 9:28–36), the eschatological discourse in Mark (Mark 13:3), and the agony in the garden (Mark 14:33–36//Matt. 26:37–39; cf. Luke 22:41–44).

Peter is the only disciple whom Jesus addresses by name in all four Gospels. According to Luke 22:32, he is also the only individual Jesus is said to pray for—though, of course, in John 17 Jesus prays for all the disciples (just as in Luke 11 he also teaches them to pray). Peter evidently operates as a kind of spokesman for the disciples (not always to good effect) and most frequently is the one who takes the lead in asking questions or replying to Jesus.

For Matthew, Peter is also the only one to embody both faith and doubt, as when he walks to Jesus over the water (Matt. 14). Glancing forward from the NT, the pastoral scope of this unique homiletical vignette came to the fore in its early effective history; it echoes perhaps as early as the *Odes of Solomon*, a late first-century hymnbook that encourages confidence that Jesus's footsteps are still on the waves and believers too can walk in them (*Odes Sol.* 39.10–13). In the earliest surviving picture of Peter, on the wall of a Syrian house church at Dura Europos on the Euphrates, we find him in a scene that appears to represent either the stilling of the storm or (perhaps more likely) the walking on the water.

One of the most familiar and prominent Petrine narratives is his messianic confession at Caesarea Philippi (Mark 8:27–30//Matt. 16:13–19//Luke 9:18–22).[12] Peter's acclamation that "you are the Messiah" evokes very different responses. In Mark, Jesus orders silence; in Matthew, by contrast, Jesus praises Peter as the very foundation of what will become the invincible messianic assembly (*ekklēsia*), its gatekeeper, and the arbiter of its binding and loosing (Matt. 16:18–19). We will need to return in a later chapter to the meaning of this passage in its Matthean

---

12. This may be taken along with its Johannine parallel at the end of the Bread of Life discourse, where Peter affirms that the disciples will not abandon Jesus as others have done because only he has the words of eternal life (John 6:66–69).

setting; for now we should note only that Matthew's Jesus here connects Peter's role with the significance of his name: he identifies Peter (*Petros*) as the rock (*petra*) on which he will build his church. In light of my earlier observation about the relationship between the names Peter and Cephas, it may be significant that Matthew's Jesus does not say "from now on you will be called Peter" or anything of the sort, but merely "you *are* Petros, and it is on this *petra* [rock] that I will build my *ekklēsia* [church]."

In John, as we have already seen, the naming of Peter appears nearer the beginning of the gospel ministry, at the time of Peter's initial call. Aside from that, there are both similarities and intriguing differences, including the extent to which Peter's call is dependent on Andrew's. As we saw earlier, the Johannine account implies that Jesus applies to Peter the Aramaic name Cephas rather than the name Peter, which in all the Gospels is the name by which he already appears to be known from the start. Matthew's episode, therefore, may imply an Aramaic conversation that runs something like this: "They call you *Petros*—what an appropriate Greek nickname. You will indeed be the *Kēpā'* on which I will build my church [*ekklēsia*, perhaps *qahălā'*]."

Peter in the Passion Narrative

Shortly before his arrest, Jesus asks that preparations for the Last Supper be made by two of his disciples—who are named by Luke as Peter and John (Luke 22:8). Peter also, and uniquely, features twice during the course of the Johannine Last Supper, consistently misinterpreting Jesus's intentions: first, by his rejection and subsequent overly effusive acceptance of Jesus's washing of his disciples' feet (John 13:1–11), and second, in urging the Beloved Disciple to discover the identity of the betrayer (13:24).

During the course of that evening, Jesus, in all four Gospels, predicts Peter's denial before the rooster crows, despite Peter's protestations to the contrary. In Luke, though, Jesus again affirms the special pastoral leadership of Peter; once Peter repents, he is to act as one who strengthens the other disciples (22:31–32). This is a unique and crucial passage—reaffirmed, in a sense, in John 21—and a theme to which we will return in the final chapter.

At the arrest of Jesus in Gethsemane, John tells us that the anonymous disciple of the Synoptics who cuts off the ear of the high priest's servant is, in fact, Peter (18:10). In all the Gospels, Peter shows a greater courage than the rest of the Twelve, who scatter from the scene; only Peter follows the soldiers who take Jesus to the house of the high priest and gains entrance. According to John, Peter manages this because the Beloved Disciple, apparently based in Jerusalem and not one of the Twelve, was known to the high priest's household (18:16).[13] In the courtyard

---

13. The second-century apocryphal *Gospel of the Nazarenes*, known to us only from fragmentary patristic quotations, apparently affirmed that this was possible because the Beloved Disciple's family were the fishmongers to the high priest's household, an interesting notion that not only

there, Peter is challenged three times as one of Jesus's followers, and he denies three times that he knows Jesus. For Mark and Matthew, it is the cock's crow that reminds Peter of Jesus's prediction, and he repents bitterly (Matt. 26:74–75//Mark 14:72; in Luke 22:61, the Lord turning to look intently at Peter is the pivotal point of recall). But, like all the Twelve (yet unlike the women and, in John, the Beloved Disciple), Peter escapes and witnesses neither the crucifixion nor the burial.

After the resurrection, Peter is singled out, by the Markan angel instructing the women at the tomb, as a recipient of the Easter message that Jesus is risen and will go before the disciples to Galilee (Mark 16:7; so also Matt. 28:7). In Luke and John, Peter rushes to the tomb as soon as the women report that it is empty (Luke 24:12; similarly John 20:2–6). Luke, for whom all the resurrection encounters take place in or near Jerusalem, also mentions an appearance of the risen Lord to Peter (Luke 24:34)—an event that, for Paul, becomes the first defining apostolic appearance (1 Cor. 15:5).

For John, finally, a special focus on Peter emerges when Jesus appears to Peter and certain other disciples at the Sea of Galilee (John 21). Peter again casts discretion to the wind by plunging into the lake to swim to Jesus, who is standing on the shore. In the conversation that follows, Peter offers a threefold confession of his love for Jesus, and each time he alone receives in response the unique pastoral charge to feed Jesus's sheep. The episode also predicts Peter's martyrdom in terms of his stretching out his arms and being compelled to go where he does not wish to—an image widely recognized in recent scholarship as hinting at crucifixion (John 21:15–18).

In relation to John 21, it is worth flagging a point to which we will return: this remarkable restoration of Peter takes place in the context of an account in which Peter not only has recently denied Jesus but has repeatedly come second to the Beloved Disciple in attentiveness, access, and proximity to Jesus. This theme is sufficiently recurrent in the second half of the Gospel to be more than incidental, even if the evidence does not support the notion of a specific conflict between the two disciples, let alone an anti-Catholic stance.

Peter in the Acts of the Apostles

Luke's distinctive image of Peter is resumed in Acts, although with interesting changes. After the ascension, Peter immediately appears as the leading apostle. He proposes to appoint Matthias by lot as the successor of Judas (Acts 1:15–22), and throughout the first half of Acts it appears that Peter is the main human protagonist, the prince of apostles. He is the public spokesman for the believers in both evangelistic and conflict situations and the chief miracle worker among the

---

would make sense of the clear priestly, temple, and festival connections of the Fourth Gospel but also would confirm the impression that this disciple was based in Jerusalem, not in Galilee.

Twelve. Peter pronounces judgment on Ananias and Sapphira (5:1–11) and is the first to oversee outreach to the Samaritans (8:14–25) and missions to the gentiles (10:1–11:18). When Herod Agrippa comes to power (AD 41), Peter is imprisoned and, upon a miraculous escape, leaves Jerusalem "for another place" (12:17).

From now on, as chapter 15 and 21 make very clear, the leading figure of the Jerusalem church is undeniably James the brother of Jesus. While some have described this as a kind of coup or power struggle, recent scholarship recognizes here a difference of style: James's governance resembles more that of an oriental caliph (one who governs as the prophet's relative)[14] than that of Peter, who even before his departure is clearly much more of a pioneer evangelist, a kind of missionary-cum-prophet as well as a healer. (In that respect too, Peter is more like Paul than like James.) Peter appears once more in a position of some influence at the apostolic council of Jerusalem (15:7–11), but the deciding vote there is evidently cast by James rather than Peter—and this is the last we hear of him.[15]

Peter in the Letters of Paul

It seems telling, puzzling, and infuriating all at once that outside the Gospel narratives the rest of the NT tells us so little about Peter. We can derive remarkably little direct evidence for him in the Epistles, even those attributed to his authorship. It is worth bearing in mind here that, unlike 2 Peter (and many would include 1 Peter), the letters from Paul himself are generally dated a good deal earlier, and certainly no later, than the Gospel narratives about Peter.

Paul's letters do at least yield a little more that is worth knowing. Above all, they grant us glimpses of an important counterpoint to the picture of Acts, even if, despite some scholarly protestations to the contrary, there is not nearly enough here for an alternative narrative. We hear, for example, that Peter received a visit from Paul not long after the latter's dramatic conversion experience on the road to Damascus. It appears that Paul regarded Peter as a key figure in the church at Jerusalem, since he includes Peter among the so-called "pillars" (Gal. 2:6–10); and three years after a dramatic conversion on the Damascus road, Paul visited Jerusalem apparently for the sole purpose of spending a full two weeks "to get acquainted with Peter," rather than, say, to meet any of the other apostles (Gal. 1:18–19 NIV).

Paul also relates Peter's visit to Antioch (Gal. 2:11–21). We cannot be certain that this was Peter's first visit to that city, although it may have been.[16] In Antioch,

14. So, famously, Stauffer 1952 (contrast von Campenhausen 1950–51); cf. Limberis 1997.
15. The implications of the subsequent silence of Acts about Peter will be discussed in chapter 4.
16. One of the perennial difficulties here is the question of whether or how Paul's catalog of visits in Galatians can be correlated with the narrative of Acts. Detailed discussion of that question cannot detain us here. Suffice it to say, there remain continued grounds for debate between those scholars, on the one hand, who see Acts 15 as Luke imagining an apostolic conference and decree after the event (when the reality looked rather more like Gal. 2:6–10) and those, on the other

Paul sharply rebukes Peter for what he sees as a mere pretense in reaching out to gentiles and as giving in to Jewish Christian (or possibly non-Christian Jewish nationalist) demands "for fear of the Jews" (Gal. 2:12). For centuries, this episode was considered indicative of Paul's call for a law-free gospel; it was a central passage for Marcion and for later post-Reformation polemics, as well as in arguments both against Judaism and against rival Christians, including Catholics. Whatever the merits of the conflict or later interpretations, the language clearly suggests an intensely felt altercation that still burdens Paul at the time of writing, quite possibly all the more for being quite a recent memory.

Within five years or so of Galatians, Paul sounds much more positive about the role of Peter. For instance, 1 Cor. 1:12 reports what seems to be a Cephas party in Corinth, but far from treating either this party or that of Apollos as rival factions to be defeated, Paul seeks to unite them.[17] Paul here speaks quite deliberately of Peter and Apollos in positive terms as his fellow "servants of Christ and stewards of the mysteries of God" (1 Cor. 4:1–2 ESV). So also in 1 Cor. 9:5, Cephas is the only figure named among the apostles and siblings of the Lord who are traveling missionaries accompanied by their wives. In chapter 15, Peter is again singled out as the first apostolic resurrection witness (note Mark 16:7; Luke 24:34) and is clearly regarded as something of a key figure. That appraisal is quite in keeping with Gal. 1:18. It is the Antioch incident that constitutes an evidently temporary exception to what appears to be a relationship of friendly respect, if not necessarily of cordiality.

Other than in Galatians and 1 Corinthians, Paul does not mention Peter. This need not be surprising if the two apostles pursued a different missionary geography and strategy, as Gal. 2:7–8 implies. The one place where it might matter is in Paul's letter to Rome, where many have seen the absence of any reference to Peter as proof that, at least until the time of writing (AD 57?), neither apostle had ever been to that city and, perhaps, that Peter never went there. This is possible, but it is by no means the only plausible interpretation. As an outsider, Paul treads extremely carefully from the start in what he can assume about Roman Christianity, proposing his visit in unusually tenuous terms (Rom. 1). This topic will be taken up again in chapter 4 below.

The Petrine Letters

Other than what we have seen so far, Peter is mentioned by name only twice more in the NT: in the first verse of each of the two letters attributed to him.

---

hand, who would regard Galatians as written before the conference of Acts 15 and preparing the way for it. There are mediating positions, but interpreters are widely agreed that the differences in approach to this question matter significantly for how one reads early Christianity as a whole. My own view is that the date of Galatians is highly likely to be quite early, either about AD 48 (if it precedes Acts 15) or else around 50, in proximity to 1 Thessalonians (if it follows that conference).

17. So, rightly, the argument of Mitchell 1991, correcting a widespread, earlier scholarly view.

One of the difficulties in understanding the nature of Petrine memory here is that these two letters differ significantly from each other in content and flavor. These differences include issues such as their place of origin, language, theology, date, and probably authorship. Above all, perhaps, even their presentation of Peter varies in interesting ways. From the start, the apostle is introduced simply as "Peter" (*Petros*) in 1 Peter but as "Simeon Peter" (*Symeōn Petros*) in 2 Peter, using a Semitic form of Peter's name that recurs only in Acts 15:14. Unusually, the identification of differences between the two epistles and their authorship is not merely a modern critical judgment but was recognized in antiquity, and it led to widespread doubts about the authenticity and canonicity of 2 Peter until the fourth century. This is an important factor to bear in mind in a survey of the first-century profile of Peter.

1 Peter

The authorship of 1 Peter was never questioned in antiquity, and its attestation in patristic literature is widespread and early, from 2 Peter via Papias (in Eusebius, *Eccl. Hist.* 3.25.2), 1 *Clement*, and Polycarp to Irenaeus, Tertullian, and Hippolytus.[18] Specific personal or biographical allusions[19] are remarkably limited in 1 Peter; yet the Petrine attribution suggests that the epistle repays close reading for allusions to the apostle's profile—regardless of authorship, as Thomas Söding (2009b, 12–30) has rightly stressed. The most influential argument here relates to the apparent reference to Peter's presence in Rome while he was writing this letter in the company of both Mark and Silvanus (5:12–13).[20] More tentatively, there may be hints at a prior mission to the parts of northern Asia Minor addressed in the prescript, including Bithynia, Pontus, and Cappadocia, that were apparently not reached by Paul (1:1).[21] Whether this mission was historical or not, it matters for our purposes that a Petrine mission to Pontus was widely presupposed in subsequent Christian sources, although it is unclear whether this is based solely on 1 Peter 1:1 or also on other traditions.[22]

Another recurrent suggestion on 1 Peter is that there may be a biographical touch in the reference to the Passion Narratives of Jesus, where Jesus is specifically

18. For recent discussion of the second-century reception, see, e.g., Norelli 2004. The absence of 1 Peter from the Muratorian Canon points more to the latter's lack of representative character than to the obscurity of 1 Peter.

19. This may be an appropriate point to acknowledge that throughout this book I use terms such as "allusion," "tradition," and "echo" in a non-technical sense, without wishing to assert or imply a relationship subject to historical or literary precision.

20. Theories about Silvanus, in particular as a relatively free amanuensis, have long been debated; Mark, too, occasionally surfaces as a candidate for this role (e.g., implausibly, Moon 2009).

21. See also Acts 16:7, where the Spirit "did not permit" Paul to enter Bithynia—perhaps on grounds similar to Rom. 15:20.

22. E.g., Epiphanius, *Pan.* 27.6.6; Pseudo-Hippolytus, *De Duodecim Apostolis* (PG 10:952); Jerome, *Vir. ill.* 1.

remembered as silent when unjustly abused in his trial (2:23–24). This is significant in that it links specifically with Mark 14:61 and constitutes a consistent feature of the Markan tradition. The interpretation of Christ's suffering as exemplary, and indeed the letter's general theology of the death of Christ, has repeatedly been linked to the Synoptics and, interestingly, perhaps also should be linked to the Petrine speeches in Acts.

While exhorting the elders in 1 Peter 5:1, the author claims to be a "fellow elder" (*sympresbyteros*) and a "witness" (*martys*) of Jesus's sufferings. The point is sometimes made that the term here is not "eyewitness" (*autoptēs*) and that, according to the Passion Narratives, Peter himself was *not* personally present after the trial before Caiaphas, and he was certainly not at the crucifixion. So it could be that this means "one who bears testimony" rather than "eyewitness" (so also in Revelation, passim). On balance, however, and regardless of the authorship question, the contrasting absence of any claim to be a "fellow" witness alongside "fellow elder" (and "fellow shepherd," 5:2, 4) does seem to single out the Petrine author as a witness in a more specific sense (i.e., a *martys* as specifically an *apostolic* witness; see Acts 5:32 or Luke 24:48).

Regardless of how we may assess its actual authorship, 1 Peter is, in subtle but significant respects, deliberately cast *in character* (see, similarly, Doering 2009). This also becomes clear in the idea of Peter as "fellow shepherd of the flock" laboring under the "chief shepherd" (5:2, 4). It does not seem particularly far-fetched to suspect echoes of a tradition rather like the pastoral charge given to Peter by the risen Christ in John 21 (a passage to which we will return).

Finally, perhaps the single most influential passage about Peter in the letter's reception history is the cryptic reference to the author's location in the church of "Babylon" in the company of Mark and Silvanus (5:12–13). If these two are identical with the characters known elsewhere in the NT, as patristic interpreters consistently believed, then both Mark[23] and Silvanus (or Silas, as he is known in Acts)[24] had long-standing connections with the Jerusalem church and also with the mission of Paul. This in turn suggests for this "Petrine" document the memory of a more harmonious working relationship between Peter and Paul than some ancient and many modern interpreters suspect based on Gal. 2:11–14. The identification of Babylon with Rome (rather than a place in Mesopotamia or a small Roman garrison near modern-day Cairo) is widely agreed upon today and was certainly understood this way in antiquity. What remains disputed, in some circles, is whether that designation makes sense before the year 70 (many would now agree that it does)—even though that is not the only consideration affecting the date. If the letter's composition was in fact posthumous, there is still the open question of whether 5:12–13 generated Christian traditions about Peter

---

23. See Acts 12:12, 25; 15:37–40; Col. 4:10; 2 Tim. 4:11; Philem. 24.
24. See 2 Cor. 1:19; 1 Thess. 1:1; 2 Thess. 1:1; cf. Acts 15:22, 27, 32, 40; 16:19, 25, 29; 17:4, 10, 14–15; 18:5.

in Rome or instead reflected and corroborated them. While these are certainly relevant issues for the shape of Petrine memory, they can here safely be left for consideration in chapter 4.

2 Peter

In stylistic and theological flavor, 2 Peter is strikingly different from 1 Peter and seems, in some ways, to fit well in the ambience of early second-century Petrine memory. Unlike 1 Peter, this document contains no indication of its place of origin, and we can only guess whether it was composed in the West (e.g., Rome) or the East (e.g., Asia Minor). Nevertheless, its millenarian theology, dependence on the (probably) Palestinian Epistle of Jude, and definitive appeal to the transfiguration (as in the *Apocalypse of Peter*)[25] may well indicate an origin in Syria or Asia Minor, though it is difficult to get beyond speculation. The spelling "Simeon" (1:1) is not intrinsically impossible, although it is unusual, since it appears elsewhere only in Acts 15:14.

We cannot derive much of specific import to a memory of Peter from this letter. It places a great deal of emphasis on the readers' memory of Peter and of "your apostles" (1:12–18; 3:2), and this seems to focus especially on the narrative of the transfiguration as the defining moment of Peter's authentic apostolic gospel. It is interesting that this episode is emphasized rather than the confession at Caesarea Philippi or the passion and resurrection, but the emphasis reveals a good deal about the importance of the transfiguration in early Christian thought. Second Peter 3:15–16 draws credibly on the relationship with Paul, which is arguably remembered as both cordial and fraught, given that Paul's writings are, in part, difficult and lend themselves to distortion by false teachers.

Some Preliminary Conclusions

All in all, then, the NT's formative picture of Peter is surprisingly vague and incomplete in biographical terms, considering his prominence not only in the original circle of the Twelve but also for the mission and expansion of the first-century church. Yet there is enough here to identify Peter as the premier disciple of Jesus, however flawed, and as a leading figure in the Jerusalem church and in Christianity's outreach beyond Palestine.

It is notable, however, that the NT is markedly silent about what happens to Peter. We will return to that question before long, but the tradition connecting Peter with Rome is early and unrivaled, although from time to time scholars have tried to deny it. The identification of Babylon in 1 Pet. 5:13 with Rome seems unquestionable; and regardless of date or authorship, this asserts knowledge of a

---

25. Though the *Apocalypse* places the transfiguration after Easter; see also Norelli 2007.

tradition about Peter's presence in Rome with Mark by the late first century. (As we will see later, an argument can be made that the mysterious silence of Acts, together with the tantalizing reference to Peter's departure "to another place" in 12:17, points in the same direction.) The tradition of Peter's death in Rome seems well established by the time of Clement of Rome (*1 Clem.* 5), who, in ca. AD 96, has Peter and Paul as the outstanding heroes of the faith "among us" and most likely affirms that Peter suffered martyrdom (*martyrēsas*). Shortly afterward Ignatius too writes to the Roman church (Ign. *Rom.* 4.2) implying that Peter and Paul had taught the Roman church authoritatively. There is much additional second-century evidence to be examined later in this book.

We must turn now to the period of "living memory" to see how this profile was remembered and augmented, contested and fictionalized, in the 150 years after the events surrounding Peter's disappearance from the narrative of Acts.

PART 2

Peter in the "Living Memory" of East and West

3

The Eastern Peter

Second-century images of Peter in the East are a confusing mix of tradition, collective memory, and proliferating legend. Peter the apocalyptic visionary or the martyr; the recipient of privileged secret post-Easter teaching or the faithful representative of orthodox faith; an observant Jew or a pioneer missionary to gentiles; the bearer of the Jesus tradition culminating in the Gospel of Mark—all these conflicting views and more can be found in second- and third-century texts from Syria. Full analysis of these far-flung traditions exceeds the limited scope of what we can achieve here, and we will necessarily have to be quite selective.

To gain a better perspective of what the tradition looked like in its developed form, we shall begin by moving the clock forward to engage in an opening thought experiment set in the middle of the fourth century. The newly Christianized Roman Empire had begun to generate large numbers of religious tourists to the Holy Land. But to travel from dusty, bustling Jerusalem to the scenic Galilee of Jesus was to confront an unexpected mental challenge. Fourth-century Jerusalem presented itself as the rigorously redesigned Roman colony of Aelia Capitolina, thriving as a Christian city centered on the new Constantinian Church of the Holy Sepulchre. Human and architectural reminders of Jerusalem's Jewish past, by contrast, were now hardly prominent. For over two centuries, Jerusalem's established and successful Christians had had no personal continuity with the church of the apostles, even though the contemporary gentile bishops continued to claim succession of worship and governance. Any surviving gospel sites and remains were either recently "rediscovered," like the true cross, or else were piles of rubble, like the temple. A narrative of Christian triumph and displacement of Judaism—supersessionism—was not hard to sustain.

But that was Jerusalem. To visit the Sea of Galilee was a perplexingly different experience. Various sites were visited, but Capernaum in particular stood out as unexpected. This small Jewish commercial center had never been destroyed and continued to be dominated by Jewish culture. Jews of rabbinic and of Nazarean persuasion intermingled in commerce, culture, and religion. A large, impressive synagogue faced a smaller Christian (possibly Jewish Christian) house church across the street—somewhat uneasily, we may imagine. Rabbis condemned Capernaum as a center of liberal heretics. Christian theologians too seem to have downplayed it despite its intimate links with the ministry of Jesus—perhaps because the sheer fact of Capernaum's continuing survival and prosperity seemed to pour scorn on Jesus's prophecy of its destruction (Matt. 11:23).

A fourth-century Gallic nun, Egeria, kept a pilgrimage journal for the benefit of her community at home. Arriving in Capernaum in AD 382, she commented on the architecture she encountered, including the synagogue (which she took to be the one Jesus had known) and a church "made out of the house of Peter, whose walls stand to this day as they were then."[1] Excavations of that church and the remains underneath it have revealed that Christian pilgrims had been coming to visit this same place for at least two centuries, leaving graffiti scrawled on the walls that Egeria saw.

But was this really Peter's house? And what should we make today of the relationship between the archaeological landscape of Capernaum and the textual landscape of the Synoptic references to Peter's house? Certainty eludes us.[2] Reading second-century memories of Peter is a bit like trying to make historical sense of the graffiti in the so-called house of Peter. In fact, some of our second-century sources date from around the time that people apparently began to scrawl names and prayers on the walls of that house in Capernaum. What is history or living memory, and what is devout tradition or imagination? Too often we cannot pry them apart, and to abandon one is to lose our grasp of the other.

In these next two, substantive chapters, we will necessarily have to be selective; a fuller impression of the fascinating breadth of sources may be gained from the online table of sources,[3] which I hope may stimulate further reading and study. For the traditions singled out, my aim will be to try to anchor the discussion in terms of *geographic* as well as historical setting. To be sure, this approach has its own problems, too.[4] But by situating these early Christian sources in their broad geographical settings and reading them dialectically, we may be able to distinguish ambiguities and tensions intrinsic to the contested memory of Peter and, in at least

1. In Petrus Diaconus, *De Locis Sanctis* 5.2.

2. Note, however, Breytenbach's (1999, 84) cautiously positive assessment that this is Peter's house.

3. http://simonpeter.bodleian.ox.ac.uk.

4. See the circumspect remarks of Grappe 1995, 31.

some cases, to the character of the man himself. Analysis of the extant sources for the first two centuries shows that the Petrine tradition flourished above all in Rome and Syria, and to a rather lesser extent in Asia Minor, Greece, Egypt, and North Africa.

It goes without saying that the nature of these sources rarely yields precision or certainty about the geographic origins of particular traditions. The early church grew up in an age of global information exchange, where even long-distance travel had often become relatively fast, safe, and inexpensive. Jews and Christians from Palestine frequently traveled to Rome, Asia Minor, and Egypt. Here, I am applying to Petrine memory a geographic point advanced in somewhat different ways by Henry Chadwick (1966) and Jaroslav Pelikan (1980), who both stressed early Christianity's twin foci of the Holy Land and Rome (see also Guijarro 1991; Karrer 1992).

We must note that the undeniable value of historical caution does not here justify a thoroughgoing skepticism or relativism about this way of proceeding. More than a few applications of this approach turn out to inject useful local color and definition into an otherwise abstract literary analysis. Tracing Petrine memory in broadly geographic terms may point a way out of a number of familiar analytical cul-de-sacs and should do justice to the often locally rooted nature of memory. Writing on a related topic, Doron Mendels (2004, 43) captures this point well:

> A tourist who wandered through the cities of Asia Minor, or other places in the Empire, would soon have discovered that these different local fragments of mythological memory clearly distinguished one community and city from another. These local memories, . . . probably written down and stored in archives, defined the nature of one's belonging to a place, and existed alongside the collective memory imposed by the emperor.

Simon Peter was one of the few apostolic figures whose Christian memory spanned from Jerusalem via Syria, Asia Minor, and Greece to Rome.

Local Memory of Peter in Syria?

It is a striking fact that so few local Petrine traditions survive from greater Syria in the period of living memory, or even among those who wrote about the period in the century or two that followed. Outside the NT there are no identifiable memories of Peter from Jerusalem or Judea in this early period, despite the patristic claim that an apostolic church and succession of bishops existed in Jerusalem between the two Jewish revolts. We have worthwhile hints of an early awareness of the house of Peter at Capernaum, but nothing at Bethsaida.

Even Antioch produces remarkably little. In the fourth century, John Chrysostom (ca. AD 347–407) managed to preach a long sermon about Ignatius without ever revealing much local tradition, except to claim that Ignatius was consecrated by Peter and that his bones had by now been relocated to the Daphne gate (*Homily on St. Ignatius* 5; cf. Jerome, *Vir. ill.* 16). The sixth-century local chronicler John Malalas, often unreliable but occasionally invaluable, records the ministry of Paul and Barnabas in Singon Street next to the Pantheon, but for Peter he knows only that he stayed in Antioch for a while, that he did not mix with gentiles at first, and that he appointed Euodius and, at a later point, Ignatius as bishops[5]—a tradition that is equally attested by Eusebius and other Syrian texts but otherwise has very few specifics about it.

The third- or fourth-century *Pseudo-Clementine* literature (discussed further below) provides a little more for Antioch, as it does for a number of other legendary encounters of Peter in Syrian towns, but none of this material is datable to our window of living memory. We are told that Theophilus of Antioch dedicated his house for the use of the church and that a chair was placed in it for the apostle Peter (*Ps.-Clem. Rec.* 10.71). These are cosmetically attractive details, but their late date means that, in the absence of earlier attestation, they yield little for our purposes. The same goes for the Church of St. Peter, shown to modern pilgrims in a cave at modern Antioch (Antakya), for which apparently no attestation prior to the Crusades can be established.

There are other early Christian traditions and legends surrounding great Syrian cities like Apamea and especially Edessa, but these tend to be associated with other apostles, most notably Thaddaeus and Thomas. We will in a moment discover a lively late second-century interest in Peter and Petrine literature in the nearby town of Rhossus. Once again, however, at this late date that connection demonstrates at least as much about the disappearance of living memory as about its occasional and tenuous persistence.

Shortly after the period here in view, we find what is probably the earliest surviving picture of Peter in art. He is depicted on a badly worn painting, apparently of Jesus walking on the water or calming the storm, that is in the Christian chapel at Dura Europos on the Euphrates, datable to the first third of the third century—an important place too, because Christians lived in close proximity with Jews and may, on one interpretation, still have prayed in Hebrew.[6]

Very little can be said about this with confidence, except that the appearance of Peter seems already to be stylized in interesting ways toward an iconography that soon became standardized in Rome and elsewhere. Sarcophagi, mosaics, and frescoes tend, with exceptions, to develop Peter as a rustic-looking man with a round head, short curly hair, and a beard; his eyes are large and round, his cheeks broad, and his nose short but pronounced. Even that more developed typology, of course, remains remarkably undifferentiated, suggesting the elaboration of a cliché rather than the preservation of an actual tradition of visual memory. Its even

---

5. Malalas, *Chron.* 242.10–22; 246.22; 252.8, 12.

6. So Teicher 1963, on what he deemed a supposedly "Eucharistic" liturgical text resembling the *Didache*, but the identification is rather more uncertain.

more rudimentary implementation at Dura Europos cautions against any notion that a specific visual memory of Peter's actual appearance is here being kept alive.

At the same time, the mere fact that a recognizable visual typology of Peter did exist in the early third century, however tenuous and general it may have been at this stage, suggests that the emerging Petrine profile may not have been a matter of wholly disparate and competing ad hoc creations. Instead, it appears to express, in a recognizable fashion, the early churches' collective memory of Peter, as informed by Scripture and later tradition. Philip Esler, among others, has emphasized the need to take more seriously the continuity in these early iconographic traditions (see esp. Esler 2001). The sometimes fanciful sixth-century chronicler John Malalas of Antioch writes of the apostle's appearance,

> St Peter was an old man, in stature of average height, with receding short hair, both hair and beard completely grey, fair but rather sallow skin, wine-coloured eyes, a good beard, a long nose, eyebrows that met, upright in posture; he was sensible, swift to anger, changeable, timorous; he spoke through the Holy Spirit and he was a miracle-worker.[7]

Depictions of the apostles existed in Rome as early as the late second century. Irenaeus reports disapprovingly of Carpocratian Gnostics, who appeared in Rome during the time of Pope Anicetus (ca. AD 155–166), saying that they venerated paintings and other likenesses of Jesus (and major philosophers) and believed that Pontius Pilate produced a first image of Jesus (*Haer.* 1.25.6). Later, a statue of Christ stood outside Antioch, near the gate leading to Daphne.[8] In Caesarea Philippi, her hometown, the hemorrhaging woman healed by Jesus (Mark 5:25–34 and pars.) was long commemorated in an old bronze statue, which Eusebius saw in his youth, although it was later destroyed under Julian the Apostate. Eusebius also knew of other gentile Christian paintings of Paul and Peter and of Christ himself (*Eccl. Hist.* 7.18.1–4).[9]

Peter in Early Syrian Literature

In order to grasp a sense of Petrine memory in the East, I would like to begin by looking in a more focused way at three identifiable second-century authors who wrote about Peter at the beginning, the middle, and the end of the second century—Ignatius, Justin Martyr, and Serapion. We will approach the evidence

---

7. Malalas, *Chron.* 10.266 (ET, Jeffreys et al. 1986); for text, see Schenk von Stauffenberg 1931.
8. So, e.g., John Moschus cited in Downey 1961, 206 and n. 27.
9. Somewhat more fancifully, the conservative journalistic study of Peter's tomb by Michael Hesemann (2008) includes a computer-generated forensic facial reconstruction (pp. 261–66 and plate facing p. 161), matching skull fragments from the "graffiti wall" discovered under St. Peter's in Rome to the stylized iconography of the catacombs.

from back to front, beginning at the end of the second century as the latest survival of claims to personal memory of the eyewitnesses of the apostles. The three named individuals are singled out as a way of anchoring what can otherwise look rather like a kaleidoscope of images connected by topical but ahistorical "axes," as Grappe puts it (e.g., 1995; 2007).

The chapter closes with a specific look at the key NT evidence from Syria, indicating the shape of Petrine memory in the East up to about the year 100. Again, this represents only a selection of the relevant material surveyed in chapter 2 above, but it does provide ease of access to what is a bewilderingly complex set of sources.[10] We will see that Eastern memory is, on the one hand, remarkably limited and often unspecific, adding little either to supplement or to subvert the NT and the mainstream Roman tradition. On the other hand, Eastern evidence is diverse and less centralizing in its account of Petrine memory.

Serapion of Antioch

We begin with a late second-century episode that illustrates both the decline and tenuous survival of the phenomenon of living memory at the end of the chronological window here in view. What survives is not eyewitness testimony but an appeal to functional collective memory in the adjudication of competing images of Peter. Serapion served as the bishop of Antioch about 190–211. The church historian Eusebius quotes from a letter Serapion addressed to a church in his diocese, at Rhossus in Cilicia (*Eccl. Hist.* 6.12.3–6). Serapion here withdraws his earlier agreement to grant approval for a group of Christians in that church to read the so-called *Gospel of Peter* in private. Why has he changed his mind? After investigating the matter further, he has come to the conclusion that the document in question is heretical and not suitable to be received by orthodox Christians. Serapion's letter is frequently cited to illustrate early Christian views of pseud-epigraphy (works falsely attributed to famous persons). For present purposes, I am more interested in the question of whether at the very end of the second century Serapion is, in this dispute about Peter, still in any sense able to appeal to surviving individual or collective memory of the apostle. He begins by outlining what appears to be an agreed-upon position on the principle of distinguishing authentic from pseudonymous apostolic writings:

> We, brothers, accept Peter and the other apostles just as Christ; but as experienced people we reject the writings falsely written in their names, knowing that we did not receive such things.

In reflecting on a recent pastoral visitation to deal with a dispute at Rhossus, Serapion concedes that he may have been naïve in assuming that the orthodox

10. For a fuller list of the relevant sources see the online table at http://simonpeter.bodleian.ox.ac.uk.

faith itself was not at issue there and that no careful examination of that "gospel in the name of Peter" was therefore necessary. The dispute appeared on the surface to be a petty one. So Serapion agreed, without further ado, to permit the (apparently private) reading of the *Gospel of Peter* by the group in question. In the meantime, however, indications of a heresy among that group at Rhossus had come to light, and Serapion, having then read a copy of the text carefully, found it to be orthodox in most respects, "but some things are additions." Unfortunately, Eusebius's quotation breaks off at this point and does not preserve for us Serapion's promised elaboration of what might be meant.

What sense can we make of this? As we have seen, Serapion clearly thinks it important to distinguish authentic from pseudonymous apostolic texts. Only the former are suitable for public reading. As for Peter, Serapion stresses his apostolic authority but denies that it extends to any pseudonymous sources. Although we cannot be certain if the text known to us as the *Gospel of Peter* is the one in question, the extant fragments we have do seek to speak in Peter's name.[11]

Beyond such basic questions of authenticity, the bishop deploys a remarkably complex set of criteria for appraising the authority of what is a somewhat ambiguous document. Beginning with the problem of whether writings in the name of an apostle have been "received" in the catholic tradition, Serapion adds to this a question about the orthodoxy of their *content*. On this basis, the *Gospel of Peter* is evidently not part of what "we" (the church of Antioch?) "received"; thus it holds no apostolic authority.

As it happens, Serapion's assessment did not immediately prevail everywhere: the *Gospel of Peter* remained popular in parts of Syria and Egypt, and it has sometimes been argued that ecclesial documents, like the third-century *Didascalia* and certain early Syrian lectionaries, show signs of dependence on it.

A number of interesting tensions surface in Serapion's reaction to this text. Most particularly, Serapion feels compelled to reject a popular Petrine text in spite of his explicit commitment to Peter's authority—a difficult tightrope to negotiate. Evidently there was in late second-century Syria an ongoing disagreement about what might constitute an appropriate part of Simon Peter's received profile.

So what can we conclude from this for our purposes? Primarily two things. First, it is noteworthy that Serapion does *not* appeal to *any* independent and specific memories of Peter. No such contemporary memories appear to be available to him in the church at Antioch or Rhossus or, for that matter, from any other orthodox or heretical circles. Serapion's criteria of authority for a doubtful text in the apostle's name are precisely those we would expect to find in most later patristic texts: orthodox doctrine and catholic reception. By contrast, an appeal to Petrine memory or even Petrine tradition plays no explicit part. This is striking,

---

11. The *Gospel of Peter* itself is probably a mid-second-century text that presupposes the final form of all four canonical Gospels. See, e.g., Brown 1987; Green 1987; cf. Foster 2007; and now, most fully, Foster 2010.

given Peter's known ministry at Antioch, even if the apostle's presence there was brief and a great deal of time had passed since then.

Second, however, it is possible to rephrase the same point in more positive form. In order to do this, it is worth pausing for a moment to reflect on the implications of the bishop's insistent use of the first-person plural: while "we" receive Peter and the other apostles as Christ himself, "we" are, on the other hand, experienced in rejecting falsely attributed writings because "we" know that "we" did not receive such things. The evidence of Irenaeus suggests that, until just before the year 200, it remains legitimate to assume that Serapion's statement could still bear something of the force of a living memory at Antioch. Conflicting profiles of Petrine memory at Antioch and Rhossus here come to be adjudicated by articulation of the common local testimony to what "we" have received. In its second-century context, then, Serapion's judgment carries a vital rhetorical force. He appeals to apostolic reception in the same decade when, in the far western Mediterranean, Irenaeus, as an old man, appeals to his vivid memory of Polycarp as one of the last surviving contemporaries of the apostles. Though Serapion has no such *personal* memory to draw on, he articulates an interpretation of the *collectively* remembered Peter (drawing on what "we have not received"), which is about to become tradition's consensus. We may speculate that, at this time, at most a tiny handful of surviving elders in the church of Antioch could in principle, like Irenaeus in the West, still have retained childhood memories of an individual who had been one of Peter's last living eyewitnesses.[12] Serapion himself, however, appeals to criteria of apostolic tradition, whose distillation of personal and corporate memory was effectively becoming an established norm.

Justin Martyr

A native of the Palestinian city of Neapolis (Nablus), the philosopher Justin (ca. AD 100–165) moved to Rome via Ephesus after adopting Christianity around the age of 30. We know very little about the circumstances of his conversion, although he does describe personal contacts with Christians while he was still a Platonist,

---

12. Cook 2011 doubts this argument, elaborated in Bockmuehl 2010a, on overly demanding grounds of arithmetic and probability. If the aged Irenaeus of the AD 190s really did as a little boy meet an octogenarian Polycarp, then the latter might indeed have met apostles or their pupils who survived to the mid-70s of the first century. Ten years earlier, a similar case is feasible for those who lived until the 60s, like Peter. Conversely, if (as gerontological studies suggest) 5 percent of first-century children who knew the apostle Peter in the 60s could be expected to live to old age, then 5 percent of those children who, in their turn, met these apostolic eyewitnesses in the 120s or 130s would have done the same. In the case of famous church leaders like Polycarp, the number of individuals entailed in that 5 percent may well be more than negligible. Absolute dates and windows are always open to debate, but for "living memory" to have meaning in the second century, a priori probability calculations are irrelevant as long as in a given location even one influential individual in his 70s or 80s (like Irenaeus) did, as a child, know even one identifiable aging apostolic eyewitness (like Polycarp).

conceivably among the Samaritans, whom he calls "my people." Justin knows Jewish Christians (*Dial.* 120.6; *2 Apol.* 12; cf. *Dial.* 7–8; 47.4) and, although he can claim no personal memory of eyewitnesses, his Syrian and Roman connections make him interesting as someone who writes about Peter within that window of living memory.

Justin's sparse statements about Peter the apostle are sometimes cited by skeptical historians to suggest that little was known of Peter's supposed presence in Rome by Justin or anyone else until the late second century. Such arguments from silence are, however, significantly weakened by the fact that Justin also has very little to say about Paul, whose activity in Rome few would doubt. The *Dialogue with Trypho* is normally thought to be set in Ephesus around AD 135 (cf. Eusebius, *Eccl. Hist.* 4.18.6). If indeed that setting is somewhat realistic, we would not necessarily expect Justin to be closely familiar with Roman memories of Peter prior to Justin's move to the capital. It is true that Peter does not feature in the two Roman apologies, but neither deals with subjects that call for such mention. Interestingly, the *First Apology*'s reference to a statue of Simon Magus, probably to be dated around AD 155, may well be drawing on ill-informed local Christian lore about Peter's archetypal enemy at a time when Justin had not long been resident in the capital.

While Justin is thus not a prime source of Petrine living memory, there is nevertheless one important exception to his relative silence about the apostle. One famous passage in the *Dialogue* provides evidence that Justin understood the Gospel of Mark to represent Petrine memory. Justin sees all four Gospels as "memoirs of the apostles" and their pupils, potentially eyewitness remembrances analogous in some respects to Xenophon's *Apomnēmoneumata* ("Reminiscences") about Socrates. Writing about Jesus's relationship with his disciples, Justin (*Dial.* 106.3) notes:

> It is said that he changed the name of one of the apostles to Peter; and it is written in his memoirs that this so happened, as well as that he changed the names of two other brothers, the sons of Zebedee, to Boanerges, which means "sons of thunder." (*ANF* 1:252, adapted)

This passage has furnished plenty of fodder for scholarly debate. But in the context of Justin's repeated references to the apostles' memoirs both here and elsewhere, he does seem to designate the Second Gospel as the memoirs of *Peter*.[13]

How can we be sure of this? Although scholars have sometimes thought to link Justin's comment to the apocryphal *Gospel of Peter*, the passage concerned is unambiguously identifiable. First, *only* Mark 3:16 refers to Jesus "giving Simon *the name*" Peter, which Justin takes (I think mistakenly) as a *change* of name—apparently drawing here on early tradition. And second, *only* Mark 3:17 gives us the Aramaic or Hebrew nickname of the sons of Zebedee, "Boanerges." In other words,

---

13. Justin's view of these "memoirs" is much discussed. See the recent treatment of Luhumbu Shodu 2008.

we have here two pegs that suggest Justin knew the Gospel of Mark specifically and uniquely as "the memoirs of Peter," just as he already identified the Gospels in the preceding context as written by the apostles and their followers (*Dial.* 103.8).

This may well suggest something of the place of Mark's Gospel in the Roman church's thought world and its role in shaping Roman memory of Peter. It is particularly interesting to note the rhetorical ease with which Justin raises this Petrine link for Mark in the Ephesian context. In Justin's discussion with Trypho, this is evidently not a contested or apologetic idea but one that is wholly uncontroversial. Critical scholars have long tended to belittle any connection between Peter and Mark as an unlikely theme of apologetic romance, but for this and other reasons it seems to me well worth revisiting. The idea of Mark as representative of Petrine memory is, in Justin, assumed to be a consensus position that is not contested among Christians or doubted by their Jewish or pagan opponents. Justin, of course, claims no personal memory of Mark or Peter to support this assertion, but in making it he represents what is evidently a geographically widespread Christian consensus concerning their relationship during the period of living memory.

Ignatius of Antioch

For our third and final introductory illustration, we turn to Antioch, specifically to Ignatius (ca. AD 35–110), a bishop of Antioch at the beginning of the second century.[14] Ignatius was arrested, and while being transferred to Rome for trial and eventual execution, he composed a number of letters to churches along the route of his journey. While they are important and engaging in many ways, these writings remain surprisingly taciturn about Antioch or Antiochene memories of Peter, even though in subsequent centuries he was consistently revered as one of that church's founding apostles.[15]

It may be that Ignatius, like Justin, represents more than just Syrian views. It has often been noted that his writings may reveal at least as much about the church in Asia Minor as they do about Syria, as indeed his letter to Rome offers important perspectives on the situation in the capital. It is true, in fact, that Ignatius is somewhat coy about mentioning Antioch (Ign. *Phld.* 10.1; *Smyrn.* 11.1–3; *Pol.* 7.1–2), perhaps because his views about church governance and relations with Judaism had not won the day there.

Ignatius's very limited Petrine references are relatively bland and "catholic" sounding, as in his rhetorical setting one might expect them to be. On the traditional dating, Ignatius could have been a child when Peter and Paul first came

14. Interestingly, Polycarp's letter to Philippi knows Ignatius but never calls him a bishop.

15. In what follows, I cannot engage in the continuing controversy about the authenticity of these letters, which has carried on for the last four centuries (see, e.g., Munier 1992 for a survey). I will here assume the mainstream position that the "middle" recension of seven letters is authentic, and composed perhaps in the second decade of the second century. For a slightly fuller bibliographical justification, see the references cited in Bockmuehl 2010a, 86–87.

to Antioch. Yet his letters offer no hint of any personal memory of Peter or, for that matter, of Paul. Ignatius is therefore a good example of someone who may be writing out of a lively acquaintance with older Christians in Antioch who themselves have known the founding apostles, even if Ignatius himself has not. It is possible that Ignatius was the first gentile bishop of Antioch, and perhaps the first to be appointed in that city after the First Jewish Revolt.

▫ *Ignatius's Letter to Smyrna*

Here I would like to concentrate on two passages in the letters to Smyrna and to Rome, which for present purposes I take to be authentic. First, in a much-discussed section of his letter to Smyrna, Ignatius either quotes or paraphrases an early gospel tradition about the bodily resurrection of Jesus:

> For I know and believe that he was in the flesh even after the Resurrection. And when he came to *those around Peter* he said to them: "Take and feel me, and see that I am not a disembodied ghost." And straightaway they touched him and believed, mingling with his flesh as well as his spirit. For this reason they held even death in contempt, being proved to be above death. Now after the Resurrection he ate and drank with them as a man of flesh, even though he was in spirit united to the Father. (Ign. *Smyrn.* 3.1–3)

Although scholarship has worried about the possible docetic adversaries in view here, I am more concerned with the implications of his statement about Peter. Ignatius evidently draws on the Pauline and Synoptic (rather than Johannine) profile of Peter as the leading representative of the disciples, both before and after the resurrection. Jesus appears "to those around [*hoi peri*] Peter," some of whom may have been known at Antioch. Peter's place among the resurrection witnesses is also affirmed in Paul, in all four canonical Gospels, and in Acts. The fact that Peter and his associates "despised" death implies a possible knowledge of his martyrdom.

Despite the similarity of this passage with Luke 24:39, the source of the gospel tradition that Ignatius cites has long been disputed. Origen proposed a document called *Doctrina Petri* (*Doctrine of Peter*); Jerome suggested the *Gospel according to the Hebrews*, while Eusebius remained agnostic. Both Ignatius and Luke may have been paraphrasing an early tradition of Petrine association that identified the risen Jesus as "flesh" rather than an incorporeal ghost. The affirmation that Jesus ate and drank with them after the resurrection (Ign. *Smyrn.* 3.3) has both a general parallel in Luke 24:41–43 (cf. 24:30, 35) and an intriguingly Petrine one in Acts 10:41.

We cannot find in this text any firm conclusions about Ignatius's ability to draw on personal, or even secondhand, memories of Peter. Nevertheless, it remains significant that, well within the period under review, a specifically Petrine gospel tradition was confidently and, it seems, uncontroversially adduced against docetic interpretations of the resurrection. In that respect, Ignatius's appeal to Peter resembles Justin's: the memory of Peter, quite possibly as an apostolic martyr ("despising even death"), underpins the apostolic gospel and guards it against misinterpretation. Evidently Simon Peter represents the center of the gospel tradition like no other figure in the early church; and his association with a tradition appears to carry particular weight.

□ *Ignatius's Letter to Rome*

In our second passage, we find Ignatius explicitly appealing to local memory of the apostles. He expects this reference to the communal Roman memory of Peter and Paul to serve as an effective engagement of the readers' goodwill, while also positing his own example to emulate the apostles' fate:

> I do not give you instructions, as Peter and Paul did. They are apostles; I am just a condemned man. They are free, but I am still a slave. But if I suffer, I shall become the freedman of Jesus Christ; and I shall rise, free in him. (Ign. *Rom.* 4.3)

Ignatius immediately concedes that his own position is very different from that of the apostles—a point similarly made elsewhere (e.g., Ign. *Trall.* 3.3; *Eph.* 3.1; cf. 12.2). At the same time, Ignatius feels able to presuppose that their ministry continues to be remembered in Rome.

There is no suggestion, either here or anywhere else in early Christian literature, that Peter too, like Paul, "instructed" the Roman church in *writing*. But that means Ignatius must be speaking about apostolic instruction in *person*. The natural, almost incidental tone of Ignatius's language makes clear that he could safely take for granted such memory of the apostles' ministry when writing to the capital. The Syrian Ignatius reaches out to his Roman fellow Christians in a strikingly catholic appeal that draws on orally transmitted memory shared by Eastern and Western churches alike.

□ *What Might Ignatius Remember?*

These two texts, though often underrated, still leave us wondering what Ignatius himself might have known about Peter. While the fourth-century interpolator of the Ignatian text (who produced the so-called long recension) attempted to compensate for the author's silence by introducing a number of intriguing Petrine assertions,[16] Ignatius himself says very little even about Paul when writing to a Pauline church like that in Ephesus (but cf. Ign. *Eph.* 12.2). Might not the claim to be the imitator of Peter and Paul have been strengthened by drawing a little more deeply from the well of his own or his community's memory of these apostles?

No obvious answer to this question escapes the charge of guesswork, especially in relation to Peter. One observation may nevertheless be helpful. Peter was widely

---

16. See, e.g., Ign. *Trall.* 7.4 (Stephen assisted James, Linus helped Paul, and Anencletus and Clement served Peter); Ign. *Magn.* 10.2 (Peter and Paul laid the foundation of the church at Antioch); cf. further Ign. *Tars.* 3.3 (Peter was crucified; Paul and James were killed by the sword); and Ign. *Letter to Mary* 4.1 (Linus succeeded by Clement, a hearer of Peter and Paul).

regarded as a figure of considerable importance among Jewish Christian groups, including those with whom Ignatius found himself at odds. We have few specifics about these opponents, but their ideas have been variously associated with writings ranging from the Gospel of Matthew to the *Pseudo-Clementine* literature. In regard to Matthew, some studies have noted in Ignatius a preference for the First Evangelist's special material (M), which appears to make up a larger proportion of Ignatius's gospel traditions than even of Matthew's. This is despite the fact that Ignatius sometimes employs this source *against* the thrust of its Matthean redaction. Indeed, it has often been noted that the views of Matthew and Ignatius seem to be at loggerheads in some ways, for example regarding the Jewishness of Christian faith and practice, the importance of OT prophecies, and the locus of authority in the church. The contrast is such that some scholars have supposed Matthew to be close to the position of Ignatius's opponents, whose praxis and self-understanding were more Jewish or Judaizing.[17]

If there is anything of value in this interpretation, then it may explain Ignatius's silence even about Petrine traditions that were known to him. Matthew and the churches of Antioch and Syria plausibly regarded Peter's form of Christianity as an encouragement neither to a monoepiscopal hierarchy of governance nor to a radical break with Jewish praxis and identity—positions that Ignatius clearly favors. Although Ignatius's dates are notoriously difficult to pin down, he was most likely one of the first gentile bishops of Antioch—possibly *the* very first—appointed perhaps (as Eusebius thought) soon after the First Jewish Revolt. If there is any truth to this, then it becomes pertinent to bear in mind the implications of Antioch's severe anti-Jewish pogroms in AD 69. A gentile bishop appointed in the aftermath might well recognize an urgent need to develop the church's image in the city as a peaceful and non-threatening religious group, which would include dissociating it from the recent riots in the city and downplaying the church's Jewish origins. Analogous considerations might account for the surprising silence about the precise circumstances of the apostles' deaths in Rome in other early Christian sources, including in Mark or Luke, Acts, or *1 Clement*. In these cases, political discretion motivated by fear of reprisals might well have played a part.[18]

Like Justin and Serapion, then, Ignatius appeals to a shared, catholic memory of Peter. There are particularly strong reasons to suspect that Ignatius's appeals to the apostles are rhetorically geared to appeal to his readers' goodwill and consent rather than to blow his own or Antioch's particular trumpet. Ignatius may well be less than representative of mainstream Christian memories of Peter in Syria or perhaps even in Antioch. Nevertheless, Ignatius's Peter appears, in the company of Paul, as an apostle and martyr in Rome and functions as the leading source and authenticator of the apostolic gospel. On this front, Ignatius endorses a widely supported tradition that unites the Eastern and Western churches and draws on the NT itself.

17. See, e.g., Trevett 1984; 1992; and Sim 1998, 270–87, referencing earlier studies.
18. This is a point also argued to good effect by Bauckham 2006, 183–201.

What Did Other Syrians Remember?

For an exhaustive treatment, even of explicit sources, we would need at this point to include detailed discussion of a wide range of other documents, most of which make interesting but only passing reference to Peter. We might begin with Papias's citation of John the Elder, who asserted Mark's discipleship of Simon Peter. Other second-century Syrian sources are exceedingly difficult to pin down with confidence, either geographically or chronologically, but there are a number that help shed light on the astonishingly diverse images to which the memory of Peter gave rise. As the NT already intimates, Peter is not only a bearer of tradition but also, at times, a visionary and a representative of apocalyptic expectation. In the *Apocalypse of Peter*, composed perhaps during the Bar Kokhba revolt (AD 132–135) and subsequently influential in Eastern churches,[19] Peter instructs Clement about a range of apocalyptic topics concerned with rewards and punishments. Throughout, Peter's function as narrator gives him a privileged position, though this is not equally clear in each manuscript tradition. In the Ethiopic tradition, Christ speaks directly to Peter as the representative of the disciples (e.g., *Apoc. Pet.* 2; 15). Going a step beyond this representative role, Peter is specially commissioned by Christ to "spread . . . my gospel throughout the whole world in peace" (14). We learn in the same scene (14.4) that Peter arrived in Rome under Nero and was martyred, which in turn hastened the emperor's end.[20]

By contrast, the *Gnostic Apocalypse of Peter* (VII,3), discovered at Nag Hammadi in Egypt, represents a pro-Petrine but anti-orthodox appropriation of the apostle as a recipient of secret Gnostic revelations. Among the examples of a remarkably different account of Petrine theology are the document's polemic against views of repentance and forgiveness like those attested in the *Shepherd of Hermas* (78; cf. *Herm. Vis.* 2.2.4), against bishops and deacons (79), and especially against any theology of the crucified Christ ("a dead man"; "the first-born of the house of demons, who is under the law"; e.g., 74, 82). However, like the so-called orthodox presentation of Peter, he has again been specially chosen by the Savior to be the beginning of "the remnant" called to knowledge (71) and glorified in knowledge (*gnōsis*; 73). Peter is presented as a visionary who receives his instruction from the Savior (72–73, 82). As noted above, other Gnostic sects also asserted a direct line from Peter: Basilides claimed to have learned from Glaucias, who was, like Mark, a disciple of Peter (Clement of Alexandria, *Strom.* 7.17). What is notable is that even for "heretical" groups, Peter is the tradent of authentic faith in Jesus, however that is construed.

---

19. It is already cited in the later second century by Theophilus of Antioch, *Autol.* 2.19. Sozomen (*Hist. eccl.* 7.19) reports that it was read in Palestinian churches annually on Good Friday.

20. Unfortunately, the textual tradition is muddled at this point. The Ethiopic tradition contains a reference to Rome ("the city in the west"), but it lacks any reference to martyrdom, which is instead preserved in the Rainer Fragment. See Schneemelcher 1991–92, 2:637n43.

The Gnostic *Apocryphon of James* presents James's letter to Cerinthus about a secret revelation to Peter and James from the risen Christ, 550 days after the resurrection. Here too we find an allusion to Peter's crucifixion (5.9–20), but the document's general tenor is to subvert the traditional appeal to any apostolic memory of Jesus by appealing instead to Gnostic teachings (3, 5, 12; see also Schneemelcher 1991–92, 1:290).

In a mid-century reaction against the rise of Gnostic ideas, the *Epistle of the Apostles* portrays an orthodox and collegial rather than authoritarian Peter among the college of apostles. He is the last-named of the eleven apostles (chap. 1), and in chapters 11–12 Peter and Thomas are jointly restored as resurrection witnesses when they both put their hand in the side of the risen Jesus. In an interesting twist on Acts 12:3–9, Peter is said to have been imprisoned twice, the first time at Passover (chap. 15).

We may also mention the early Christian redaction of the *Ascension of Isaiah*, which appears to allude to the martyrdom of Peter in Rome (4.2–3). An early date, perhaps around AD 80–140, has sometimes been questioned, especially in German scholarship, alleging Christian interpolations into an originally Jewish document.[21] A Jewish Christian origin, though, seems at least equally plausible. Even if the document were interpolated, it is not clear why this should make it either late or invalid as a source, let alone dependent on the *Acts of Peter*.[22]

□ *Syrian Noncanonical Gospels*

Several noncanonical Gospels also reference Peter during our period of living memory. Among these, the eponymous *Gospel of Peter*, an early- or mid-second-century text of probably Syrian provenance, might seem to be the most plausible candidate for significant analysis, since it appears ostensibly to employ Simon Peter as what Pierre Nora calls a *lieu de mémoire* (a landmark of memory) and what Jan Assmann identifies as an *Erinnerungsfigur* (a figure constitutive of a community's cultural memory).[23] The narrative voice seems, at least implicitly, to be that of Peter, although there is very little first-person reflection. At the end of the second century, the *Gospel of Peter* featured controversially in the episcopate of Serapion at Antioch, as we saw above; it was known in the third century to Origen and appears to have affected a variety of later writers.[24] Its account of the passion is interesting for its anti-Judaism and heightened interest in miraculous features as well as for its apparent (but contested) docetism. Nevertheless, this work is dependent on all four canonical Gospels and asserts little or no distinctive knowledge of Peter, being shaped instead by martyrological, anti-Jewish,

---

21. Most recently by Zwierlein 2009, 34–35.

22. As is claimed by Zwierlein 2009, 34–35; cf. Müller 1992.

23. So, e.g., Assmann 1982, 30–38, and passim (cf. 4th ed. 2002; ET: Assmann 2012); for the application to the *Gospel of Peter*, see Kirk 2007, 142–44, 156.

24. For the recent debate on this question, see the contributions in Kraus and Nicklas 2007, 183–261.

and anti-heretical conflicts of the second century.[25] Somewhat unexpectedly, the crucifixion, burial, and resurrection of Jesus are narrated here by Peter, even though, according to the canonical accounts, he was not an eyewitness of any of these events. All the while, it eliminates *dramatis personae* such as the Roman executioners. In significant respects, then, the *Gospel of Peter* manifests not only cultural memory but also a collective *forgetting* of the inconvenient or irrelevant— a partial Christian analogy to Imperial Rome's political practice of *damnatio memoriae* (erasing memory).[26]

One unusual first-person reflection, however, occurs at 7.26–27 (in the Akhmim manuscript), where the narrator recalls that he and his associates were being sought as potential threats to the temple:

> I with my fellows was in grief, and we were wounded in our minds and would have hid ourselves; for we were sought after by them as malefactors, and as thinking to set the temple on fire. And beside all these things we were fasting, and we sat mourning and weeping night and day until the Sabbath. (M. James 1924)

Although it might appear to run against the grain of the Gospel narratives, this theme does perhaps reflect a credible awareness of the factors behind the persecution and imprisonment of Peter described in Acts 12. (There is the interesting twist of a fear of arson, possibly informed by a knowledge of the temple's demise in AD 70.) The apostle's only other explicit appearance is in the Akhmim fragment's last sentence (14.60), which reports that Peter and Andrew and "Levi the son of Alphaeus" returned to fishing. At this point the extant fragment breaks off; it may or may not be significant, therefore, that what we have of the *Gospel of Peter* contains no resurrection appearance.

All in all, this text represents a second-century popularization of the Gospel narratives with surprisingly little direct relevance for the memory of Peter, who is shown even to engage in a Good Friday fast (presumably at Passover!). Few fresh prosopographical features emerge; the narrator sticks to narrative generalities and, aside from his literary poise, neither claims nor demonstrates access to distinctive personal or collective memory.[27] At the same time, it is significant that the document does underscore this apostle's specific role as an acknowledged broker of Jesus tradition—indeed, this is why, despite the lack of concrete "memories," it represents itself in Peter's narrative voice (Foster 2007; 2010). In short, the *Gospel of Peter* has attracted considerable attention in recent years and contains much that is of interest for an understanding of second-century Christianity—but its anemic figure of Peter is little more than a flag of ecclesial convenience adorning its derivative account of the passion.

---

25. The evidence is summarized in Kirk 2007, 156–57.

26. Again, Kirk 2007, 157; also citing Assmann 1982, 224; and Schaeffer 1991, among others. I am grateful to David Lincicum for the evocative analogy with *damnatio memoriae*.

27. So also, rightly, Mara 2006, 154–55.

Several other apocryphal gospels also mention Peter only fleetingly, although one or two of these do offer additional narrative details that enhance the profile of the remembered Peter during our period. The *Gospel of the Nazarenes*, for instance, situates Jesus's logion of the camel passing through the eye of a needle (Mark 10:25 and pars.) as addressed to "Simon son of Jona," his disciple "who was sitting next to him [Jesus]" (16). More intriguingly, this gospel supplies a fascinating additional detail to the story that, as John 18:15–16 twice asserts, Peter was able to gain access to the high priest's courtyard because Peter's companion (often identified by commentators as the Beloved Disciple) was "known to the high priest." The *Gospel of the Nazarenes* claims to know that this was because this disciple supplied fish to the household (33). It is, nevertheless, impossible to decide whether this reflects a Jerusalem-based memory of local tradition or merely a romantic speculation based on the assumption that the disciple concerned was John, junior partner and joint heir of Zebedee's fishing business on the Sea of Galilee.

Among other Jewish Christian sources, Epiphanius cites the *Gospel of the Ebionites* to the effect that Jesus *narrates* the call of his first disciples at the house of "Simon surnamed Peter" (frag. 2). This passing but intriguing comment reinforces an impression, initiated by the Gospels and confirmed by the reception history and archaeological remains of Capernaum, of the importance of Peter's house in the ministry of Jesus.

The extant *Gospel of Thomas*, whose origins are probably in second-century Egypt or Syria, mentions Peter once in passing as having called Jesus "a just messenger" (13). The only other occurrence is in the very last logion (114), perhaps an appendix, where a startlingly misogynistic-sounding Peter says to Jesus,

"Make Mary leave us, for females don't deserve life." Jesus said, "Look, I will guide her to make her male. . . . Every female who makes herself male will enter the kingdom of Heaven."

We cannot here enter into a discussion of the unusual gender theories of *Thomas* (cf. 15, 79–80; 61); suffice it to say that the theme of a misogynistic Peter finds expression in other Gnosticizing sources. Among these, the post-Easter dialogues of the *Gospel of Mary* feature Andrew and Peter doubting Mary Magdalene's report of the risen Jesus's secret revelation to her; this distrust reduces Mary to despair. Levi, in turn, challenges Peter as always having had a hasty temper and speaking like an "adversary."[28]

A puzzling Jewish tradition of doubtful origin and rather later date is nevertheless worth mentioning. In the early medieval *Toledot Yeshu* traditions (which take up a number of much earlier polemical traditions), Simon Peter surfaces as a righteous Jew who craftily feigns conversion to Christianity and uses his position of influence to protect the Jews from gentile attack. It may be of interest,

28. For further discussion, see Tuckett 2007, 19–20, 72, 185–203; also cf. Heckel 1999, 65.

though hardly compelling for our purposes, that this tradition already occurs in
the very earliest recension of the *Toledot* (ca. AD 500) and recurs in a variety of
other later documents. A positive picture of Peter also surfaces in Jewish traditions that attribute to him the composition of synagogue prayers such as the
Nishmat Kol Hay (Soul/Breath of all that lives), and various *piyyutim* (liturgical
poems).[29]

A Syrian origin of many of these texts remains plausible, though very difficult
to establish; in several cases, scholars have instead seen indications for Egypt (e.g.,
Gospel of Mary). Many, indeed most, of these texts presuppose knowledge of
all four Gospels; in some cases they are also familiar with the longer ending of
Mark or other later developments.[30] Specific interest in Simon Peter is difficult to
confirm, except perhaps in the case of the *Gospel of Peter* and the *Apocalypse of
Peter*, and negatively in certain Gnostic anti-Petrine passages. These sources do
attest the memory of Peter in the second century, even though there may be few if
any biographical or other details of historical interest. All in all, it is interesting
how few of the Petrine texts—like the *Gospel of Peter*, the *Apocalypse of Peter*,
or the *Preaching of Peter*—reveal much for Petrine memory, except the *fact* of its
importance.

One important set of texts remains to be discussed more fully, namely, the
Pseudo-Clementine writings. Discussing these texts is important not because they
give a clear view of special Petrine memory but because of the way these texts
have been treated by previous scholars in reconstructing early Christianity and
the reception of Peter.

□ *The Pseudo-Clementines*

The *Pseudo-Clementine* writings, a voluminous pseudepigraphal collection
associated with Clement of Rome but probably originating in Syria,[31] have long
been viewed by scholars as the classic source for a particularly pro-Petrine and
anti-Pauline Jewish Christianity. F. C. Baur (1792–1860) considered the *Pseudo-
Clementine* writings to be clear proof of his theory that early Christianity was
marked by a deep rift between Pauline and Petrine factions:

> From a work written in the second half of the second century, the pseudo-Clementine
> Homilies, we gather that even then the Jewish Christians had not yet learned to
> forgive the harsh word which the apostle Paul had spoken of the man whom they
> regarded as the chief of the apostles. (Baur 1878, 55)

29. Among Jewish Palestinian texts, it has also been suggested that rabbinic polemic against
a mysterious figure known as Ben Stada, occasionally linked with Jesus or Jewish Christianity,
may in fact have in view Simon Peter; but this suggestion has not thus far gained widespread
support. See Schwartz 1995; cf. Bockmuehl 2010a, 136–37.

30. On an earlier note, those who believe in the sayings source Q, which is usually thought
to be Syrian, may find it interesting that Peter does not feature here at all.

31. For a more detailed treatment of the *Pseudo-Clementine* writings, see Bockmuehl 2010a,
94–113.

In this reading, the polemical attacks on Simon Magus (Acts 8:9–24), who is presented in these texts as a heresiarch and Peter's main opponent, are seen as thinly veiled attacks on Paul.[32] Further, Baur and many of his sympathizers considered it obvious that the *Pseudo-Clementine* writings, as anti-Pauline and Jewish Christian, were connected with the Ebionites (cf. Irenaeus, *Haer.* 1.26.2). However, recent discussion of this point places such a connection in serious doubt (e.g., Carleton Paget 2010; Jones 2003).

The texts that comprise the *Pseudo-Clementine* writings are complex and display several stages of development, even if the exact shape of this development is not clear.[33] The collection includes the so-called *Homilies* and *Recognitions*, which seem to be two different recensions of a common base text (often dubbed "*G*" for *Grundschrift*) that was most likely composed in Syria around AD 200–250. Appended to the *Homilies* were three shorter writings: two epistles to James the brother of Jesus (one from Peter [*Epistula Petri*] and one from Clement [*Epistula Clementis*]) and a description of the reception of Peter's letter called the *Contestatio* (*Cont.*). The G source evidently already contained both the Petrine narrative frame and the polemic against Simon Magus. In the third and fourth centuries, the *Pseudo-Clementines* were heavily redacted by a pro-Arian scribe, and the texts we have today manifest a variety of Jewish Christian concerns. For our purposes, however, what is important is the presentation of Peter and his conflict with Simon Magus, the false prophet or false messiah.

In these texts, Peter is presented as the authorized apostle of Jesus Christ, the "rock" that grounds the church, and is described as one who "has penetrated most deeply into the divine wisdom" (*Ps.-Clem. Rec.* 1.12.6). Peter's teaching ranges widely across theological and moral topics, presenting Jesus as the true prophet in the line of Adam (*Ps.-Clem. Hom.* 1.19; 3.21.1–2; 3.26.1–6). The Petrine ministry is traced from Caesarea to Rome as he opposes Simon Magus and preaches the gospel (*Ps.-Clem. Hom.* 7.1–8.7). Interestingly, the *Epistula Petri* and the *Contestatio* are particularly replete with anti-gentile rhetoric, perhaps in connection with the gentiles who rejected Peter's preaching in favor of "the man who is the enemy" (*Ps.-Clem. EP* 2.3). This stands in contrast to the position espoused in *Ps.-Clem. Rec.* 1.27–71, widely reputed to be a separate Jewish Christian source, a kind of alternative "early Jerusalem church history." There the gentiles are explicitly called *into* the people of God and the preaching of the kingdom is sent into the whole world (*Ps.-Clem. Rec.* 1.42, 50). The frequency with which Peter refers to relations between Christians and Jews suggests that he was himself a key figure in this discussion, both during and after the period of living memory. Although Peter is often portrayed as following the law in teaching and practice, he is also critical at certain points: sacrifice was a temporary concession to be supplanted by baptism (*Ps.-Clem. Rec.*

---

32. For a recent statement of this position, see Strecker 1992, 490–91, who also incorporates this view into the structure and content of his translation (535–36).

33. See Drijvers 1990; Jones 1995; Strecker 1992.

1.36–37, 39) and Satan caused several "false pericopes" to be included in the writing of the law after Moses's death (*Ps.-Clem. Hom.* 2.38.1–2; 3.48.2; 3.50.1–51.3). In sum, Peter is presented as *the* center of the Christian movement, the deference to James in the *Epistula Petri* and the *Epistula Clementis* notwithstanding.

In the treatment of Peter's conflict with Simon Magus, Peter is portrayed as the chief opponent of heresy, which is effectively represented by Simon. While this conflict is also preserved in the *Acts of Peter*, Justin, Irenaeus, and Hippolytus,[34] it is here that scholars have long seen an anti-Pauline polemic at play, as noted above. The subject of the conflicts between Peter and Simon concerns theology, cosmology, and moral, or even halakic, practice. Peter accuses Simon of falsely claiming to be a temporary apostle based on visions of the risen Jesus (*Ps.-Clem. Hom.* 17.13.1; 19.4), a point that is often alleged to reflect Paul's own account of his commissioning (Gal. 1:1, 11–12). Further, the fact that Peter claims that Simon "resisted" him and called him "condemned" has commonly been seen as an obvious allusion to Gal. 2:11–14 (*Ps.-Clem. Hom.* 17.194–96). In light of these passages, then, the reference to "the man who is the enemy" (*Ps.-Clem. EP* 2.3) is typically taken as another reference to Paul, who is then seen as leading the gentiles astray from the truth (cf. *Ps.-Clem. Hom.* 2.17.3–5). Further, Simon Magus lacks authority because he is not supported by James in Jerusalem, another oft-cited link with Paul (e.g., Ehrman 2006, 79–80; Stanton 2007, 314).

However, while an anti-Pauline bias is possible, there are a number of impediments to the Simon–Paul equation. First, the texts themselves nowhere make this connection. The one place where there is a clear reference to Paul (*Ps.-Clem. Rec.* 1.70–71) presents him as the pre-Christian *Saul*, who primarily opposes James, and Peter only secondarily. Indeed, in this scene, which to be sure does not portray Saul in a positive light (he is introduced as "a certain hostile man"), Simon Magus and Saul are explicitly *differentiated*; Saul himself condemns Simon as a sorcerer (*Ps.-Clem. Rec.* 1.70.2). This explicit differentiation between Saul and Simon has implications for attempts to find Paul behind the phrase "the man who is the enemy" in *Ps.-Clem. EP* 2.3, especially if one takes seriously the integrity of the epistle's placement alongside the *Pseudo-Clementine* romances that feature Simon Magus as the clear antagonist.[35]

Second, Simon's preaching, opposed by Peter, contains little that could be construed as Pauline. Most of it seems generally Gnostic rather than Pauline and

34. Justin, *1 Apol.* 26; 56; *2 Apol.* 15; *Dial.* 120.6; cf. Irenaeus, *Haer.* 1.23.1–4; Hippolytus, *Haer.* 4.51.3–14; 6.7–20; 10.12.

35. In *Ps.-Clem. EP* 2.3, "Peter" refers to the lawless and trifling doctrine of *tou echthrou anthrōpou* ("the hostile man" or "the enemy," with the definite article). For *Ps.-Clem. Rec.* 1.70.1, we do not have a Greek original, but the ancient translations both speak of "a certain hostile man" or "a man who was hostile / an enemy" (Syriac *ḥd 'nš' d'twhy B'lzbb'*; Latin *homo quidam inimicus*) and who appears in the temple with a group of followers. More strikingly, while Peter's enemy in the later narrative of the *Homilies* and *Recognitions* is clearly Simon Magus, the devilish opponent of *Rec.* 1.70–71 is unmistakably Saul, who opposes James and castigates the church as a group "deceived by Simon, a magician."

lacks any Jewish apocalyptic framework, so important for Paul, or consistent references to Scripture. Simon rejects basic Pauline positions such as the resurrection from the dead (e.g., *Ps.-Clem. Rec.* 1.54), the goodness of the creator (e.g., *Ps.-Clem. Rec.* 2.37, 53), and the divine sonship of Christ (*Ps.-Clem. Rec.* 2.49), and he even sets himself up as the Messiah (e.g., *Ps.-Clem. Rec.* 1.72; cf. 2.49; 3.47). These positions are difficult to square with any other known picture of Paul, "orthodox" or "heretical."

Thus, the dispute between Peter and Simon Magus functions to imbue previous traditions of this conflict (in, e.g., *Acts of Peter*) with the paradigmatic force of an anti-heretical treatise. Simon Magus is a fictionalized literary type who combines elements of heresiarch and antichrist, a view further supported by the evident relation between the *Pseudo-Clementines* and the ancient novel.[36] In the end, Peter is remembered as the keystone of the early Christian movement who concerns himself with the unity and purity of the church. His teaching is normative, and he faithfully interprets and passes on the law, fighting the threat of heresy embodied in Simon Magus. For the *Pseudo-Clementines*, Peter is both the repository and embodiment of the apostolic gospel tradition.

Peter in John and Matthew

We turn now to the Gospels of John and Matthew, in that order. These texts contain our fullest narrative accounts of the way Peter was remembered in the East at the end of the first century.

Peter according to John

Writing perhaps in Asia Minor not long before Ignatius, the author of the Fourth Gospel nevertheless has a rightful place in any discussion of Petrine memory in greater Syria. While the actual narrative of this Gospel shows few if any demonstrable connections with Asia Minor, it does manifest many such links with Judea, Samaria, Galilee, and Gaulanitis. The Fourth Evangelist's repeated and explicit appeal to apostolic eyewitness memory of Jesus begins, interestingly, with the temple cleansing, which John introduces as soon as the disciples are called to faith and to witness the revelation of his glory at Cana (1:35–51; 2:11): "After he was raised from the dead, his disciples remembered that he had said this; and they believed the scripture and the word that Jesus had spoken" (2:22).

More important still, the Gospel's rhetorical stance relies crucially on repeated appeals to the Beloved Disciple and his *personal memory*—especially, perhaps exclusively, of events and locations surrounding the passion and resurrection in the vicinity of Jerusalem. A good many of these reminiscences involve Simon

---

36. See Edwards 1992; cf. Barilier 2008, esp. 21–22.

Peter; in fact, there are only two stories about Peter before the Last Supper, one involving his call and the other his confession (1:40–44; 6:67–69). For the Gospel's author, the only identified source of Petrine memory remains the Beloved Disciple himself, who may plausibly be the final editor's teacher.

But what might this mean? Clearly, the Gospel is well aware of rival ways to remember and tell the story of Jesus (1:11; 6:66; 7:25–52; 9:24–34). The evangelist's explicitly self-involving, unreservedly invested testimony must be heard *as such* in order to be intelligible. This is a task to which classic biblical scholarship's historicism has amply shown itself to be ill-suited—though Richard Bauckham and others have attempted over the past decade to do justice to the testimony and witness aspects of this Gospel (Bauckham 2007).

□ *Peter in John's Book of Signs (1–12)*

As we noted a moment ago, Peter appears only twice in the entire first half of the Gospel. Both of these passages adapt episodes known from the Synoptic tradition. Indeed, it appears that the Fourth Evangelist assumes his readers' familiarity not only with Peter but also, at least in outline, with the Synoptic Jesus tradition. This relatively familiar point has been taken further by Richard Bauckham in an important analysis of "John for Readers of Mark" (Bauckham 1998b), showing the range of circumstances and individuals whose familiarity is similarly taken for granted and who therefore need no introduction.

Peter's call (1:40–44). Familiarity easily dulls our eyes to Peter's surprising entry onto the Johannine stage. This Gospel's most prominent named disciple is never introduced at all, but assumed to be familiar: "One of the two who heard John speak, and followed him, was Andrew, Simon Peter's brother" (1:40). Peter himself, it seems, is already known: the point of the reference here is that, as in 6:8, Andrew is most easily identifiable in relation to his more famous brother. Thus, far from Peter being sidelined in favor of actors like Andrew or Philip, as some have suggested, Peter's position is a point of reference that can be taken for granted from the outset, as the implied readers know him already. This deceptively simple point is of great significance for our purposes. The Fourth Evangelist sees Simon Peter as a familiar character before the narrative even begins. The only others previously treated in this way are God, Jesus, and Moses (but not, for example, John the Baptist [1:6]).

At the same time, it is Andrew who leads Peter to Jesus as "the Messiah" (*ton Messian*, 1:41). This constitutes an interesting departure from the Synoptic tradition—a conflict already noted by Origen (*Comm. Jo.* 10.6). In the Synoptic account, it is Peter who first articulates the disciples' faith in Jesus as Messiah. In John, Andrew, rather than Peter, is the first disciple to be called.

At this point, Peter remains silent. Jesus greets the man called "Simon Peter" with the words "You are Simon son of John. You shall be called Cephas." The most natural way of reading this is to suppose that Jesus already knows Simon and that Jesus himself first applies the name Cephas. This would be consistent with my earlier suggestion that Simon already had the name Peter but that Jesus first called him by the otherwise unparalleled Aramaic name Cephas.[37]

John's interpretation of Peter's name remains more allusive than Matthew's, but early modern translations quite reasonably assumed *hermēneuetai* in 1:42 to denote *meaning* rather than *naming*—hence "Cephas, which is by interpretation, a stone" (so the KJV; cf. Luther). John wants his readers to understand Jesus's naming of Simon as "Cephas," "rock." The otherwise unparalleled epithet Cephas, in other words, is here a name of programmatic significance: what Peter will be called designates what he will be.

The Aramaic form of the name Cephas, then, along with the episode's unexpectedly early and non-Galilean placement, suggests that the Fourth Gospel here fills out the partial Synoptic parallels (Matt. 16:18; Mark 3:16; Luke 6:14) by taking up an independent Palestinian Petrine account of its own.[38]

Peter's confession (6:67–69). At the end of the controversial "Bread of Heaven" discourse, many of Jesus's own followers turn away and abandon him (6:66). At first, the scene is somewhat reminiscent of the Synoptic narrative of Jesus's question about his identity at Caesarea Philippi (Mark 8:27–30 and pars.).

Here, Jesus turns to the Twelve (6:67, 70, 71) and asks them the rhetorical question, "Do you also wish to go away?" This passage is the Fourth Gospel's first mention of them and the only time the Twelve are explicitly in view as a group, just as nowhere does John speak of "apostles" (though note 13:16). As C. H. Dodd (1963, 220–22) already noted, the tension of this passage could reflect an authentic reminiscence of a deep crisis in the ministry of Jesus.

In reply to Jesus's query, it is Peter who speaks for the Twelve, in a confession of Jesus's messianic identity that is at once strongly reminiscent of the Synoptics and yet at some remove from them. Quite apart from certain notable differences in form and narrative context,[39] Peter's response is deeply Johannine: the Twelve have nowhere else to go because there is no one but Jesus who has "words of eternal life," whom they have "come to believe and know" as the messianic "Holy One of God" (6:68–69). At the same time, unlike the Synoptics, John does *not* use the term *Christos* in this connection.

The biggest surprise, however, comes in Jesus's response. He gives no direct reply to Simon Peter at all. Nor, however, does the Johannine Jesus predict his passion (unlike all three Synoptic parallels) either here or at Peter's rebuke of that prediction (like Mark and Matthew). Instead, we are confronted with a reaction by Jesus to Peter that is hard to relate to the Markan and Matthean accounts: "Did

37. For Peter's names, see the discussion of Matt. 16 below and chap. 2 above.

38. We can be less certain how closely familiar the Fourth Evangelist is with the apparently Galilean name of Peter's father Yonah, which is not otherwise attested as an abbreviation of Yoḥanan.

39. As Bauer (1933, 102) rightly observed, the closest similarity in narrative context is with the account in Luke 9:18–22, where the confession follows immediately after the feeding of the 5,000 near Bethsaida (9:10–17; cf. John 6:1–14).

I not choose you, the Twelve? Yet one of you is a devil [*diabolos*]" (6:70). Could this be some thinly veiled, polemically garbled literary echo of Jesus rebuking Peter as Satan in Mark 8:33 (cf. Matt. 16:2), censuring him without praise? That seems far-fetched in view of Peter's wholly undiabolical confession here—not to mention the obvious fact that on this reading the Johannine tradition would end up disowning itself in 6:71. In other words, the "devil" of John 6:70 cannot be the Peter of Caesarea Philippi. If a memory is represented here, it is not of Peter but of Jesus's dawning realization that even the Twelve will not support him unconditionally: one of them will turn on Jesus and make common cause with his enemies. The Twelve are handpicked, but even they can be unreliable.

□ Peter in John's Book of Glory (13–21)

Up to now we have seen a largely literary and theological reflection on Petrine memory, with few indications of fresh or independent reminiscences. In the second part of the Gospel, John turns both to more intimate instruction of the disciples and to the public declaration of Jesus having "finished" his work in public view now that his "hour" has come. The theme of memory is here most explicitly associated with Jesus and the work of the Paraclete, but it is explicitly mediated too by the testimony of the Beloved Disciple.

The footwashing (13:6–10) and the identity of the betrayer (13:23–24). The Last Supper, though not overtly concerned with Passover, turns out to be an episode of crucial importance for Petrine memory in that it is the first to feature both Peter and the Beloved Disciple, the stated guarantor behind the Fourth Gospel's Jesus tradition. While the Beloved Disciple has remained in the background thus far, two exchanges—over the footwashing (13:6–10) and over the identity of the betrayer (13:23–24)—bring this disciple into the picture in a way that has famously preoccupied commentators, artists, and popular writers ever since.

In the first episode, about the nature of Christlike service, Peter appears in his customary combination of reluctance and zeal, as someone who gets it right the second time around. The reference to Passover purity is unmistakable and may possibly have relevance for the Gospel's view of the Torah's purity legislation, in which case there could be a Petrine echo with similar concerns in Acts 10. But on balance that seems far-fetched. The point of the passage is neither Petrine nor halakic, as the exposition in 13:12–20 shows.

In the second vignette, Peter motions to the disciple "whom Jesus loved" and who "was reclining next to him" to ask Jesus who would betray him (cf. v. 21). That question, which in the Synoptics is asked by all the disciples (Matt. 26:22// Mark 14:19; cf. Luke 22:23), receives an answer that is similar and yet more specific than in Mark and Luke: it is Judas Iscariot, and the sooner he gets on with his plan, the better (13:26–27).

Once again, the Fourth Gospel's privileged picture of the Beloved Disciple's relationship with Jesus makes issues of historicity impossible to resolve with certainty, and Peter's evident dependence on this disciple's intervention with

Jesus seems altogether in keeping with the author's tendency to reduce Peter's prominence. It is also true that the Synoptic disciples' ignorance and confusion on this point might be found conducive to a characteristic scenario of Johannine one-upmanship, in which the Beloved Disciple's proximity to Jesus supplies what is wanting in Peter and the Twelve.

That disciple's relationship with Jesus, of course, lies at the heart of the Johannine claim to authenticity and truthful witness. For all its apparent predictability, therefore, the picture of 13:23–24 is not easily explained away. The Fourth Evangelist wants to show himself conversant with the Synoptic tradition and affirming of Peter's episcopal role in the larger church (21:15–19). Given this ultimately non-sectarian rhetorical and ecclesial stance, however, the truthfulness of assertions about well-known episodes in the Passion Narrative must inevitably impinge on the Gospel's success among the writer's own community and a wider Christian readership. It may be, as has been suggested, that the Beloved Disciple was one of the leading Jerusalem-based followers of Jesus during the earthly ministry. He may have had priestly connections (hence 18:15–16) and perhaps even served as the host at the Last Supper in the upper room, as some have argued.

This situation shows that during this period, claims of alternative tradition could still be, and were in fact, liable to challenge and correction, not only from authoritative written sources but also by appeal to personal living memory. In this respect, it is important that no significant evidence of mainstream suspicion against the Fourth Gospel's account emerges in the period we are studying. Twentieth-century scholarly theories about the Gospel's supposed unpopularity in orthodox circles should finally be laid to rest: despite some Gnostic interest in the Gospel and its apparent rejection by the anti-Montanist sect of *Alogi* in the late second century,[40] it was an integral part of the fourfold Gospel in orthodox circles from at least the mid-second century.[41]

This implies that the Beloved Disciple's special relationship with Jesus likely constituted an authentic part of the Johannine community's living memory, which went uncontested by the tradition of the wider church. The Gospel's claims about this disciple's relative precedence over Peter in certain aspects of the Passion Narrative therefore merit sympathetic interpretation.

Following Jesus (13:36–38). After Judas's departure from the Last Supper, Simon Peter again fails to understand Jesus when, after leaving his disciples the "new commandment" of love, he tells them he is going "where you cannot come" (John 13:33–35; cf. *Gos. Thom.* 24). Somewhat reminiscent of Synoptic parallels (cf. Mark 14:29–31 and pars.), Peter is told that he cannot "follow" Jesus now; although here, uniquely, we also learn that he will in fact "follow later." This latter phrase evidently alludes to Peter's martyrdom, which is confirmed by the comparison of 13:37 and 21:19. Despite Peter's misunderstanding, the author does not demean

---

40. Cf. Irenaeus, *Haer.* 3.2.9; Epiphanius, *Pan.* 51.3.1–3, passim.
41. Charles E. Hill (2004) has persuasively demonstrated these points.

his significance. Indeed, the very shape of Peter's question expresses a praiseworthy desire to be a true disciple. Instead, the contrast is between Jesus's perfection and Peter's slowness to grasp the divine purpose for which Jesus has been sent; at this stage, far from giving his life for Jesus, Peter will in fact deny him (13:38).

The predicted martyrdom of Peter seems to be the primary Johannine contribution for our purposes. The evangelist may simply wish to reflect on the significance of the familiar mainstream tradition here. Something like what Peter claims in Mark ("even if I must die with you, I will not deny you") has been recast by the Fourth Evangelist so as to bring out a double significance: although at present false, this promise will eventually come true. It is precisely here that twentieth-century NT scholarship's customary dichotomizing between the supposed flimsiness of "tradition" and the bold editorial hand of "redaction" shows up its methodological inadequacy. As Dale Allison once noted about this dynamic, "We cannot separate chemical compounds with a knife. Nor can we tell at the end of a river what came from the fountainhead and what from later tributaries" (Allison 1998, 33). In this respect, the more plastic evidence for living memory turns out to be useful in providing color and depth to source-starved, two-dimensional snapshots of authenticity in the Jesus tradition. The Johannine narrative relates the events in terms of their effective significance—reading the beginning from the end, and each part in light of the whole story, as this emerges in the memory of the living witness.

In the high priest's courtyard (18:10–27). We turn next to the events surrounding Jesus's arrest and Peter's denial in the courtyard of the high priest. The Fourth Gospel uniquely reveals what readers of the three Synoptics (Mark 14:47 and pars.) will not already know: the anonymous disciple who cuts off the ear of the high priest's servant is none other than Peter. The attacker is rebuked somewhat, as in Luke (22:51), but less elaborately than in Matthew (26:52–54). This Gospel uniquely reveals the victim's name as Malchus, although unlike Luke (22:51), it does not suggest that Jesus healed him.

Commentators tend to see no obvious reasons to deny the essential facticity of this narrative. "Malchus" is a well-attested Palestinian name, and while the identification of Peter as the sword-bearer certainly suits the Gospel's penchant for exposing Peter's tendency to get things wrong at the first attempt, no particular anti-Petrine conclusions appear to be drawn. Here, the Fourth Gospel merely supplies what readers of the Synoptics might not have known.

Peter himself reappears a few verses later in a role that is more familiar from the rest of the Jesus tradition. As in the Synoptics, Peter has followed Jesus from a distance into the courtyard of the high priest (though here this is Annas, the emeritus and the present incumbent's father-in-law), but once again we find that the Fourth Gospel introduces considerable additional detail. Here Peter evidently enters the courtyard with the help of another unnamed disciple. This disciple's possible identification with the Beloved Disciple is an attractive possibility, but this remains contested among commentators. The unnamed person arranges Peter's entry into the courtyard through connections with the high priest's household or at least, we may surmise, with the female servant in charge of the door: nego-tiations with her lead to Peter's admission (18:16–17).[42] This same doorkeeper immediately turns out to be the woman who, as in the Synoptics, first challenges Peter as one of Jesus's disciples, apparently as soon as he walks through the gate (unlike Mark 14:67; Luke 22:55); only then do other bystanders follow suit as he joins them by the warming fire. Evocatively interlacing this episode with Peter's failure just a little earlier in the garden, the Fourth Evangelist identifies the last questioner before the cock's crow as a relative of the hapless Malchus (18:26).

The fact that all three of Peter's denials here (18:17, 25–27) are less fiercely insistent than in Mark and Matthew allows few conclusions about Petrine memory, though it seems compatible with theories that consider this Gospel to have been available to Luke.[43] As in the Synoptic parallels, the focus throughout is clearly on Jesus, with Peter's denial serving more as a minor counterpoint. Where Jesus confesses, Peter denies, and what he denies is not so much his earlier confession of Jesus as Messiah but rather his own desire to follow the only one who has the words of eternal life (cf. above on 6:67; 13:36–37).

John omits any mention of the Synoptic Peter's sudden self-awareness or re-morseful departure from the scene. The apostle simply drops out of sight, to reappear only after the resurrection, and his repentance is also left until chapter 21.

At the empty tomb (20:2–6). Two post-resurrection settings involve Peter: the first is his visit to the tomb with, and a few paces behind, the Beloved Disciple (20:2–6); the second is the extended encounter with the risen Jesus at the Sea of Galilee (21:2–7, 11–21). Neither has exact Synoptic parallels, although we must note that in the first episode, it is again Luke who offers the closest link with a note about Peter's "running" (*edramen*) to the empty tomb and "stooping" (*parakypsas*) to find only the linen grave clothes (*othonia*); all three of these terms are unique to the resurrection accounts of Luke 24:12 and John 20. Since Luke is the only Synoptic evangelist to offer any explicit post-resurrection story of Peter, it seems appropriate to wonder whether Luke has drawn on a Johannine and more Jerusalem-based memory, regarding it as valuable for his own project of conveying the carefully investigated truth through an "accurate and orderly" account (Luke 1:3–4).

Once again Peter lags a little behind the Beloved Disciple in several respects, though not systematically so. Peter runs more slowly and thus reaches the tomb after his companion but enters it before him and is able to confirm that the grave cloths are folded up separately (20:6–7). Only of the Beloved Disciple is it said that upon entering the tomb, he "saw and believed" (20:8)—a classic Johannine phrase. (It is, of course, also the case that unlike Peter and the Twelve, only the Beloved Disciple and the Marys witness the crucifixion [19:25–27].)

---

42. See above for the suggestion in the *Gospel of the Nazarenes* that this disciple was in fact the high priest's fishmonger.

43. See, e.g., Morgan 2002; Gregory 2006, on Luke as the last Gospel.

As in all three Synoptic Gospels, it is Mary (elsewhere together with other women) who becomes the first resurrection witness (also note Mark 16:9).[44] Peter and the Beloved Disciple do *not* meet the risen Lord at this point, although they presumably do so in the episodes reported later that same day and again a week later (20:19–25, 26–29). *None* of the Gospels affirms the Petrine primacy of creedal formulations like 1 Cor. 15:5 (unless perhaps Luke 24:34 hints at it),[45] but this is not anti-Petrine or anti-patriarchal; instead, the exuberance and complexity of post-resurrection memory[46] are intelligible in dialogue with the requirements of the apologetic and creedal contexts that may have laid greater stress on the formally authorized witnesses beginning with Peter and the Twelve.

With the risen Jesus in Galilee (21:2–7, 11–21). The last Petrine narrative in the Fourth Gospel occurs in the extended resurrection appearance of chapter 21, an apparent appendix that is without parallel in the Synoptics (despite possible echoes of 21:2–14 in Luke's Petrine call narrative: Luke 5:1–11; cf. 4:38; 6:13–14). Seven disciples are present: "Simon Peter, Thomas the Twin, Nathanael of Cana in Galilee, the sons of Zebedee, and two others of his disciples" (21:2). Speculation has long kept scholars busy explaining the significance of this group, above all because one of them must apparently have been the Beloved Disciple (21:20, explicitly identified as the same one who featured in the Last Supper). Both the unambiguous (if unspecific) Galilean lakeside location and the identification of the previously unmentioned sons of Zebedee presuppose familiarity with Mark (14:28; 16:7) or Matthew (26:32; 28:7, 10, 16), though not Luke (who has no post-Easter place for Galilee).

Simon Peter seems cast in a pragmatic role. It is Peter who makes the first move to go fishing, and the others join in, though contrary to many commentators there is no decision here to return to his former life. What follows is a story with elements reminiscent of the miraculous catch of fish in Luke 5: Jesus, who is here on the shore rather than in the boat, tending the distinctively identified coal fire,[47] instructs Peter after a night's unproductive fishing to "cast" the net on the other side (rather than "let it down"). They immediately enclose a great quantity of fish—for Luke, enough to break the nets and swamp even the boat that comes to help (5:6–7), and for John, 153 fish, which cannot be hauled in but must be dragged to shore (21:6, 8, 11). If there is a link between Luke and John on this point, it seems likely to be oral rather than written, possibly based on shared tradition.

As before, it is the Beloved Disciple's insight that prompts Peter as the action man: the person on the beach "is the Lord" (21:7). Peter casts off inhibition and swims a hundred yards back to shore, where, prompted by Jesus, he helps to haul in the catch (21:10–11).

44. On this issue, see, e.g., O'Collins 1987.
45. Note also Mark 16:7; contrast Mark 16:9, in the longer ending.
46. See also my remarks in Bockmuehl 2001a, 110–11.
47. The NT has the word *anthrakia* (charcoal fire) only here and in John 18:18, at the scene of Peter's threefold denial. Cf. 4 Macc. 9:20; Sir. 11:32.

After breakfast, Jesus turns to Peter to effect their reconciliation and Peter's special commission, which, unlike in Matt. 16, is introduced here for the first time. Peter's appointment (*not* restoration) to a pastoral role by his threefold fireside declaration of love is clearly Johannine in its carefully designed literary cast, evoking not only Peter's earlier threefold fireside denial (18:18) but also Jesus's first address to him in 1:42 as "son of John." And the scene shows the chief shepherd of John 10 entrusting the care of his sheep[48] to the one who, for all his failings, remains the leading member of the Twelve. As such, does Peter love Jesus "more than these" other disciples (21:15)? Peter now understands, at long last and with sadness (21:17), that this question is not answerable by his customary protestations of unswerving loyalty, since these have too recently proved hollow. Instead, three times he avoids the comparison and answers transparently, from the heart. And three times that transparent bareness is clothed by the charge to follow Jesus by tending and feeding his flock.

What does this charge mean? In this context, it certainly does not intend to make Peter the sole "Vicar of Christ on earth" to the exclusion of all other disciples, as some older Roman Catholic exegesis fancied. But neither does it make his commission simply identical to that of any other Christian leader, then and now, as has sometimes been the preference of conservative Protestant exegetes. In Jewish and OT texts, the theme of God as shepherd delegating authority to human religious or political "shepherds" is a commonplace (see, e.g., Jer. 23:1–5; Ezek. 34:2–24; Zech. 11:3–17), and within this received imagery, any singling out of just one divinely approved shepherd of Israel usually concerns specifically the Davidic messiah rather than one of his servants (2 Sam. 5:2; 7:7; 1 Chron. 11:2). The NT likewise affirms this derivative role for Christian leaders as shepherds more generally, including in 1 Peter.[49] In this respect, there is no implication here that Peter is the *only* proper shepherd; nor is there any hint of a succession of Petrine ministry so defined.

All this leads one to wonder whether we are dealing here with a literary type-casting intended merely to reconcile the Johannine Peter with the supposedly more "catholic" or "ecclesial" Petrine tradition, as has often been supposed. Three considerations, however, must nevertheless give us pause. First, for all the perceived narrative parallels with the denials of chapter 18, the threefold repetition of the pastoral commission remains unique in the entire gospel tradition, and it clearly carries considerable weight for its explicit association in this context with the remembered testimony of the Beloved Disciple (21:20–24). Second, adding to this is the fact that the charge is addressed to someone of Peter's stature and profile. Not only has he been prominent throughout this Gospel, but the archaic-sounding address "son of John" appears to link this text by way of *inclusio* to his

48. Despite unnumbered sermons to the contrary, no discernible significance appears to attach to the variation of the expressions for love and the feeding of sheep in 21:15–17.

49. E.g., Acts 20:28; 1 Pet. 2:25; 5:3–4; 1 Tim. 3:4–5; Heb. 13:17, 20. See also Culpepper 2010 on Peter in John 21 as the *exemplary* disciple.

first appearance in 1:42, where he was identified as the one who "will be called Cephas."[50] And third, none of the other six disciples present is included in this charge, not even the Beloved Disciple, whose inclusion as witness would have carried significant authority in the community. We must not underestimate the rhetorical implication of this singling out of Peter as the chief apostolic shepherd.

The closing scene, comparing the different fates of the two disciples, also explicitly contains the Fourth Gospel's concluding appeal to living memory (21:23). Peter is told not to concern himself with the question of whether the Beloved Disciple will survive until the *parousia*, the return of Christ (21:22). Peter's own future, as commentators are generally content to acknowledge, will involve crucifixion in old age (21:18), an interpretation well understood in sources as early as the mid-second century.[51] In 21:19, the evangelist nicely alludes to the community's memory of this prophecy's fulfillment. A wealth of ancient pagan as well as Christian texts associated the "stretching out of the hands" with crucifixion, as indeed the sequence of verse 18 appears to reflect the prisoner's arms being tied to the cross-beam before being led to execution.[52]

The answer of the Beloved Disciple's fate is one that the final author immediately finds himself having to explain, evidently in light of this founder figure's recent demise: he will remain alive if that is Jesus's will (21:22–24). Peter's responsibility, now, is simply to follow his master all the way as a shepherd laying down his life (21:19, 22; cf. 13:36–37 with 10:11).

□ Summary: Peter in the Fourth Gospel

Peter's role throughout the Gospel is that of the representative leader of the Twelve, who are here seen as close to Jesus but emphatically not the only authoritative source of his teaching. Peter is a sympathetically fallible man of resolve, eager to demonstrate commitment but slow to grasp the spiritual point at issue. It is easy to see how Johannine memory and theology concur in juxtaposing (rather than opposing) the contemplative witness of the Beloved Disciple with the active leadership of Peter.

For all the debate about the implicit one-upmanship between Peter and the Beloved Disciple in the Gospel's concluding chapters, in the end there is no doubt about Peter's role in the author's vision of the church. The Beloved Disciple may be closer to Jesus in some respects, his distinctive knowledge and eyewitness is clearly foregrounded, and he is also recalled as having been mysteriously singled out for longevity (21:21–23). Yet, it is also true that, despite somewhat preliminary and incomplete description of Peter across nearly twenty chapters,[53] the pastoral charge for the Good Shepherd's flock is in the end entrusted uniquely and without

50. The new name Cephas, although duly translated as *Petros*, is never actually *explained*. A pastoral commissioning of Peter is also implied in Luke's Passion Narrative of 21:32.

51. See *Acts of Andrew* 20; Tertullian, *Scorp.* 15.

52. Cf. recent commentaries; also Bauckham 1992, 547.

53. This is nicely highlighted by Hartenstein 2007, 171–73.

any relativizing comment or justification to the rehabilitated Peter, whose exercise of this ministry is known in Johannine memory to have ended faithfully in martyrdom. The undershepherd too was remembered to have laid down his life for his flock on a cross.[54]

Peter according to Matthew

□ Matthew's Mark and Date of Origin

I will assume here that Matthew used Mark, although possibly in a form that slightly predates the canonical one. I am agnostic about the existence of Q and increasingly skeptical about our ability to know in detail what it did or did not contain, if it did exist. Beyond that, I am wholly unpersuaded that we can know anything worthwhile about its different redactional stages, let alone its "community." Arguments that Luke used Matthew without Q have gained a good deal of support in recent years. Matthew's use of Luke without Q, by contrast, has not been widely affirmed, even if some of the arguments may merit further discussion. Neither of these alternatives offers a secure peg for early or "late" (i.e., second-century) dating of Luke.[55]

The famously cryptic tradition preserved in Papias offers little specific help with the search for the evangelist's individual identity or memory: "Matthew compiled the sayings [logia] in the Hebrew language; but everyone interpreted [hērmēneusen] them as they were able" (Eusebius, Eccl. Hist. 3.39.16). Whatever Papias may have meant with Matthew's collation of Hebrew logia, that collation must be something other than the extant Gospel now before us.[56] Perhaps it does mean a collection of teachings subsequently worked into our Gospel, whether or not it was anything like Q.

The important point here is that this evangelist's identification as "Matthew" was never in doubt in subsequent tradition, beginning well within the period of living memory. Here it matters relatively little whether the writer is Papias's "Matthew" or someone who represented or "interpreted" (hērmēneusen) an apostle, as Mark was said to have done in relation to Peter and as, perhaps, the

---

54. On this mainstream view of the balance between Peter and the Beloved Disciple, fuller discussion is offered in the commentaries and, e.g., in Blaine 2007.

55. See the account in Goodacre 1996; 2002; Goodacre and Perrin 2004. Note also Derrenbacker and Kloppenborg 2001 in reply to Goulder 1999. The alternative argument that Matthew used Luke is made most prominently by Hengel 2000 (and most fully in Hengel 2008, 274–353). See further Powell 2006 and also, rather differently, the arguments of Baltes 2011 or Edwards 2009 for a Jewish Christian source other than Matthew.

56. It is interesting, however, that Matthew is discussed *after* Mark in this context; might this point to some awareness of the latter's priority? Leaving aside that question, the canonical Matthew does incorporate a great many more "sayings" than Mark, although it is difficult to say whether these derived from the sayings source Q, from the parallel in Luke (so, e.g., recently Hengel 2000, 68–70, 169–207), or from another compilation or compilations originally in Aramaic.

Fourth Evangelist claims in relation to the Beloved Disciple. (An internal hint at the apostolic Matthew's importance for the First Evangelist might arise from the observation that after the opening call narrative of 4:18–22, he is the only one of the Twelve whom Jesus recruits personally [9:9].)[57] In that sense, we may rightly follow the ancient convention that saw here the Gospel "according to Matthew": it is a named, late first-century Syrian reflection on Petrine memory.

The consensus that until very recently favored Antioch and a date in the 80s AD[58] as the place and time of composition seems to me almost wholly unfounded on evidence. A scenario of this sort is *possible*, but several considerations render it not merely unwarranted but positively unlikely, especially as far as Antioch is concerned. The only really cogent arguments adduced in support of a post-70 date are Matthew's dependence on Mark and the First Evangelist's supposed presupposition that the temple has been destroyed. Neither of these is finally compelling, and the destruction of the temple is no clearer in Matthew than in Mark.[59] Far from dwelling on the recent destruction of the temple, Matthew inserts into his Markan text a number of fresh redactional additions that presuppose the *continued operation* of the temple system.[60] All this does raise questions about what is often a curiously untroubled consensus.

Markan priority, therefore, remains by far the strongest argument for a somewhat later date, but since Mark's date is also uncertain, the criteria here are exceedingly elusive. The time required to transport Rome's Petrine gospel to the East and edit it for local use need not exceed a few months, and if, as has been plausibly argued, Matthew is a kind of "authorized edition" of Mark, there would be incentive to produce it without undue delay.

□ Matthew's Place

A post-70 date becomes more problematic if Matthew is specifically associated with Antioch;[61] and it is to this question that we must now turn. Antioch's main advantage as a setting for Matthew is that it was a large Syrian city with a sizeable Jewish population, among whom Christianity did indeed gain an early foothold.[62]

---

57. See also Dschulnigg 1996, 33.

58. Stanton (1994, 11) thinks the Antioch consensus is "crumbling," but Sim 1998 and others have since restated the case in favor.

59. The evidence usually cited includes 22:7; 21:41; 23:38; and 24:15–16. None of them, however, speaks of the temple's or Jerusalem's fate in terms more specific than those of ancient commonplace regarding siege and destruction, especially as linked to OT prophetic texts about the first temple's demise. Predictions of the second temple's destruction were not uncommon in the first century; see, e.g., Bockmuehl 1994, 63–68.

60. So, e.g., 5:23–24; 17:24–27; 23:16–22.

61. Irenaeus (*Haer.* 3.1.1) claims that Matthew wrote while Peter and Paul were in Rome, i.e., before AD 70.

62. A virtually unchallenged consensus holds that Matthew was produced somewhere in greater Syria. The Gospel enjoys particularly strong and early attestation in Syrian sources (e.g., *Did.* 7.1; 8; 10.5; 16; Ign. *Smyrn.* 1.1; *Phld.* 3.1).

Beyond that, however, the arguments in Antioch's favor seem rather tenuous, as is increasingly coming to be recognized.[63]

Antiochene Christianity in the NT and in Ignatius is notable for its inclusion of gentiles, and Josephus tells us that even the Jews of Antioch had gained large numbers (*poly plēthos*) of sympathizers and adherents among their fellow citizens (*J.W.* 7.45; cf. 2.463). Yet Matthew, although he embraces the gentile mission, neither envisages a mixed Christian polity nor sees as yet any need to address any of the major practical issues such a polity would entail. On the contrary, his Jesus has no truck with those who would claim him in support of anything but full law observance, and non-proselyte gentiles are shunned rather than invited to dinner.[64]

If the conventional date is adopted, Matthew also stands at a considerable remove from the sorts of positions that the bishop of Antioch embraces a mere decade or two later, as in his interpretation of the OT or in his surprisingly developed view of ecclesial order.[65] And given what we know about Antioch's Jewish community, Matthew's emphatic redactional development of the dispute with Pharisaism also seems curiously melodramatic on the assumption of a *Sitz im Leben* in the Syrian capital. Even if some Pharisees may well have lived there, especially after 70, Antioch was never known as a center of Pharisaic-rabbinic Judaism.[66]

Antioch's experiences during and after the First Jewish War also militate against the composition of Matthew's Gospel there. After initial calm,[67] the city saw anti-Jewish rioting in AD 67 (instigated in part by the betrayal of an apostate Jew) and a vicious pogrom and massacre in AD 69–70.[68] On two successive visits, the triumphant Titus resisted a popular petition either to expel the Antiochene Jews or at least to abolish their citizenship.[69] Nevertheless, to mark their public humiliation, Titus presented to the city a part of the spoils from the Jerusalem temple for permanent display outside the city gate on the road to Daphne. And on the gate itself, facing Jerusalem and adjacent to the Jewish quarter, Titus erected a patently pagan bronze figure of the Moon with four bulls. He also had Jewish captives

---

63. For a balanced discussion, see Davies and Allison 1988–97, 1:138–47.

64. A somewhat overstated case to this effect is argued by Sim 1998, 247–55.

65. Sim (1998, 59–60, 270–87, and passim) addresses this point by suggesting that Matthew and Ignatius belonged to different Christian factions within Antioch; indeed, he proposes (271) that two parallel developments are confirmed by the tradition in *Apos. Con.* 7.4.46 that Paul ordained Ignatius as bishop but Peter ordained Evodius. Ignatius, however, repeatedly uses Matthew as authoritative. Sim's argument of *rival* episcopal lines of succession likewise comes to grief on the complete absence of evidence; on the contrary, the *Apostolic Constitutions* make analogous claims for Antioch and Rome and are clearly concerned to involve both apostles in the founding of both churches.

66. On this point, the remarks in Sim 1998, 61, are largely speculative.

67. Josephus, *J.W.* 2.479.

68. Josephus, *J.W.* 7.46–53, 54–62.

69. Josephus, *J.W.* 7.96–111; cf. *Ant.* 12.121–24.

killed in celebratory games held throughout Syria.[70] On the usual supposition of a Jewish or Judaizing Matthean community in Antioch in the 80s AD, would one not expect either a more recognizable attitude of relief at the horrors now past or else (on the theory of a church now separated from Judaism)[71] a more articulate sense of vindication, not to say internecine *Schadenfreude*, against "the Jews"?[72]

Syria was a bigger place than NT scholarship's focus on Antioch tends to allow. Apamea, Edessa, Tyre, Sidon, and even Caesarea all had significant Jewish and early Christian communities, and there is little or nothing in Matthew that requires a large metropolitan setting.[73] If anything, the Gospel's territorial perspective hints at a self-understanding not far removed from Galilee. Quite possibly, Matthew speaks for Jewish Christian churches[74] in the largely gentile regions that were part of the promised biblical tribes of Zebulun and Naphtali, where, we are told, Jesus first made his home when his fame spread throughout Syria (4:13, 15, 23) and where he later appeared risen from the dead. This is important because, among other reasons, it constitutes Matthew's Petrine memory as self-consciously located in the same biblical promised land in which Jesus walked and from which Peter came.[75]

If Mark represents the Petrine gospel for Roman Christians, then Matthew arguably constitutes its enhanced revision for a Greek-speaking Syrian readership of believers in Jesus who saw themselves as Jewish. In other words, Matthew is designed to take the place of Mark in Syria and perhaps more generally.[76] This would explain not only Matthew's uniquely close dependence on Mark's wording and sequence but also why, in spite of significant alterations and additions, it was indeed Matthew rather than the largely neglected Mark that came to be far more commonly used and expounded among the early church fathers.

□ *Matthew's Memory of Peter*

What, however, does all this mean for a memory of Peter? Does the author know him to be dead at the time of writing? Does he claim any firsthand, "living" memory? All these are difficult questions to which the evidence permits no unambiguous answers.

70. Josephus, *J.W.* 7.96.

71. So, e.g., Roloff 1993, 145–62; Stanton 1993, 167; and Stanton 1996. Cf., more recently, Foster 2004.

72. Even Matt. 21:43 or 23:38, which are sometimes adduced in this connection, are by no means clear and are in any case rather tame by standards of oriental rhetoric.

73. This is a point rightly noted by Theissen 1992, 251 (German ed., 1989, 262–63).

74. Graham Stanton has rightly urged a move away from a single, clearly defined "community of Matthew" to a network of "loosely linked communities over a wide area" (so, e.g., Stanton 1994, 12, reiterating earlier arguments). A somewhat different argument for a more "public" interpretation is offered in Bauckham 1998a.

75. This much, at any rate, might of course also be argued in relation to Antioch, as I attempted to do in Bockmuehl 2003, 49–83; but it is a point not normally considered by advocates of Matthew's composition there.

76. Cf. the fuller arguments in Heckel 1999, 62–80.

Matthew's portrait of Peter generally follows that of Mark: Peter is the first to be called (4:18–20) and the first in the list of Twelve disciples (10:2). Compared to Mark, though, the name "Peter" appears to have gained in importance.[77] Peter serves repeatedly as spokesman for the disciples as a whole, and Matthew enhances this role in a number of respects.[78] So in the Syrian setting, Peter becomes both a paradigm believer and the uniquely appointed custodian of the church. In that sense, Matthew, together with the Fourth Gospel, represents the most thorough-going Petrine portrait in the NT.[79]

□ Peter's Calling

In the call narrative in 4:18–22, Matthew follows Mark closely. The fishers Simon and Andrew are called while casting their nets into the Sea of Galilee and summoned by a famous wordplay to the eschatological task of "catching human fish," which could be a play on the name of Bethsaida and which in Isaiah means the restoring of Israel to the land.[80] One small but possibly significant difference is that Simon is from the start "the one called Peter" rather than being given that name by Jesus (4:18//Mark 1:16). This is carried through consistently in the list of disciples (10:2; contrast Mark 3:16), and in the Matthean context it makes better sense of Jesus's declaration in 16:18, as we shall see. (That idea of an existing epithet or nickname also seems to be assumed in the second-century *Gospel of the Ebionites*, where Peter is always "Simon surnamed Peter.")[81] The Fourth Gospel, as we saw earlier, gets it right: Simon is called Peter from the start, and Jesus then proceeds to say that he *is* Peter and, as "son of John," *will* be called (*klēthēsē*) by the distinctive Aramaic equivalent Cephas (*Kêpā*).[82] In other words, Matthew here seems to preserve a sound Palestinian memory.

□ Healing of Peter's Mother-in-Law

The healing of Peter's mother-in-law (8:14–15) appears here in a more condensed form than in Mark, highlighting Peter's family and their relationship with Jesus. As is confirmed in the later archaeological and pilgrimage record, the site associated with Peter's house evidently became a memory of particular interest to Syrian Christians.[83]

77. He is usually called "Peter" (22x), but sometimes "Simon" (4:18; 10:2; 17:25), once "Simon Peter," and once with his native Aramaic patronym, "Simon Bar Jonah" (16:17; cf. John 1:42).

78. Note the introduction of Peter as the questioner in Matt. 15:15 and the reduced emphasis on James and John (though their mother appears twice: 20:20; 27:56).

79. So Berger 1981, 274; Schenk 1983 even views Matthew as "the gospel of Peter."

80. The image's OT background in Jer. 16:15–16 is often overlooked: the Lord himself will send fishermen to catch all the exiles, for redemption but apparently also for judgment (cf. similarly Ezek. 29:4–5; 38:4; Amos 4:2).

81. Frag. 4, in Epiphanius, *Pan.* 30.13.3.

82. John 1:42, 45; see above, and cf. my fuller discussion in Bockmuehl 2010a, 135–57.

83. For references, see Bockmuehl 2010a, 73–75.

□ Peter as Mission Leader

In the list of the twelve apostles[84] sent on their exclusive mission to Israel, Matthew further enhances Peter's leading role by making it explicit: "*first* [*prōtos*] Simon, the one called Peter" (10:2). Here, Peter leads the mission to the twelve tribes. In view of the apostles' role as eschatological judges of the twelve tribes in 19:28, it is interesting to note that Matthew envisages this apostolic mission under Peter's leadership to the lost sheep of the house of Israel as continuing uninterrupted "until the Son of Man comes" (10:23). This suggests a relatively early state of Petrine memory, within a generation of the apostles. At the same time, Peter's leadership of the particularist mission to Israel might seem to introduce a tension with the universal mission of 28:19. That tension is not fully resolved in Matthew and perhaps remains latent in Peter's own ministry.

□ Peter Walks on Water

Peter's walking on the water (14:28–31) clearly serves a paradigmatic and homiletical purpose. It is the first episode in which Matthew adds anything of significance to Mark's portrait of Peter, and it seems particularly important to note its appearance in this central section of the Gospel, which is Matthew's distinctive composition on the church. As Davies and Allison put it in their commentary, Peter's Matthean prominence often "seems to be a function of ecclesiology" (1988–97, 2:649). When Jesus comes to the disciples to save them in distress at sea, Matthew uniquely adds Peter's venturing forth at Jesus's invitation to join him on the water. Faith in Jesus lets him walk, but taking his eyes off his master makes him sink. When Peter calls on the Lord to save him, Jesus takes hold of him and rebukes him for his "little faith" and his hesitation.[85] When the wind dies down as they enter the boat, the disciples worship Jesus as the true Son of God. We are dealing with a homiletical vignette that reflects Matthew's own preferred vocabulary and his interest in Peter. Without wishing to deny an earlier point of reference, it is clearly difficult to retrieve an identifiable memory of Peter from this story.

Nevertheless, the passage fits Matthew's pattern of introducing additional traditions about Peter (16:17–19; 17:24–27). In particular, Peter's walking on the water first develops a liturgical or homiletical theme that resurfaces in subsequent texts like the late first-century *Odes of Solomon* (39.8–13) or in the early third-century wall paintings of the church at Dura Europos (noted earlier).

□ Peter and the Purity Question

Interestingly, it is Peter who here requests clarification of Jesus's teaching about purity: "Peter responded by saying, 'Tell us the meaning of this parable'" (15:15).

---

84. This is Matthew's only use of the otherwise primarily Lukan term *apostolos* (10:2); cf. Mark 3:14 (textually uncertain); 6:30; Luke 6:13; 9:10; 11:45; 17:5; 22:14; 24:10 (and 28x in Acts); John 13:16.

85. NB *distazō*, a word the NT uses only here and in Matt. 28:17.

No specific memory seems immediately to lurk behind this change, even though Peter came to be frequently associated with the problem of the observance or non-observance of purity laws by Jewish and gentile Christians alike.[86] Whatever we think about that, the notion that Peter should ask for clarification is remarkably consistent with Matthew's overall presentation of him (not least in 16:17–19) as the authoritative bearer of the Jesus tradition. It is through him that light is shed on the substance and the meaning of the Jesus tradition. For Matthew, whose Jesus observes and upholds the Torah against the Pharisees (note 15:20), Peter is not a taboo-toppling revisionist but is concerned to understand Jesus's teaching.

□ Peter's Confession

We come, then, to the pivotal passage of Peter's confession, elevation, and rebuke in 16:13–23. Matthew deliberately links Peter's appointment as foundation stone and holder of the keys of the kingdom with the received Markan episode (8:27–30) of Peter's confession (and subsequent rebuke) near Caesarea Philippi.

We will confine ourselves here to Peter's role. He appears as the spokesman for the disciples: it is they whom Jesus asks collectively (as in Mark), but it is Peter who answers for them all. He acknowledges their trust in Jesus as "the Messiah, the Son of the living God" (16:13–16). Matthew adds to Peter's Markan confession the qualifying phrase "the Son of the living God" to make explicit the *divine sonship* of this Messiah.[87] In verse 17, Jesus responds by pronouncing Peter blessed for having made this confession not by human wisdom but based on a revelation from the Father.

The most surprising feature of this passage has long been the term "my church [*mou tēn ekklēsian*]" used in verse 18 to describe the building whose foundation Peter becomes. For some commentators, this clinches what seems clear on other grounds: the passage is a late composition reflecting prior Pauline and other early Christian usage and is designed to give a seal of dominical approval to a separate Christian church of Petrine flavor and orientation. Most, however, will note the strong OT connotations of the term *ekklēsia*; it is used over one hundred times in the Septuagint (most typically to translate *qāhāl*) and usually denotes the congregation of the people of God.[88] We know from other sources that the early Christians, not unlike the Qumran sect,[89] viewed their community in analogous terms as representing the eschatological counterpart of the people of God at

86. Galatians 2 and Acts 10 most obviously come to mind, and some of the second-century fathers still maintain a memory of Peter as an observant Jew (see, e.g., Irenaeus, *Haer.* 3.12.15; 3.13.1; cf. Tertullian, *Marc.* 4.11).

87. As such, this is clearly also a Markan theme: see, e.g., Mark 1:1, 11; 3:11; 5:7; 9:7; 12:6, 35–37; 13:32; 14:62; 15:39.

88. For further discussion, see, e.g., Horbury 1997, 1–9.

89. Note especially 1QSa 2.4 with its explicitly messianic setting (e.g., 1QM 4.10; CD 7.17; 11.22; 12.6).

Sinai, gathered now around the leadership of the Messiah.[90] This is an important point for the OT's vision of the congregation of Israel: the nation is specifically envisaged as united around its leader, whether Moses or the one who is to come.[91] Whether Jesus said precisely these words may be impossible to prove (that is not a question we need to settle here), but the statement has a natural home in the context of first-century messianic hope.

The key point in this connection, then, is the affirmation of Peter as the foundation on which the Messiah will build the "house" or "temple" of his eschatological community. This is not some late and apologetic agenda devoid of genuine Petrine memory. What is said here makes good first-century sense, and it was apparently remembered elsewhere: not only are Peter's Greek name Petros and Aramaic name Cephas traced back to the mid-30s AD in the earliest Pauline letters (Gal. 1:18; 2:7–8), but Paul strongly implies Peter's position as the most important representative of the Jesus tradition in Judea. Indeed, the rhetorical context of Gal. 1–2 makes clear that Paul echoes and emulates Peter's apostolic credentials. Like Peter, Paul *too* has received a revelation of the Messiah Jesus, the Son of God, not from flesh and blood but from God himself (1:12–16), and he too, like Peter, has been entrusted with a gospel to proclaim.[92]

What is more, in two early letters written around the year 50, Paul designates the original community—among whom Peter and others were not foundations but "pillars" (Gal. 2:9)—as "the churches [*ekklēsiai*] of Judea that are in the Messiah" (Gal. 1:22) and as "the churches of God in the Messiah Jesus that are in Judea" (1 Thess. 2:14). Ephesians 3, as well, talks of an apostolic "foundation" to the building of the church, an image partly echoed in 1 Pet. 1 with its talk of "living stones." Whatever one makes of Matthew's precise wording or meaning, a memory of Peter as the foundation or support on which the congregation of Jesus would be built seems to breathe the same air as Paul's reported visits to the Jerusalem church in the 30s and 40s AD.[93] Given the rhetorical situation of Galatians, Paul would certainly have preferred to say less about Jerusalem and Peter if it had been

90. See, e.g., 1 Cor. 10:1–5; Heb. 12:18–24; and cf. Berger 1976; and Davies and Allison 1988–97, 2:629. Judas Maccabeus, similarly, had an "*ekklēsia* of the faithful" gathered around him (1 Macc. 3:13).

91. Note especially Horbury 1997, 8–9. See also Schlatter 1929, 508, who notes "of my congregation" (*mi-qehali*) versus "of your congregation" in *Pesiq. Rab Kah.* 4.9 (cited according to Buber 1868, p. 41a; see also Mandelbaum 1962).

92. A correlation between these two passages has been argued by a number of scholars, sometimes in explicitly antithetical terms; see, e.g., Riesner 1998, 240–41, and the literature cited there.

93. It might be objected that Matthew's use is singular and Paul's plural, but once the usage of *qāhāl/ekklēsia* was adopted, the appearance of additional "congregations" (either within or outside Jerusalem) would naturally lend itself to the plural. (The same usage, incidentally, is attested in rabbinic literature; see, e.g., *y. Ber.* 7, 11c on Ps. 68:23; *y. Yebam.* 8, 9b speaks of *four* "congregations" [*qehilot*] in the one "congregation of the Lord" in Deut. 23:2–9; cf. *b. Qidd.* 73a.)

possible to do so without endangering his message. But evidently Paul's gospel and apostolic identity cannot bypass Peter.[94]

All this, incidentally, makes it more likely that Paul in Gal. 1–2 plays on an existing tradition echoed in Matt. 16:17–19, rather than that Matthew specifically invents this to combat Paul after the fact, as is sometimes supposed. Peter's unique commission by Jesus was part of what the Syrian church remembered about him, and the *fact* of his commission may well have been remembered more acutely than the chronology.

A number of interesting issues surround Peter's connection with the "gates of Hades." Most straightforwardly, this is a promise of the messianic congregation's steadfast endurance even in adversity, perhaps especially in the eschatological battle with the powers of the underworld. Whatever one's precise interpretation of this disputed phrase, the general sense is illustrated by parallel usage at Qumran and elsewhere.[95] Commentaries offer a fuller discussion of the numerous exegetical positions and bibliographical contributions.[96]

Of particular importance for the question of Petrine memory is the further elaboration of Peter's role in verse 19. The imagery changes slightly from the foundation and construction of a building to the custody of its gate: Peter is given the "keys of the kingdom of heaven." Numerous biblical and traditional Jewish parallels suggest that we are dealing with a statement of considerable significance for the constitution of Jesus's kingdom in Matthew. Not only Hades has gates (v. 18), but heaven does too (cf., e.g., Gen. 28:7; Ps. 78:23; *1 En.* 9.2); and the holder of the keys is sometimes identified as Christ, Michael, or another angel.[97] In a passage reminiscent of verses 18–19, the keys of the house of David are entrusted to Eliakim son of Hilkiah in Isa. 22:20 with the further words "he shall open, and no one shall shut; he shall shut, and no one shall open" (v. 22), a passage applied to Christ in Rev. 3:7. Peter's role is at the same time conceived in contrast to, and perhaps in succession to,[98] that of the scribes and Pharisees: although they evidently

94. Indeed, if Paul had intended and been able to omit his implicit emulation of Peter and extended fortnight's interview (*historēsai Kēphan*), it might have suited his purpose better. But even where he is on a rhetorical knife's edge in Galatians, Paul evidently considers his connection with Peter indispensable, precisely in the context of his own authenticity in the gospel of Jesus Christ. On the likelihood of a connection with Gal. 1:18, see, e.g., Grappe 1992, 108.

95. Davies and Allison (1988–97, 2:630) rightly draw attention to 1QH 14 (= 6), where the psalmist approaches the "gates of death" but looks for shelter by leaning on the truth of God, "for you place the foundation upon rock" in an eschatological city that is fortified against its enemies (14.24–26). Similarly, Gnilka 1986–88, 2:62.

96. E.g., Davies and Allison 1988–97, 2:630–33, who evaluate twelve different interpretations before settling on the last.

97. Rev. 1:18; cf. *3 Bar.* 11.2; *4 Bar. (Par. Jer.)* 9.5; *3 En.* 18.18; 48 C 3.

98. Cf. Davies and Allison 1988–97, 2:639, although their case may be somewhat overstated. They note especially the critique of the scribes and Pharisees preceding our passage in 16:11–12.

hold the key, through their teaching they lock the door and prevent anyone from entering.[99] As the pioneer and representative of faith in the Messiah's kingdom ministry, Peter is entrusted with opening access to that kingdom.

How does he do this? It would appear that the opening and closing of the door to the kingdom of heaven is about *teaching authority* and how it is exercised. That is an impression confirmed in the second half of verse 19. Peter's role consists not only in the uniquely appointed guardianship of the kingdom's keys but also in authoritative "binding" and "loosing." Numerous interpretations of this latter terminology are discussed in the commentaries. The majority view among exegetes, which draws on widespread Jewish parallels, is that Peter exercises the unique teaching authority within the community to declare what is permitted and what is not permitted,[100] probably including the exercise of discipline and excommunication.[101] Peter, then, assumes in these verses the role of an empowered representative, who is entrusted with the charge of his master's business—the kingdom of heaven. Matthew's Peter alone is unique among the Twelve as the one on whom the Messiah's church is founded, and his teaching is the authoritative basis for the life of believers.

Some of these aspects of Peter's role are reflected in other NT documents (including John 21; Acts 1–11; and Gal. 1–2), but nothing either here or elsewhere implies the establishment of a formal, let alone autocratic, office. Indeed, chapter 18 shows Matthew's ecclesiology to be strongly resistant to such a notion. The function of binding and loosing in 18:18 is vested in somewhat analogous terms in the community of disciples as a whole. So it seems important not to misread Peter's appointment in monarchic or autocratic terms. It suggests, rather, that Peter's role is *both unique and paradigmatic* at the same time (so, e.g., Kingsbury 1979).

By founding his building on the rock, Jesus *himself* is, in Matthean terms, the epitome of the wise man in Matt. 7:24–25 who built upon the rock (*epi tēn petran*)[102]—the floods and storms do indeed come, but they cannot prevail against the house. In chapter 16, of course, Peter is both "rock" and foundation and yet dramatically rebuked as a "stumbling block [*skandalon*]" just a few verses later (16:23). Matthew's Peter is at once authoritative and fallible, whatever may be

99. Matt. 23:13//Luke 11:52; also cf. *b. Šabb.* 31a–b. Many interpreters have followed Streeter (1936, 515) in suggesting that Peter here becomes a kind of "chief rabbi" (so, e.g., Davies and Allison 1988–97, 2:639; Dschulnigg 1996, 43).

100. Commentators offer extensive lists of Jewish parallels (e.g., Josephus, *J.W.* 1.111; *T. Levi* 18.12; *T. Sol.* 1.14); for later rabbinic usage, see also Strack and Billerbeck 1922–61, 1:738–47. See the comprehensive discussion in Davies and Allison 1988–97, 2:623–41; Gnilka 1986–88, 2:60–67; Luz 1985–2002, 2:461–66.

101. See the reapplication of the image in these terms in 18:18; cf. Acts 5:1–11. See also Luz (1985–2002, 2:466), who considers both church discipline and the authority to forgive sins to be implicit in the general use of the designation *ho ean*, confirmed in 18:18.

102. The slight grammatical variation between *epi* taking the dative here and the accusative in 16:18 does not, in my view, carry any precise significance in Matthean Greek (which also liberally employs the genitive).

asserted for those who claimed the mantle of his successors. (We will come back briefly to the question of a Petrine succession.)

Nevertheless, it remains the case that Peter alone is the recipient of the messianic revelation, the rock of foundation, and the holder of the keys, and it is significant that these are *not* qualities assigned equally to the other disciples in 18:18. Peter is, in Matthew, the uniquely authorized representative of Jesus's kingdom community.[103]

One issue of special significance, to which Ulrich Luz rightly draws attention, is the fact that some memory of Peter's unique foundational role appears to have found virtually universal reception in the NT and beyond: Peter alone of all the apostles is remembered as the founding figure of the church of Jesus *as a whole*.[104] Where he remains controversial is only in a small number of later writings associated with his name, primarily in Gnostic circles.[105] This is despite the fact that first-century Petrine literature is so remarkably limited in scope, even on a generous interpretation. Indeed it is remarkably difficult to identify distinctive theological themes associated with Peter—unlike James, John, or Paul. Documents like 1–2 Peter do tend to stress mainstream Christian commitments to the death and resurrection of Jesus as redemptive and as fulfilling messianic prophecy in Scripture. And Peter is presented as both a bearer of tradition and a mediator of apocalyptic revelation. But these particular themes do not seem to be unique to Peter in the early church.

Matthew's Peter as the founding rock remains compatible with virtually all other Christian traditions in the period of living memory: his uniquely authorized teaching role in the early church bridged the gap between Jewish and gentile Christianity in a way that neither Paul nor James could. Neither of them approximates Peter's role as foundation, key-holder, or authoritative teacher to the church as a whole.[106] More than that, indeed, this Matthean profile of Peter's place in the universal church closely dovetails with the significance of the Jesus tradition itself in all mainstream Christian circles.[107] In other words, Matthew's remembered Peter uniquely guarantees that what Jesus calls "my church" will indeed remain his (see p. 85 below for an excursus on Peter's successors).

103. Davies and Allison rightly caution against a hasty relativization of the Matthean Peter's role in light either of his failures or of the authority given to all the disciples in chapter 18: "An overlap in function does not entail an identify [*sic*; read "identity"] of status or office" (1988–97, 2:650).

104. Luz 1985–2002, 2:469–70. Even occasional criticisms of Peter in the Synoptics, in John, in Galatians, or in a number of Gnostic texts never really call this into question.

105. Smith 1985 usefully surveys some of the Petrine controversies of the first two centuries. Unfortunately, he inclines throughout to a maximalist interpretation of such controversies, without acknowledging sufficiently the extent to which almost without exception they presuppose a position remarkably like that which Matthew presents.

106. This casts doubt on Luz's claim that there is nothing in Matthew's portrait of Peter that cannot be applied to all other disciples (Luz 1985–2002, 2:482).

107. Again, Luz 1985–2002, 2:470, although he states the case even more strongly; see also Davies and Allison 1988–97, 2:651.

□ Peter's Rebuke

Returning to Mark's script, Matthew now offers a somewhat fuller version of Peter's objection to the first passion prediction and Jesus's rebuke of him. Jesus's passion prediction in 16:21 is, for Matthew, the first of many and clearly a turning point (note *apo tote*). Jesus's impending suffering is particularly associated with Jerusalem, whose citizens reject him and turn him over to the gentiles (27:25; 20:19; etc.). As in Mark, Jesus here predicts not only his suffering and his death but his resurrection "on the third day."

Peter resists this prediction, for reasons that remain unclear. Indeed, Matthew strengthens and expands Mark's wording with a quotation in direct speech: "God forbid it, Lord! This must never happen to you" (Matt. 16:22). Peter's inherited vision of what it means to be Messiah and Son of God cannot cope with what Jesus has said.[108] Matthew's Peter seems to infer that "the gates of Hades" ought to be powerless against the Messiah, not just against his church. It is clear from early Christian apologetics that the crucifixion of Jesus constituted for many Jews a grave impediment or even invalidation of his messianic claims. (Luke 24:21 plausibly presents even the disciples on the road to Emmaus as feeling compelled by recent events to abandon their previous hopes about Jesus.)

Despite the exalted position to which Peter has just been appointed, Matthew does not mitigate Jesus's harsh rebuke in Mark but strengthens it and reduces its application to the other disciples.[109] Peter's objection gives voice to the opposition of Satan, the tempter and accuser, who resists the divine plan and must be forcefully dismissed, as in Jesus's wilderness temptation (16:23; cf. 4:10). And just as Satan's instruments place traps and impediments (*skandala*) in the way of God's plan (13:41), so Matthew here elaborates the statement by identifying Peter as a *skandalon*, a tempting trap and obstacle.

The effect of the authoritative Peter being immediately rebuked is to reinforce the point that, despite his unique teaching authority, he remains paradigmatic as both a positive and a negative example—a fallible, weak disciple who in no sense detracts from the role of Jesus or occupies a pedestal. He, like all other disciples, is called to "deny himself and take up his cross" (16:24–28).

□ Peter at the Transfiguration

The dual role of Peter as foundation and failure is taken further in the next episode, Jesus's transfiguration on a high mountain, perhaps implicitly still in the region of Caesarea Philippi. Peter is again the first named of the threesome of disciples singled out to witness Jesus's heavenly confirmation as Son of God (17:1). Matthew follows Mark quite closely, although the account is structured

---

108. This interpretation goes back at least as far as Irenaeus, *Haer.* 3.18.4, and continues to find the support of many commentators.

109. Note the omission of "looking at his disciples" in Matt. 16:23; cf. Mark 8:33. Similarly, see Dschulnigg 1996.

more carefully and places the heavenly voice, rather than the vision of Jesus, at the center of the narrative.[110] A number of small changes shared by Matthew and Luke may indicate their use of a slightly different version of Mark's account (Luz 1985–2002, 2:506). Peter's suggestion to the Lord about the construction of tabernacles for Moses, Elijah, and Jesus is not specifically characterized as showing that Peter "did not know what to say" (Mark 9:6). Instead, the heavenly voice that confirms Jesus as Son of God, attested by the Torah (Moses) and the Prophets (Elijah), leads the disciples to fall down in fear and worship (Matt. 17:6–7, a Matthean addition).

Peter's role is not specially highlighted beyond his response to the vision, but it is clear that as the leader and spokesman of the inner circle, he is implicitly charged with the narration and transmission of this vision "after the Son of Man has been raised from the dead" (17:9).

□ Peter and the Temple Tax

The intriguing episode of Jesus's payment of the temple tax is unique to Matthew 17:24–27. Peter, again apparently as the perceived spokesman for the Jesus movement, is asked in his hometown of Capernaum whether Jesus does not pay the annual two-drachma tax. He answers, "Yes," but Jesus later instructs him "at the house" (presumably Peter's own) about the believers' freedom in principle from religious taxation, since they are not God's taxable subjects but his children. Nevertheless, in order to settle the matter amicably, Peter is instructed to catch a fish and told that he will miraculously find a stater coin with which to pay the tax for himself and for Jesus.

Numerous historical and literary puzzles remain, not least about the surprising *absence* of the implied, somewhat folkloristic miracle story at the end. Once again, it is not our purpose here to excavate the story's original historical setting in the life of Jesus, if any. Three points are worth noting for the perspective of Petrine memory. First, the story effectively involves a private conversation between Peter and Jesus, for which only Peter himself can stand as the implied source of transmission.

Second, with most commentators, we must conclude that the only plausible *milieu* for the passage is the period before AD 70, when the temple tax was in fact collected. An interpretation in relation to the Roman *fiscus Iudaicus* offers a potentially interesting reapplication at a later time, but the reference to "children" or "sons" in 17:27 seems firmly to rule out an original reference to a collection on behalf of the Roman emperor.[111] Jesus's skepticism about the temple tax, moreover, is quite in keeping with his recurrent critique of Pharisaic halakic innovations, with his emphasis on a relationship to God as Father rather than as king, and potentially with his explicit critique of the current temple establishment's collection

110. Cf., e.g., Dschulnigg 1996, 46; Luz 1985–2002, 2:505.
111. Bauckham 1986, 219; see also Davies and Allison 1988–97, 2:739–41; Horbury 1984.

of the tax in overturning the moneychangers' tables (cf. Bauckham 1986, 230–32). The Qumran sectarians too may have rejected an annual collection of the temple tax (cf. 4QOrd^a 1.ii.6–7).

Third, the figure of Peter is here introduced in the resolution of a matter of public ethics that had considerable practical consequences for Jewish Christians but none for gentile Christians. This has implications not only for the implied setting of Matthew's Gospel but almost certainly also for the continuing importance of Peter in connection with the Jesus tradition in Jewish Christian communities during the period following his departure from Jerusalem. If Peter was remembered in connection with this initially private conversation on the question of the temple tax, it is easy to see how his authority may in turn have assisted in shaping the Christian response to this and perhaps related issues. He is remembered as having been encouraged to take an attitude of critical detachment but practical cooperation.

□ Peter and Radical Forgiveness

Following the uniquely Matthean discourse on church discipline (18:15–20), Peter asks Jesus how many times one needs to forgive a person who sins against another. Peter's own proposal of seven times seems quite radically generous in itself.[112] Jesus's answer, whose parallel in Luke 17:4 is unconnected with Peter, is effectively that forgiveness must be unlimited. (The contrast with 18:15 appears to be that here the offense is only a private matter, whereas there it was sufficiently grave to be a public concern to the church.)[113] If the tradition itself derives from Q, as many scholars would argue on the strength of the Lukan parallel,[114] the Petrine link could be merely a matter of Matthean redaction. The form of Luke 17:4 is, however, quite different, and the case for wide-ranging redactional adaptation less than cogent.[115]

The primary implication for our subject seems to be that it is again Peter's question that prompts a dominical instruction. Peter, in other words, exercises his instrumental role as mediator of the Jesus tradition in a practical matter of church life. He speaks, however, not on his own authority but as the one who has access to the word of Jesus.

□ Peter and the Rich Young Man

In this episode, Peter raises a question that prompts Jesus's teaching on a subject of import to the believer's life. If the rich young man cannot follow Jesus unless he

---

112. Cf. Davies and Allison (1988–97, 2:793) for the suggestion, not least in light of *b. Yoma* 86b–87a, that perhaps a limit of three times was usually suggested.

113. So also Dschulnigg 1996, 49.

114. See the discussion in Luz 1985–2002, 3:61; Gnilka 1986–88, 2:144.

115. Neither Peter's question nor Jesus's answer is wholly redactional (Davies and Allison 1988–97, 2:792–93), and the conflation of Matthew and Luke in *Gospel of the Nazarenes* 15 (in Jerome, *Pelag.* 3.2) may imply that two different versions of the logion were in circulation.

sells all he has and gives to the poor (19:16–22), and if it is nearly impossible for the rich to enter the kingdom of God (19:23–26), what assurance can even the disciples have, who have after all "left everything" to follow him? Matthew follows Mark's lead in having Peter ask the question (19:27//Mark 10:28). The Matthean answer, however, differs primarily in the insertion of a strikingly concrete eschatological promise: "Truly I tell you, at the renewal of all things, when the Son of Man is seated on the throne of his glory, you who have followed me will also sit on twelve thrones, judging the twelve tribes of Israel" (19:28). The twelve disciples, in other words, have risked all to become the Messiah's emissaries to the lost sheep of the House of Israel (10:6), and their reward in the day of the Messiah's triumph will be to serve as the judges of the restored twelve tribes of Israel.[116] The remainder of the pericope continues along largely (if somewhat simplified) Markan lines to promise the disciples a "hundredfold" reward for the sacrifices they have made.

A number of important corollaries emerge from the connection of Peter with Matt. 19:28 in particular. The affirmation and appropriation of Peter for Jewish Christians in the Holy Land is again evident, despite the fact that the Markan *Vorlage* makes relatively few concessions to such a point of view. Given the seemingly irenic introduction of this material, it would appear that the supplementation of Roman with Palestinian memories of Peter was wholly uncontroversial for Matthew. (A connection with Q [cf. Luke 22:30], at least in substance, is possible, but again the differences are sufficiently complex and significant that one cannot speak of a straightforward "insertion," *pace* many commentators.) Without interruption, Jesus then continues to address the theme of eschatological reward in the parable of the laborers in the vineyard (Matt. 20:1–16). The nature of the rewards here is equally surprising—more for their startling uniformity than for any exalted role assigned to the disciples.

As in 17:24–27, Peter once again becomes the mediator of a tradition uniquely relevant to a Jewish Christian audience. (The apostles will not judge the gentiles, who will be liable to the Messiah's own judgment.)[117] The importance of the twelve tribes to the ministry of Jesus is especially reflected in the Gospel of Matthew. We find here significant indications of a concern for the mission to the twelve tribes and indeed for Jesus's outreach to the lost sheep in the *land* of the long-lost twelve tribes, including Galilee and the region of Syria to the north of it, "the land of Zebulun and Naphtali" (4:13).[118] Despite Matthew's openness to the gentile mission, this outreach is not sidelined here (as if it were merely the sectarian concern of conservative Jerusalem Christians around James the Just). Instead, the Matthean *chreia* links it centrally with Peter himself in what becomes his last appearance before his dramatic anticlimax in the Passion Narrative.

---

116. For the specifically Jewish setting of this passage in the traditions about the twelve phylarchs, see especially Horbury 1986.

117. Rightly, Dschulnigg 1996, 50n64, with reference to 24:30; 25:31–32.

118. See my passing remarks in Bockmuehl 2003, 76–77; see also Riesner 1998, 238–39; and Giesen 2001, esp. 31–37.

□ *Peter's Denial Predicted*

Just as Peter resisted the first passion prediction, so he still resists on the eve of the crucifixion, thereby sowing the inevitable seeds of his tragic downfall. Following the Passover meal at a friend's house in Jerusalem (26:17–29), on the way to the Mount of Olives, Jesus once more announces his impending death, now with the specific prediction that all the disciples will take offense and fall away because of him that very night. But once again this is combined with a prophecy of the resurrection and the future appearance in Galilee. As in Mark, Peter voices his objection and declares his readiness to die with Jesus, the other disciples chiming in. Matthew's main change to the Markan source is the heightening of Peter's objection in 26:33: "I shall *never* fall away [*oudepote skandalisthēsomai*]."[119] Even in Matthew's simplified form,[120] Jesus replies to Peter's "never" with an equally emphatic assurance that "amen, *tonight*" Peter will deny him not once but thrice (26:34; cf. Mark 14:30).

□ *Peter in the Garden*

Peter's promise, of course, begins to sound hollow in the very next pericope, which also closely follows Mark. Although accompanied by James and John, Peter is the only *named* member of the trio invited to join Jesus at prayer. All three fall asleep while Jesus agonizes before his Father about the impending events. Upon his first of three returns to see the disciples, Jesus reproaches Peter by name (as in Mark), but Matthew has removed the Markan address "Simon, are you sleeping?" and extends the reproach to all three disciples.[121] Here as elsewhere, however, the evidence does not bear out a supposed redactional intention to exonerate Peter[122]—his name, after all, stands out more clearly in the absence of the other two names. Instead, the effect of Matthew's redaction is to shift the story's focus more clearly onto the example of *Jesus*, whose prayer language is brought into closer conformity with the opening petitions of the Lord's Prayer. At the same time, Matthew appears to develop the *corporate*, paradigmatic dimension of the disciples' failure to watch and pray.[123]

□ *Peter's Denial*

As in Mark, Peter is the only one of the disciples who does not flee at Jesus's arrest[124] but instead follows Jesus into the high priest's courtyard "in order to

---

119. Jesus's prediction of the denial, by contrast, is fuller and more explicit in Mark 14:30, perhaps in light of the events (cf. 14:72).

120. See, e.g., Luz (1985–2002, 4:127n26) for the thorny problem of the timing of the (one or more) cock's crows in Jewish and Roman sources.

121. *Ischysate* instead of Mark's *ischysas*.

122. Rightly, Dschulnigg 1996, 54; 1989, 178. The notion of a Matthean exoneration of Peter is still widely found in the literature (see, e.g., Goulder 1997; Pesch 1980, 141; etc.).

123. Cf. Dschulnigg 1996, 52 and n70.

124. Note that Matthew retains the statement that "all" fled (26:56//Mark 14:50), only to follow Mark's qualification of it in v. 58 (cf. Mark 14:54).

observe the end [*idein to telos*]" (26:58c).[125] Matthew does, however, tell the story in less vivid detail than Mark: Peter here does not warm himself by the fire, and the rooster does not crow twice (cf. Mark 14:54, 67, 72). At the same time, the evangelist builds on the earlier impression of Peter as a paradigm: a believer whose privilege and promise is great, whose failure is catastrophic, and whose remorse is bitter.[126] In Matthew, the apostle's denial of Jesus involves two different maids rather than just one (cf. Matt. 26:71 with Luke 22:58), and he disowns his master "before all" (26:70; cf. the warning of 10:33) and "with an oath" (26:72), all the while giving himself away by his Galilean accent (26:73). This last element, with its highly pertinent understanding of contemporary Jerusalemite attitudes to Galilee, must caution against any notion that Matthew's changes to Mark in this pericope can be straightforwardly interpreted as the implementation of a purely homiletical agenda. In Matthew's Jewish Christian Gospel, the Peter who denies that he was with Jesus[127] is the paradigmatic disciple, not despite but because of his particularity as a flesh-and-blood Palestinian Jew. Far from being flattened as a literary cipher of wavering discipleship, Peter is remembered in Matthew's Syrian context as an identifiably Galilean, Aramaic-speaking compatriot.

In the end, the cock's crow causes Peter to remember Jesus's prediction of this denial and to repent bitterly. His remembering has considerable significance in relation to Peter's post-resurrection role, as we shall see in a moment. Here, a somewhat different point about Petrine memory is worth noting. Scholars of an earlier generation sometimes suggested that the episode of Peter's denial has no basis in fact but is simply the polemical figment of anti-Petrine circles in the early church.[128] Such theories have long since been exposed as baseless, and we need not repeat the arguments here.[129] As a truthful, if brutally honest, account of Peter's most spectacular failure, this story forms part of the core of Petrine memory in all three Synoptic Gospels. And without allowing final certainty, several of Matthew's distinctive emphases suggest that the shape of that memory in Syria retained a recognizably local flavor.

□ Matthew 28:16 and Other Perplexing Omissions

Having said all this, it remains a puzzling fact that Matthew makes no further mention of Peter in the remainder of the Gospel. More specifically, it seems odd

---

125. Dschulnigg (1996, 53n73) may well be right to link this with 10:22 and 24:13: Peter observed Jesus's own faithfulness "to the end [*eis telos*]," which becomes the example par excellence for all Christian faith, including Peter's own.

126. Matt. 26:75, an important minor agreement with Luke 22:62. See, e.g., recently Luz 1985–2002, 4:213.

127. Luz (1985–2002, 4:214) nicely notes the Matthean contrast in this chapter between Peter's denial that he was "with" his Lord and Jesus's consistently being "with" the disciples both now (26:23, 38, 40, 51) and in the future (26:29).

128. So, most notably, Klein 1961.

129. See, e.g., in considerable detail, Pesch 1974.

that Matthew's is the only one of the canonical Gospels that fails to single out Peter as a resurrection witness. This cannot really be seen as an attempt to diminish the apostle's continuing significance: not only is Peter's overall Matthean profile too consistently prominent and positive, but several aspects of that profile point quite explicitly to his post-Easter role (e.g., 4:19; 16:18–19). Peter is the last disciple to speak in the Gospel, and Matthew's reference to "the eleven disciples" in 28:16 makes clear that Peter evidently remains one of the resurrection witnesses alongside his fellow disciples.

Reasons for this partial silence are difficult to ascertain and inevitably somewhat speculative. It may suffice merely to note the phenomenon rather than to try to explain it. There is no evidence of any anti-Petrine critique, but neither is Peter elevated, as in some later Syrian texts (see below), to be the exclusively privileged recipient and mediator of revelations from the risen Christ. The resurrection message, essentially christological and evangelistic in content, is instead entrusted to all the apostles *as a group*. Specially authorized by Jesus, Peter is indeed in some sense their *primus*, but he remains emphatically *inter pares* (i.e., he is first, but among equals).[130]

That said, what other explanations might there be for this post-crucifixion silence about Peter? Commentators sometimes note that Peter's apparent restoration stands in troubling contrast to the fate of Judas. Jesus predicted the failures of both (26:21, 25, 33–35), and both show remorse. Yet despite Judas's seemingly comparable change of mind and attempt to return his blood money, recounted just a few verses later (27:3), he is the one who hangs himself, whereas Peter is reinstated and commissioned by the risen Jesus (cf. Kuschel 1991). The history of interpretation offers an interesting wealth of speculations ranging from Judas being pardoned at Christ's descent into hell (so Origen) to the distinctions between Judas's merely regretful remorse and Peter's true heartfelt repentance.[131]

The issues at stake in this question are to some extent inscrutable. However, at least three unspoken factors may come into play in Matthew's portrayal: the nature of the sins involved, the relational context of the sinners, and the point of reference for their remorse. First, a categorical difference between Peter and Judas may be the difference between denial and betrayal. Only Judas contributed to Jesus's innocent death; on this, Peter's reply to the two maids had no effect (cf. Luz 1985–2002, 4:235). Second, Matthew leaves implicit (26:14, 25, 47) another factor, which in John 13:30 is graphically obvious: Judas permanently deserts the fellowship of the Last Supper and of the disciples of Jesus, while Peter does not. And third, Judas's regret appears to be largely self-referential, like that of the

---

130. This is also the burden of the balance between chapters 16 and 18, as we saw; similarly, 23:8–10.

131. See the valuable documentation in Luz 1985–2002, 4:234–35. It remains true, *pace* Luz, that the verb *metamelomai*, used of Judas's remorse in Matt. 27:3, *cannot* be shown to carry the theological force of "repentance" conveyed by *metanoeō*, whether in Matthew (21:29, 32; 27:3) or anywhere else in the NT (2 Cor. 7:8 [2x]; Heb. 7:21). See also Böttrich 2001, 128.

only other biblical figure who "went away . . . and hanged himself" (Ahithophel in 2 Sam. 17:23). What Judas regrets, it seems, is not the betrayal for money but its effect of shedding "innocent blood" (Matt. 27:3–4); his inability to undo this effect (27:5–6) makes his very life morally loathsome. Peter's compunction is described rather differently. Although in theory open to analogous assessment, it is occasioned in all three Synoptic accounts by Peter's relationship with Jesus—more precisely, by his *remembrance* of "the word which Jesus had spoken" about his denial.[132] As Böttrich rightly notes, memory of Jesus's words and deeds is one of the key qualities of the resurrection witnesses, including Peter.[133]

Nevertheless, the very seriousness of Peter's fall from the height of Matt. 16 could be one of the reasons why he no longer features prominently in the remainder of the Gospel; in that respect, Matthew represents an understatement of Peter's post-resurrection role compared, for instance, with John 21.

At the same time, the Gospel's three other omissions of Peter would appear to confirm that there is no consistent Matthean agenda either to exonerate or to denigrate Peter. The passages in question are Mark 1:36; 5:37; and 11:21. The first of these, about Peter "and those with him" searching for Jesus at prayer in the wilderness, has only a very loose parallel in Luke 4:42–43, which also does not mention Peter. In Mark 5:37—which has Jesus taking Peter, James, and John into the house of Jairus—Luke does echo his source more closely, but Matthew's version of the whole pericope (Matt. 9:18–26) is very compressed throughout, focusing almost entirely on the work of Jesus. No specific conclusions about Peter can be drawn as a result. Finally, Matt. 21:20 replaces Peter's comment about the withered fig tree (Mark 11:21) with a broadly analogous one by the disciples. Once again, the implications seem either nil or neutral.

Excursus: Did Peter Have Successors?

As we have seen, Matthew affirms a unique Petrine mandate and even office *for Peter*. This account, though, has little immediate bearing on later confessional debates, including (1) whether there might be *successors* to Peter, (2) whether such successors might inherit aspects of his mandate and office, let alone (3) whether they could ever entail the priority of one particular church (such as Rome). We will return to this question in the conclusion to this book, but it is worth noting here that, at the Matthean level, exegetes today are skeptical about any idea of succession. Matthew's conception of Peter's role does not envisage or require any substitute or successor after the apostle's death, a point that Oscar Cullmann (1953, 206–12, and passim) and others rightly have stressed. In fact, if this were a

---

132. So Matt. 26:75; similarly, Mark 14:72. Luke 22:61 adds the haunting note that Peter remembered this when "the Lord turned and looked at Peter."

133. Böttrich 2001, 129, with reference to Mark 16:7//Matt. 28:7//Luke 24:6–8.

problem for Matthew and if that death had by then occurred, it could reasonably be expected to occupy the evangelist's mind. Peter was the founding figure, but the question of a successor to his dominically appointed role is not envisaged.[134] The Matthean Peter per se has no application to the pope in Rome.[135]

Ulrich Luz (2005) rightly draws attention to the well-known multivalency of Matt. 16:18–19 in its early reception history. The first association of this passage with the office of the bishop of Rome did not surface until the mid-third-century Pope Stephen, and for most patristic interpreters, the significance of the rock ranged quite widely from Peter as paradigmatic for all believers to finding the rock as a distinctly christological one.[136]

That a figure like Peter may nevertheless have *identified* one or more successors—whether in Rome, Antioch, or elsewhere—is perhaps more likely than many contemporary critical scholars are prepared to countenance. Antiquity, like Middle Eastern societies to this day, did quite readily expect the appointment of successors and the formation of dynasties, and by the end of the second century agreed upon lists of apostolic succession were apparently accepted in Rome, Jerusalem, and other churches. At the same time, the specific Petrine predicates of the foundation, the keys of the kingdom, and the authority to bind and loose seem unique and non-transferable in Matthew. And, of course, neither Peter nor the other apostles were ever remembered to have passed on their own *apostolic* status. Specifically Petrine authority was not claimed for the bishop of Rome until much later, and the self-understanding of that church and office remained for a long time linked to the idea of both Peter and Paul as the twin founding apostles. Where the early commentators do seek a contemporary application of Matt. 16:18–19 to anyone other than the apostle Peter, they tend to see his role as paradigmatic for *all* believers or at least all bishops.[137] There is no evidence prior to the third century of a *Roman* assertion of primacy specifically on the basis either of this passage or of genuine claims to Petrine memory; indeed, everything we have seen suggests that the potential for any such appeal to living memory ceases not later than the year 200. As we will also see in the conclusion, this need not rule out a priori the potential legitimacy of a later Roman *relecture* (rereading) of Matt. 16:18–19 in papal terms, particularly when this is linked with other NT passages such as John 21, but such an argument would need to be established in open reflection on well-documented patristic alternatives.[138]

134. So, rightly, Karrer 1992, 1143.

135. Cf. Viviano 2000, 334; see also the widely accepted arguments of Cullmann 1960, 243, and passim.

136. Luz 2005, 167–72; cf. his commentary (1985–2002; ET, 2001–7).

137. So, very clearly, Origen, *Cels.* 6.77; *Comm. Matt.* 12.10–11; Tertullian, *Pud.* 21. Cyprian, resisting Pope Stephen's claims (AD 254–257) for Roman papal authority as an innovation, stressed the application of Matt. 16:18–19 to *all* bishops (*Unit. eccl.* 4–5). It may be that Tertullian and Origen already oppose the emergence of positions analogous to that of Stephen. Further, see the discussions in McCue 1974; Ludwig 1952.

138. Cf. the important discussion of Luz 1985–2002, 2:475–81.

Peter versus Paul?

We must offer a brief comment on the recurrent assertion among some interpreters that Matthew was written as an anti-Pauline tract, targeting not merely certain gentile theological tendencies of a Pauline flavor but the apostle to the gentiles quite specifically. On this reading, Matthew has Paul in mind in his references to the "enemy" who secretly sows tares among the wheat (13:28), the one who is "least" because he breaks commandments and teaches others to do the same (5:19; cf. 1 Cor. 15:9; Eph. 3:8?), and the offender who refuses to listen to the church (18:17). Other allusions, including 7:15–27 and 24:24, have also been suggested. Paul, in other words, is explicitly the enemy of the church whose foundation is Peter. In various forms, this interpretation of Matthew continues to find support, especially among intellectual heirs of the nineteenth-century Tübingen school's fiercely bipolar reconstruction of early Christian history.[139]

Such interpretations not only are exegetically unsubstantiated but are explicitly contradicted even by Matthew himself: his redactional interpretation of the "enemy" (Matt. 13:28) is explicitly given as "the devil" (13:39), in keeping with a common Jewish understanding of Satan,[140] rather than intended as ill-concealed code for an identifiable human opponent (i.e., Paul). Needless to say, no patristic interpreters read Matthew in this vein: not even Ebionites, Elkasaites, or any other anti-Pauline circles known to us came anywhere near a straightforward identification of the apostle to the gentiles with the prince of darkness. This reading of Matthew as documenting a polarity between Peter and Paul is without demonstrable foundation.

Summary: Matthew's Syrian Peter

Matthew's presentation of Peter, although clearly developed in a homiletical and pastoral accent, is by no means simply idealized and reducible to an insipid or "colorless" cipher for Christian discipleship. Simon Peter appears as a distinctly Jewish and Palestinian believer in Jesus who leads, according to the Jesus tradition, a mission of the kingdom to the lost sheep of the twelve tribes of Israel. The Jewish flavor of Peter's identity is clearly reflected, for example, in his interest in exclusively Jewish issues, such as the purity halakah (chap. 15) and the temple tax (chap. 17). At the same time, Peter's recognizably Galilean speech marks him out as an undistinguished, ordinary man. Despite his failings, Peter is the disciple whose faith in Jesus as messianic Son of God makes him the foundation rock on whom Jesus proposes to erect the spiritual temple that is his church. It is a church for which Peter exercises a definitive role in teaching and discipline, authorized to

---

139. Recent versions of this reading of Matthew include Sim 1998, 196–99, 206, and passim; Smith 1985; Goulder 1994, 31–32; Goulder 1997, 24–27; Grappe 1995, 224, citing A. Lindemann and S. Légasse.

140. Cf., e.g., Gen. 26:21 LXX; Josephus, *Ant.* 1.262.

open access to the ministry of Jesus. That church is also the place in which Peter, like his fellow believers, is called to live out the forgiveness he himself has received.

In assessing Matthew's reflection of a Syrian memory of Peter, it is important to recall that this Gospel was composed well within the lifetime and the social networks of Christians who did remember Peter. Indeed, in some places it almost certainly draws on specific memories of the earliest church in Jerusalem (as we saw, e.g., in relation to Matt. 16:17–19). Matthew's version does lose some narrative detail vis-à-vis its Markan source, but the resulting account of Peter still manifests a diversity and complexity that rules out any sort of purely redactional make-over—for example, in the service of the sort of binary agenda, *pro* or *contra* Peter, that critical NT scholarship has traditionally presumed to define the early church. Indeed, Matthew retains and in several cases significantly enhances precisely the sort of Palestinian "local color"[141] that might be expected to characterize the first generation or two of Petrine memory in Syria. Contrary to widespread assumptions, Matthew may well take us closer to Peter and his world than Mark does.

For Matthew, the narrative strongly reinforces a memory of Peter as positioned at the center of the Jesus tradition, as an eyewitness transmitter of the oral history that became the story of Jesus. As Samuel Byrskog and Richard Bauckham have shown in seminal studies of the gospel tradition, it is highly unlikely that this narrative feature is a mere literary fiction or post-Easter retrojection, but it is more likely based on genuine memory of the historical Peter.[142]

And yet, it is not Peter but Jesus who is the main subject of Matthew's Gospel. Matthew's picture of Peter, therefore, remains fragmentary and inherently open to diverse effective histories. Aspects of that ambivalence of Petrine memory come to the fore in the Gospel of John, which we discussed above.

Memory of Peter in Eastern New Testament Letters

We struggle to find very much more Petrine memory in Eastern sources from the later first or second century, a point that is readily gleaned from the rapid NT overview offered in chapter 2.

One complex of evidence, however, requires brief comment: we do have a number of NT letters *emanating from and received in* the East, some of which make reference to Peter. For present purposes, Galatians will be treated as Eastern; Romans and 1 Corinthians will be dealt with in chapter 4, on the Western Peter. Here we begin with 2 Peter, as the latest of these documents, and then turn to Galatians.

141. I am using this phrase in the technical sense of *Lokalkolorit* as employed, e.g., by Theissen 1992 (cf. the title of the German edition 1989 [2nd ed., 1992]) and Riesner 1999. Note also the classic literary exploration in the work of Truman Capote (1950).

142. See, e.g., Byrskog 2000, 71–73; cf. previously Feldmeier 1985, 60, and passim; and more recently, the fuller and in part more controversial explorations of "eyewitness" testimony in Bauckham 2006.

2 Peter

The second letter of Peter may well be the latest document in the NT. Its inclusion in the canon was contested for a very long time. As late as the fourth century, Eusebius could affirm that only 1 Peter was universally regarded as authentic and canonical, even if 2 Peter appears to have been accepted to be read along with the canonical writings in a way that other Petrine pseudepigrapha were not:

> One epistle of Peter, that called the first, is acknowledged as genuine. And this the ancient elders used freely in their own writings as an undisputed work. But we have learned that his extant second Epistle does not belong to the canon; yet, as it has appeared profitable to many, it has been used with the other Scriptures. The so-called *Acts of Peter*, however, and the *Gospel* which bears his name, and the *Preaching* and the *Apocalypse*, as they are called, we know have not been universally accepted, because no ecclesiastical writer, ancient or modern, has made use of testimonies drawn from them. (*Eccl. Hist.* 3.3.1–2, NPNF 1:133–34)

In early Christian literature, 2 Peter is also one of the most poorly attested of all NT documents. Clement of Alexandria and Irenaeus may have known it, though neither mentions it explicitly. The fact that Origen regarded it as Scripture (*Hom. Num.* 13, on 2 Pet. 2:16) matters but should not be overrated, since he was generally more willing than other church fathers to quote and accept as authoritative certain apocryphal documents.

For reasons we will advance in the next chapter, 1 Peter may appropriately be considered as part of the Western memory of Peter. By contrast, the second century provides no evidence that 2 Peter was known as part of the apostle's public profile in Rome. While a Roman origin cannot be ruled out, the document's substance and florid style have been thought to point more plausibly to Palestine or Asia Minor.[143] The earliest clear use of 2 Peter appears to be in a number of verbal and topical echoes in the *Apocalypse of Peter*, a Palestinian document dating from ca. 130, while the earliest likely Roman attestations may include Justin (*Dial.* 82.1) and, more certainly, the *Acts of Peter* (e.g., 12, 20).[144] The literary posture of the epistle is clearly Petrine, but other attestations do not confirm a close association with the apostle, either in fact or in ancient perception.

Biblical scholars have long discounted the possibility of Petrine authorship for a host of reasons, not the least of which is that the work is so unlike 1 Peter in both style[145] and content. The apparent appropriation of quasi-technical terms from Greek philosophy and mystery religions (e.g., virtue [*aretē*]; piety [*euse-*

---

143. On this point, it may be significant that 2 Peter is lacking from the Muratorian Canon, a contested list that in my view continues to have a plausible claim to a second-century Western origin. Both Petrine letters, by contrast, are present in $\mathfrak{P}^{72}$ (Bodmer VIII), dating from third-century Egypt.

144. See, e.g., Bauckham 1983, 162–63; 1988; 1994.

145. This point was already noted by the time of Jerome in his *Vir. ill.* 1. See also Kraus 2001.

beia]; eyewitness [epoptēs]; knowledge [gnōsis]) counts, for many, against Petrine authorship. Another obstacle for authenticity is the likely literary dependence on Jude suggested by numerous verbatim and sequential agreements, especially in their polemic against false teachers.[146] To the issues of style and literary dependence can be added the cryptic reference in 3:4 regarding the death of the "fathers" (pateres), which commentators often take as a reference to the apostles. Finally, 2 Peter's mention of a collection of Pauline letters that are placed on par with "scripture" (3:16; see below) indicates to many a date well after the death of Peter. It therefore seems likely that, as J. N. D. Kelly once memorably put it, "2 Peter belongs to the luxuriant crop of pseudo-Petrine literature which sprang up around the memory of the Prince of the apostles" (Kelly 1969, 236).

Must we assume, then, that 2 Peter is irrelevant for our interest in the living memory of Peter and that it instead offers testimony to the burgeoning of fictitious and imaginative literature written in Peter's name in the second and subsequent centuries?[147] Second Peter does indeed present problems in this regard, since its historical connection with Simon Peter seems to most commentators somewhat distant, and in its apocalyptic emphases it has a good deal in common with other second-century documents. Nevertheless, even if we accept non-Petrine authorship and a date in the second century, this letter yields a number of important insights for the remembered profile of the apostle. A second-century profile this may be, but it is one that came to command widespread respect and influence—more so, certainly, than the *Acts of Peter*, *Gospel of Peter*, and *Apocalypse of Peter*, as Eusebius makes clear. Despite Eusebius's report of widespread doubts, the book was eventually included in the canon, and an early manuscript such as $\mathfrak{P}^{72}$ contains both 1 and 2 Peter. Thus, for nearly a millennium and a half after Eusebius, it was highly uncommon to question Petrine authenticity.

As we have seen previously, 2 Pet. 1 majors on the transfiguration (rather than the passion, let alone the resurrection appearances!) as the chief peg of the Petrine memory of Jesus, and also, it seems, of the readers' memory of Peter. In 2 Pet. 2–3, the theme of Peter as a teacher of apocalyptic wisdom and secrets may seem at first unfamiliar, but it has a wide currency in second-century apocryphal documents, where Peter generally appears as a recipient of new revelations (especially from the risen Christ) or the guardian of tradition or as both. Over the past thirty years, this motif has been the subject of a number of scholarly studies.[148] Peter's

---

146. E.g., 2 Pet. 2:1 = Jude 4; 2 Pet. 2:10–11 = Jude 8–9; 2 Pet. 2:17 = Jude 12–13; 2 Pet. 2:18 = Jude 16.

147. My online table of sources (http://simonpeter.bodleian.ox.ac.uk) indicates something of the breadth of this material, even in the early centuries. Klaus Berger's 1981 study of Peter in Gnostic and apocalyptic literature catalogs dozens of such documents.

148. Note on this the seminal study of Berger 1981; also, more recently, Grappe 1995, chap. 6; and Norelli 2007.

portrayal as a mediator of both tradition and innovation clearly illustrates his potential as an apostle of very wide, catholic appeal in the twists and turns of early Christian movements. It is difficult to be sure about the derivation of this idea, although we may note that as early as the Gospels of Mark and Matthew we find Peter articulating the heart of the messianic faith of Jesus (Matt. 16:17 attributes the Caesarea Philippi confession to a transcendent revelation) and also present at the disclosure of Jesus's apocalyptic teaching (note especially the singular verb in Mark 13:3: Jesus's revelation is in response to Peter's question).

The letter's final chapter has an intriguing comment about the ambiguity and difficulty of Paul's writings (3:15–16):

> So also our beloved brother Paul wrote to you according to the wisdom given him, speaking of this as he does in all his letters. There are some things in them hard to understand, which the ignorant and unstable twist to their own destruction, as they do the other scriptures.

This comment may be either complimentary or instead rather guarded, a difference that is surprisingly difficult to untangle. Is Paul here a "beloved brother," whose wise and trustworthy teachings are being maliciously abused, or are his writings difficult and ambiguous and therefore prone to give succor to false teachers? If the primary emphasis is on the latter, the author here is not far removed from Tertullian's famous observation at the end of the second century: Paul was often the favorite "apostle of the heretics" (*Marc.* 3.5.4).

Does this hint at abiding tensions between the remembered Peter and the remembered Paul, perhaps justifying after all the famous nineteenth-century theory of F. C. Baur about the defining importance of their dispute at Antioch reported in Gal. 2? In my view, this would be to overread both Galatians and 2 Peter. The fact that some "heretics" liked Paul does not entail that the "orthodox" rejected him: this writer commends the wisdom of Paul's counsel about God's saving patience. The letter's closing note thus suggests instead that there is no deep-seated antipathy between the remembered profiles of Peter and Paul. We have here a testimony to the formation of a Pauline letter collection, in which this author recognizes a quasi-scriptural authority. Overall, then, the canonical recognition of 2 Peter may represent a Petrine testament analogous to the Pauline 2 Timothy (so, e.g., Pesch 2001, 19).

Galatians

As we turn to one of the very earliest documents in the NT, the first puzzle we encounter in reading Paul's Letter to the Galatians is who precisely are the recipients being addressed. The older (and in some circles still common) critical view is that Galatians is addressed to *ethnic* Galatians, immigrants from Gaul, in the north of the Roman province of Galatia, possibly near Pessinus (today in northwest Turkey).[149] This would place the foundation of this church in Paul's so-called second missionary journey and would require for the letter a date after AD 53. However, this is not the only, or indeed the most plausible, analysis. Instead, building on the arguments of Sir William Ramsay, many scholars have pointed out that the *Roman province* of Galatia was not restricted to the north but also included Pisidian Antioch, Iconium, Lystra, and possibly Derbe, cities where Paul founded churches during his first missionary journey.[150] Thus, in this "South Galatia" theory, we need not find a time for Paul to sojourn among the ethnic Celts in the north when there are other provincial Galatians close at hand. This pushes back the *earliest date* to at least the time of 1 Thessalonians and possibly even prior to the apostolic council in AD 48.

Paul's rhetorical poise in the volatile first two chapters is particularly precarious and difficult. With his apostolic authority evidently under threat in the South Galatian churches that formed the core of his first missionary journey in Acts 13 and 14, Paul faces the unenviable task of having to justify, on the one hand, his direct, unmediated commissioning with the apostolic gospel by the risen Jesus himself and, on the other hand, his good standing and concord with the original apostolic leadership of the mother church in Jerusalem. This finds him insisting that he did not have to travel to Jerusalem for approval of his ministry and yet, at the same time, confirming that he did exactly that, both to gain a personal acquaintance specifically with the tradition-bearing Peter and to receive the formal endorsement of his gentile mission from the leading triumvirate of Jerusalem apostles.

Much obviously hangs on this controversial passage for a proper understanding of the origins of Paul's mission and his self-understanding, at least for this relatively early period in his missionary activity. For our present purposes, however, it is Peter's profile in Galatians that is of greater significance. What is particularly interesting here is that, unlike most of our other sources, Galatians represents *not* settled memory benefiting from hindsight (including perhaps postmortem memory) but rather a snapshot based on Paul's relatively unseasoned recollection of three acutely felt encounters with Peter (1:18; 2:7–10, 11–15). Indeed, the last of these may (and in my view, probably does) lie in the very recent past, so that Paul is still somewhat smarting from the defeat he suffered in the aftermath of the conflict at Antioch.

First, however, we hear in 1:18 that Peter received a visit from Paul not long after the latter's dramatic conversion experience on the road to Damascus. It would appear that Paul regards him as without question a defining figure in the church at Jerusalem. For instance, three years after his conversion, Paul undertakes a potentially dangerous journey to Jerusalem, apparently for the sole purpose of spending a full two weeks "to get acquainted with Peter" rather than, say, to meet

149. At times referred to as "Celtic Galatia," e.g., Apollodorus, frag. 60.2; cf. Diodorus Siculus 5.24.1–3. See the detailed argument by Murphy-O'Connor 1996, 185–93.

150. See the commentaries for discussion; note also, e.g., Scott 1995; Breytenbach 1996; Riesner 1998.

any of the other apostles (1:18–19 NIV). Given his evident desire to downplay such contacts, it is at least worth speculating whether this is mentioned somewhat defensively in order to underwrite Paul's claims to speak competently on subjects such as the Jesus tradition, which in 1 Corinthians he claims to have transmitted verbatim to his converts. (Indeed, both 1 Cor. 11:23–25 and 15:3–7 relate to narratives in which all four Gospels assign Peter a prominent role. 1 Corinthians 15:5a does so with particular insistence, listing him emphatically as the first apostolic witness of the resurrection.)

Peter—whom Paul usually prefers to call by his Aramaic nickname, Cephas—is again cited as a key figure and Paul's evident counterpart in the apostolic agreement about the gentile mission. Just as Peter seems tasked with a particular responsibility for outreach to Israel (a mission that characterizes much of his role in Acts), so Paul affirms agreement from Cephas, James, and John for his own mission to gentiles. In a sense, then, Paul's legitimacy is equivalent to and yet also conditioned by Peter's: it is precisely the Petrine mission's primary orientation toward Jews that allows for the emergence of a parallel sphere of influence for Paul.

Paul then turns to relate Peter's visit to Antioch, where conflict nevertheless occurs (Gal. 2:11–21). Whatever the relationship between Paul's Letter to the Galatians and the so-called apostolic council, it remains the case that Paul sharply rebukes Peter for seemingly yielding to pressure from Jewish (possibly Jesus-believing) circles for loyalty to the Jewish national cause—and thus making his outreach to gentiles look like shallow pretense.

As noted earlier, Christian scholarship, especially since the Reformation, long regarded this to be a clear, if emotionally fraught, triumph of Paul's law-free gospel against the legalistic claims of "Judaizers." In recent times, however, several further considerations have seemed worth pondering. First, the flipside of Paul's strength of feeling is that his rhetoric betrays one caught on the back foot: he sounds agitated and defensive in Galatians, aware that, as he himself admits, within the Jesus-believing Jewish fellowship at Antioch, he found himself in a minority, apparently a minority of one (Gal. 2:13).

Second, the usual assumption that Paul represents the defense of a pure gospel against Peter's vacillation and compromise is only one possible reading of the event. Are we to understand that Peter abandoned a previous commitment and praxis of fellowship with all Christians regardless of their racial background? Much is unclear. In fact, Paul openly concedes that his own rejection of the request for loyalty from persecuted fellow believers in Jerusalem left him isolated: the church of Antioch, including even his senior mission partner Barnabas, disagreed with him. If that is correct, then Peter's action, whatever it may have been and however misguided in Paul's view, was evidently in keeping with the consensus of the apostolic community at Antioch. According to the outline of Acts, Antioch does not again serve as Paul's mission base after this episode, whether one places it shortly before or shortly after the Jerusalem Council (though he returns for a visit in 18:22, perhaps two years later).

Third, Paul's use of the first-person plural while addressing Peter in Gal. 2:15–21 is increasingly recognized as a candid acknowledgment of the extent to which Paul and Peter, and apparently even James, *agree* on the basic theology of the salvation of Jews *and gentiles* by faith in Christ rather than by the stringency of their legal observance. Paul respects the Torah-observant mission to the Jews and asks only for recognition of the validity of law-free praxis in the gentile mission. As Peter Tomson (1990, 227–30) comments on Gal. 2,

> Paul implies here that his "Law-free gospel" for Galatian gentiles was founded on his respect for Law-observance by Jewish Christians. . . . According to Gal. 2:11–13 the majority of Jews of Antioch, as Peter and Barnabas and also Paul, thought it possible for Jews and gentiles to eat together without transgressing the Jewish Law. . . . If Paul really would have violated the food laws and induced others to do so in the presence of Barnabas, Peter and the Antioch Jews, he would have made the agreement [Gal. 2:1–10] null and void and his apostolate impossible. . . . The conclusion is that here Paul does not urge Peter to join him again in a non-Jewish way of life. On the contrary: he urges for a Jewish life which does not force gentiles to judaize, in line with the agreement.

The salvation of gentiles without circumcision is evidently a conviction held in common by James, Peter, and Paul. Indeed, outside the indirect evidence of Galatians and Acts 15:1, it is remarkably difficult to find any Jewish or Jewish Christian sources advocating the circumcision of *gentile* believers in Christ. Certainly Peter never did so, as far as we can tell.

It is also commonly assumed that Peter's fault was to stop eating with gentile *believers*. However, the text is not at all clear whether what was contested was a practice of eating with *unbaptized* gentiles. Galatians makes consistently good sense when one reads every reference to both "gentiles" (*ethnē*) and "the circumcision" as denoting unbelievers (with "Jews" being a term that may or may not include Christian believers). In 1 Cor. 12:2, Paul himself refers to the "gentile" identity of non-Jewish believers as explicitly something *in the past*, a usage that is frequently implicit elsewhere too, with the apparent exception of Romans (cf., e.g., 1 Thess. 2:16; 4:5; 1 Cor. 1:23; 2 Cor. 11:26; Gal. 2:15; Eph. 4:17).

It is still too rarely appreciated among NT interpreters that the Torah says nothing to prohibit table fellowship with gentiles: even observant Jews in the first century in practice held a wide range of views about how to implement the practicalities of what it *does* say, for example, about matters like diet and idolatry.[151]

It is significant that Peter does not surface again in Galatians and certainly not in chapters 3 and 4, where Paul's polemic against attempts to impose the law on gentiles is fiercest. This raises significant doubts about the theory, advanced by Michael Goulder and others, that the opposition to Paul in Galatia (and elsewhere) consistently involved Peter and his agents, who were sent to subvert Paul's

---

151. See the detailed documentation offered in Bockmuehl 2003.

mission. Galatians never polemicizes against Jewish Torah observance, as 5:3, for example, makes explicit: gentiles certainly should not be circumcised, because to do so could only reinforce the false claim that the Torah remains the gatekeeper or "guardian" of the covenant (cf. 3:24–25). But conversely, those who *are* circumcised, presumably including Jews like Paul himself, do, according to 5:3, remain under obligation to keep the Torah.

Conclusion

In the end, one of the abiding puzzles about Peter's footprint in the East is that his home turf in Palestine yields so few localizable Petrine associations and memories. This situation is worth contrasting with that of James the Just, whose death features in Josephus, about whose ministry in Jerusalem the second-century writer Hegesippus relates a variety of traditions, and whose relatives continued to be remembered and revered in early Christianity for some time.[152] There is even the later tradition of a tomb of James (Eliav 2004).

However, the silence about Peter is not complete, and we should not exaggerate it. The NT sources we have discussed provide clear evidence of a stock of shared knowledge, some of which does assert the claim of a living and perhaps occasionally eyewitness memory, as Richard Bauckham and others have extensively argued. In these texts, Peter is consistently singled out from his fellow apostles as *a* (if not *the*) key figure in the early Christian movement: he alone speaks for the disciples as a group, he serves as a key witness and expositor of the Jesus movement, he is the "rock." This picture of Peter is markedly continued, and even exaggerated, in subsequent memory. For both orthodox and heretical appropriations of Peter, he remains the fountainhead of tradition and the defender of the church against false teachings.[153]

Nevertheless, the lack of early local traditions stands in surprising contrast with what pertains in Rome, as we will begin to see in the next chapter. The one significant exception to test this rule is Peter's house in Capernaum, pointed out to pilgrims in antiquity and tethered to the written gospel traditions (including the *Gospel of the Ebionites*). Other Eastern appeals to Petrine memory concern his affiliation with a Judaizing Christianity represented in the *Pseudo-Clementines*, the *Gospel of Peter*, the *Apocalypse of Peter*, or for that matter in Galatians.[154]

One other aspect of the remembered Peter's profile, largely dismissed by critical scholarship as fiction, is his evidently widespread affiliation with a particular part

---

152. See the extensive documentation in Bauckham 1990.

153. Note the very similar roles of Peter in the (Greek) *Apocalypse of Peter*, the Gnostic *Apocalypse of Peter*, and the *Pseudo-Clementines*, though the content of the guarded teaching is differently construed.

154. Though note the substantial break with this tradition represented in the Gnostic *Apocalypse of Peter*.

of the gospel tradition. Both Justin Martyr and Ignatius of Antioch explicitly link that gospel tradition with Peter's authority and testimony, referred to by Justin as Peter's "memoirs." These authors seem to believe that their claims in this regard are non-controversial, a rhetorical common ground with their audience.

Strikingly, the memories of Eastern writers, rather than claiming Peter and his apostolic authority for their own, associate him with Rome (e.g., Ign. *Rom.* 4.3). Additionally, there are several Eastern hints at his martyrdom, sometimes specified as having taken place in Rome (John 13:36–37; 21:18–22; *Apoc. Pet.* 14.4; *Ascen. Isa.* 4.3).

Thus, we have in the early period little local Petrine memory, especially outside Galilee. Unlike in Rome, there is no centralizing narrative that would encourage retaining or even generating "pegs of memory." That said, in addition to the common stock of Petrine memory presupposed by, say, Serapion, assertions of *personal* living memory are not uncommon in literary sources: in the NT these include Galatians, 1 Corinthians, 2 Peter, and the Gospel of John, among others.

Once again, it is clearly reasonable to ask *why* such appeals to Petrine memory in the East are not more numerous: in historical terms, Peter's primary sphere of activity would seem to have encompassed greater Syria, Asia Minor, and possibly Greece, well before any decisive period of final ministry in Rome.

In my view, there may be three different but complementary reasons for this relative Eastern silence. The first pertains to Peter himself. Aside from one or two fourth-century pilgrimage sites around the northern shore of Lake Tiberias, there is, as we noted, very little to point to in the early centuries. Although speculation on this matter is unlikely to get us much further, there may nevertheless be reason to wonder if Peter's relatively brief stay and early departure from Jerusalem and especially Antioch meant that there was perhaps little living memory to pass on or assert. Peter's limited Palestinian profile is in this respect comparable to that of Paul, who outside the literary sources is also rarely remembered except for a few late traditions at Antioch. Acts and the Epistles strongly imply that neither of these two leading apostles spent much time in either Judea or Galilee after the beginning of their mission away from Jerusalem—certainly by the mid-30s AD in the case of Paul and probably AD 41 in the case of Peter. Their prominence in narrative and memory alike, at least in terms of specific places, attaches overwhelmingly to locations outside the Holy Land.

A second consideration is that there is scope for doubt about how much of the modest store of *local* Petrine memory could have survived Palestinian Christianity's dramatic disruptions of AD 70 and especially the complete *personal* discontinuities of AD 135, when Jewish Christianity in Jerusalem was comprehensively displaced by a gentile church. Incentives to generate fresh "places of apostolic memory" for the benefit of pilgrims were less obvious in the second century than they would become in the fourth.

A third, more tentative, consideration relates to the second and is perhaps as speculative as it is evocative. Given the deteriorating and increasingly threatened existence of the Jesus-believing Jewish communities during the events of AD 70 and 135, silence may have a more eloquent function. The relative dearth of personal, living memory of Peter and the other apostles in the East (including, perhaps, the explicit claims associated with the anonymity of the Beloved Disciple) could be analogous to the anonymity of certain characters in the Gospel of Mark, to which Richard Bauckham has drawn attention. In the context of persecution and of the revolts against Rome, it is not difficult to see the attraction—in view of Roman and Jewish hostility—of a "protective anonymity" for those who were personally acquainted with a Christian ringleader who either was or had been a fugitive and was possibly executed as a subversive criminal (Bauckham 2006, 183–201).

For stakeholders across the spectrum of the emerging Christian faith, therefore, living Petrine memory in the East offers, in the first century and a half of the apostle's footprint, a dialectical and complex but vitally important frame of reference in the forward development of Christian tradition. A remembered apostolic anchor-figure like Peter turns out to carry a significant weight as a personal guarantor of the faith, as Bauckham among others has stressed vis-à-vis the more fluidly anonymous conception of James Dunn and others. Peter as "the rock" here represents not a polemical but a consensual principle, universally accepted as being authoritative yet without any possibility of being authoritarian. As a representative torchbearer of the foundation of apostles and prophets, Peter is indeed the first among equals.

4

The Western Peter

To move from an Eastern to a Western quest for Petrine memory is to encounter further complexities. On the one hand, the evidence here still commends that we retain the last chapter's guiding metaphor of multigenerational graffiti on the wall of Peter's house at Capernaum. Our sources are undeniably complex, diverse, and in many ways inscrutable. Nevertheless, regardless of the degree of their ideological or narrative fictionality, they presume and reward an implied reader concerned with some sense of Peter as a real, extratextual figure—one whose apostolic biographical past connects with the past of Jesus Christ and whose surviving memory these sources engage either directly or, more often, indirectly. Complex and diverse as it is, our evidence from Italy and Greece is also surprisingly extensive; one rough-and-ready count might identify twenty relevant sources up to the year AD 200 for Rome alone.[1] A full discussion could easily take up a whole volume on its own, so we must be selective. After some introductory considerations about Christianity's origins in Rome and its connection with Peter, we will take in four major points of reference as we work our way back from the end of the second century, before taking a second look at some key NT texts, including the Gospels of Luke and Mark.

1. Cf. the online table of sources compiled at http://simonpeter.bodleian.ox.ac.uk.

Christians in Rome

We know remarkably few specifics about how Christianity first got to Rome. The earliest Christian writing associated with that city is Paul's letter to the Roman Christians in AD 56 or 57, and it already assumes a diverse community, or perhaps several communities, of Jewish and gentile believers, with somewhat fraught relations between them and signs of potential trouble with the authorities. It is significant that Paul never addresses them as "the church" at Rome. Rather, Rom. 16 mentions a number of Christian house churches, among whom we may assume some of these tensions could well be represented.

Though Paul's letter is the first Christian writing associated with the Roman Christians, it is not the earliest evidence. Many scholars now agree that the Edict of Claudius in AD 48, who expelled Jews from Rome because of disorders "at the instigation of Chrestus" (Suetonius, *Claudius* 25.4; cf. Acts 18:2), seems to hint at inner-Jewish strife about the Messiah (*Christos*). As early as AD 41, his first year in power, Claudius issued a temporary cancellation of the established Jewish assembly rights, a move some suspect was caused by this unrest (Dio Cassius, *Hist.* 60.6.6; cf. Josephus, *Ant.* 14.216; 16.160–66). Augustine, citing Porphyry, accepted that the Christian gospel first reached Italy under Caligula (i.e., AD 37–41; Augustine, *Ep.* 102.8).

Several other external sources suggest a Christian presence prior to the persecution under Nero. One remarkable first-century pagan is Pomponia Graecina, a distinguished aristocratic lady whom Tacitus describes as having engaged in an extraordinary habit of grief that lasted forty years. In AD 57 she was accused of a "foreign superstition" (Tacitus, *Ann.* 13.2), which several recent scholars have seen as a secret adherence to Christianity. Later inscriptions at the catacomb of San Callisto in Rome suggest that members of her family may have been Christian. While this is an intriguing possibility, the evidence does not allow certainty. If true, it could shed interesting light on the seemingly anachronistic claims for Peter's aristocratic acquaintances in documents like the *Acts of Peter*, sometimes thought to confirm a late date for these writings.

All in all, there is surprisingly extensive and early evidence for an important Christian presence in Rome beginning before the year AD 50, perhaps even a decade earlier. How did it begin? Paul does not tell us; indeed, Romans makes no reference to the origin of Christianity in Rome except to state clearly that it is independent of Paul (Rom. 1; 15). Romans 16 mentions no fewer than twenty-six individual Christians in Rome—eight women and eighteen men—although it seems that more of the women were active in the community. Over half of them likely were immigrants from the East, suggesting either that there were not yet many local converts or, at least, that Paul had no occasion to know any of them. About two-thirds may be of slave origin (see Lampe 2003, 164–86).

Peter Lampe (2003) and others have persuasively argued that Christianity most likely came to Rome via the lively trade routes connecting Palestinian Jews with the large Jewish community in Rome. These routes might proceed by sea either to Ostia or to Puteoli near Naples, where Paul also landed (Acts 28:13). The overland alternative route would proceed along the Via Egnatia to Dyrrhachium in modern Albania and, from there, cross over to Brindisi or Otranto in Apulia, which could sometimes be covered in less than a day. Alternatively, boats might leave the harbor of Corinth and travel to Brindisi, largely along the sheltered coastline. Quite possibly this was Phoebe's route when she carried Paul's letter to the Romans.[2]

If faith in Jesus was a source of controversy in Rome no later than the edict of AD 48, it is intriguing to think that the people who first took it there were themselves eyewitnesses of the apostolic generation or perhaps even of Jesus's ministry. Acts 2 mentions visitors from Rome at the first Pentecost. The most plausible supposition is that Jewish pilgrims or traders took Christianity to Rome along any of a number of well-traveled routes from the East. It is interesting that in AD 41 and 49 Claudius twice had to deal with synagogue riots getting out of hand, both of which may possibly have had Christian connections.[3]

Peter and Rome

What does all this mean for the role of Peter in the foundation of the Roman church? A recurring patristic tradition, first attested early in the second century in the so-called *Kerygma Petrou* (*Preaching of Peter*), is that Peter left Jerusalem twelve years after the resurrection (i.e., ca. AD 41–44). Later in the second century, we are told that Peter then traveled via Antioch to Rome to preach there, quite possibly only for a relatively short time. This is asserted not only by Hippolytus of Rome and in the *Acts of Peter* but also in clearly Eastern documents such as the Syrian *Didascalia* and Eusebius's *Chronicon* for the year AD 42.[4] The possibility of an early visit of Peter to Rome is certainly interesting but very difficult to prove one way or the other.

One recurring suggestion has been that Luke hints at an early visit to Rome. When Peter flees Jerusalem in the spring of AD 41, after Caligula's death on January 24 and during Agrippa I's Passover persecution (Acts 12:3), he goes "to another place [*eis heteron topon*]" (Acts 12:17). Could this be Rome? Although at first it may sound far-fetched or preposterous, this suggestion has been argued by

2. Some traditions claim it was Peter's route too. One finds a number of Petrine legends among the ancient churches of Apulia, from which the Via Appia runs to Rome.

3. On a more speculative note, *Ps.-Clem. Rec.* 1.7 suggests that it was Barnabas who first preached at Rome. This is an interesting suggestion, which might also make sense of the association of Mark, Barnabas's cousin, with Rome. When Paul and Barnabas part company in Acts 15:37–39, Barnabas takes Mark with him to the West, initially to Cyprus, although the date of this parting is after the apostolic council and thus after AD 49.

4. The later *Acts of Philip* links Peter's mission in Rome with the apportioning of geographical mission areas by the "savior" (8.1).

a steady trickle of scholars.[5] It has been pointed out that the only other occurrence of this phrase in biblical Greek is in Ezek. 12:3 LXX, where it denotes Babylon, a convenient first-century cipher for Rome, as 1 Pet. 5 and Jewish literature both before and after the NT suggest (see below, under "Peter in 1 Peter?"). In any case, Acts finds Peter back in Jerusalem in time for the apostolic council (15:7).

Some scholars have suspected an awareness of Peter in the writings of Nero's adviser Petronius, who obeyed orders to commit suicide in AD 66. He has been thought to allude in his *Satyricon* to certain episodes in Mark, including the anointing with spikenard, the Last Supper, and an unseen cock's crow. But despite some interesting similarities, Markan allusions seem unlikely to most critics, and even if they could be established, we are still some way from any connection with Peter.

A standard argument against an early link of Peter with Rome is that he is not mentioned in Paul's letter to Rome. It is difficult to know what to make of that silence. In a sense, it means no more than that Peter was probably not in Rome at the time of writing. He may only have returned to the city in the early 60s AD. One persistent ancient tradition sees him in northern Asia Minor before that, as a missionary in the regions mentioned in 1 Pet. 1:1—most of which Paul did not visit, perhaps deliberately (cf. Acts 16:7). Even in Romans, one notes Paul's great diplomatic care not to presume his right to an acknowledgment of his ministry (1:8–12) and his concern not "to build on another man's foundation" (15:20).

The question of when—or indeed whether—Peter first came to Rome cannot be resolved here. I offer a fuller discussion of these matters elsewhere (e.g., Bockmuehl 2010a, 114–32). Nevertheless, as we will see below, several late first- and early second-century sources do affirm an uncontested memory of Peter's martyrdom, some of them explicitly in Rome. In addition to those like Ignatius and *1 Clement*, which we will discuss here, they include the *Ascension of Isaiah* and the *Apocalypse of Peter*, Eastern documents discussed in the previous chapter.

Turning now to the evidence of Petrine memory in Rome, we have to be selective. It could be instructive to discuss Irenaeus again, because he clearly represents Roman tradition on a number of relevant points, including Peter's relationship with Mark and with the Roman line of episcopal succession (*Haer.* 3.1.10; 3.3.1–3), but he also draws significant anti-Marcionite conclusions from the fact that Peter and the other apostles were positively remembered as observing the law (*Haer.* 3.12.7)—an intriguing contrast with Origen's more dismissive and patronizing view of Peter's Jewish observance (e.g., *Cels.* 2.1).

We will see that at the very end of our period we have figures such as Gaius, a Roman priest who, in dispute with the Montanist Proclus's claims for the tomb of Philip and his four daughters at Hierapolis, points out that the martyr's tomb, or "trophy," for Peter is located specifically on the Vatican hill and similarly for Paul on the way to Ostia (Eusebius, *Eccl. Hist.* 2.25.7).[6] That claim is also tacitly

5. E.g., Wenham 1972; Thiede 1986; Riesner 1998, 119; Jobes 2005, 34–36, 323.
6. The sense of competition with Montanist claims is explored in Tabbernee 1997.

acknowledged a few years earlier by Polycrates's letter to Pope Victor about the date of Easter, which insists over against Roman claims to apostolic authority that "in Asia, *too*, great stars [i.e., apostles and martyrs] have fallen asleep" (see Eusebius, *Eccl. Hist.* 3.31.3; cf. 5.24.2).

These sorts of testimonies highlight an interesting contrast between the Eastern and the Western Peter. From quite early on, Rome generated specific localities of Petrine memory, beginning with the simple marker on the Vatican hill adjacent to the gardens of Nero but later including Petrine places of hospitality, of conflict, introspection, and imprisonment. We will return to this matter, and to Gaius, briefly at the end of this chapter in relation to local memory. Hippolytus, in the late second or early third century, also takes for granted that Peter was crucified under Nero and makes passing reference to the widely attested claim that the apostle repeatedly opposed Simon Magus in Rome after Simon had abandoned his pretense of Christian faith. Other writers, such as Justin Martyr and Irenaeus, claim that Simon Magus came to Rome in the time of Claudius (AD 41–54), and Porphyry appears to have known a tradition that the gospel first arrived under Caligula (AD 37–41). The *Acts of Peter* speaks in extravagantly legendary terms about that conflict with Simon, which was becoming part of Roman lore by the mid-second century. Around this same time, Justin repeats erroneous but no doubt popular Christian views about a statue on Tiber Island supposedly honoring Simon Magus as a god. The mid-second century is also when the first archaeologically identifiable marker is erected on Peter's tomb. It is impossible to tell, however, to what extent the fully developed cycle of legend at the end of the century has a core in genuine living memory: second-century writers who do care about such memory show no detailed knowledge of that narrative.

Both Irenaeus and Justin have Roman connections, and both affirm that Peter came to Rome to build up the church and was subsequently martyred under Nero. Irenaeus knows that Simon Magus persistently opposed Peter and the apostles and that Claudius "is said to have" honored him with a statue, though the Roman location of either the statue or the conflict remains implicit (*Haer.* 1.23.1). According to Irenaeus, the Gospel of Matthew was written while Peter and Paul were evangelizing and strengthening the church in Rome, but Mark's deposit of Peter's preaching was written down only after their death (3.1.1, 10). So Irenaeus places both Peter and Paul in Rome and knows that Linus, Anencletus, and Clement are the first bishops descended from them (3.3.1–2). The Marcionites, by contrast, also appear to know both apostles, but they regard Peter as imperfect because he affirmed the Jewish God, while Paul alone (in their opinion) knew the truth, by revelation (3.12.7; 3.13.1; cf. Tertullian, *Praescr.* 23).

Justin makes no connection between Simon Magus and Peter, although we saw in the previous chapter that he does identify the Gospel of Mark specifically with the memoirs of Peter. He does place Simon Magus explicitly in Rome at the time of Claudius, and he identifies the statue he believes to have been erected in

Simon's honor as "to a holy god" (*1 Apol.* 26.2). Since its rediscovery in 1574, we know that the inscription on that statue actually read *Semoni Sanco Deo Fidio* and was thus dedicated not to Simon but to the Sabine tribal deity Semo Sancus—an understandable error on the part of Greek-speaking immigrants. We may wonder if Justin ever personally inspected this statue or merely took the local Christians' word for it. On the other hand, the fact that Semo Sancus was identified with Jupiter (i.e., Zeus) helps to understand why Simon, who was also revered as Zeus, may in the popular mind have been associated with that effigy.[7] However, Justin remains silent about the legendary Roman conflict between Simon Magus and Simon Peter as it was famously developed in the mid-second-century *Acts of Peter* and later texts.

The problems with Justin's picture of Simon Magus, which was widely followed by other early Christian writers, are well known and discussed in the relevant literature and need not detain us here.[8] For present purposes, I would like instead to focus on four other individuals within the period of living memory of Peter, three Christian and one pagan.

Dionysius of Corinth

While bishop of Corinth, Dionysius wrote to the bishop and church of Rome around the year AD 170 and also sent letters to a number of churches and individuals (Eusebius, *Eccl. Hist.* 4.23.1–13). His letter to Rome has been much debated. Here I simply want to mention it briefly as documenting that *both* Peter and Paul were by this time believed to have ministered in Corinth as well as Rome before being martyred in Italy at the same time.

> You linked the foundations of the Romans and Corinthians. For they both alike planted and taught us in our Corinth; and similarly, having taught in the same place in Italy, they experienced martyrdom at the same time. (*Eccl. Hist.* 2.25.8)

Dionysius's truthfulness has sometimes been questioned, in relation to both Corinth and Rome, on the grounds either that Peter and Paul never in fact worked together in Corinth or else that Dionysius is merely attempting to ingratiate himself with the Roman church on the basis of a scenario wholly manufactured out of 1 Corinthians and *1 Clement*.[9] It is true that existing first-century sources do not encourage the idea of a *joint* ministry of the two apostles in Corinth. However, a close reading of Dionysius shows that no such claim about Corinth is made

7. On Simon as Zeus, cf. Acts 8:10; Justin, *1 Apol.* 26; Irenaeus, *Haer.* 1.23.4; see further Logan 2000, 273.

8. Cf., e.g., Irenaeus, *Haer.* 1.27.1–3; 2.9.2; Eusebius, *Eccl. Hist.* 2.13.3; Cyril of Jerusalem, *Procat.* 6.14. Logan 2000 offers a useful survey.

9. So, e.g., most recently Zwierlein 2009, 134–40.

in the text. They are not said to have worked "hand in hand" either in Corinth or, for that matter, even in Rome but merely to have worked "in the same place" (*homose*). Their systematic twinning, typical of the idea of apostolic concord, became a dominant *topos* of Roman Christian ideology not in the second century but only in the fourth.

But what of Dionysius's claim about Peter in Corinth? Paul's correspondence with that church could be interpreted to imply that Peter had either already visited or might well be expected to do so in the future. It is not altogether clear if Paul means to identify a Cephas faction in 1 Cor. 1:11–13 (cf. 3:5–9, 22). A plausible interpretation, however, must be that different members of the Corinthian church viewed their religious orientation as "humanly" (3:3–4) conditioned by a preferential loyalty to one or another apostolic leader. Personal loyalty to Paul or Apollos evidently derived from personal experience of their ministry, and it stands to reason that the same is true of Peter. The church's awareness of his ministry and of his missionary travels with his wife (9:5) might, in theory, have been acquired elsewhere by traveling Corinthians or conveyed secondhand by visitors traveling to and from Corinth. Equally straightforward, however, is the assumption of a loyalty to Peter generated by personal acquaintance. A passing missionary visit of Peter to Corinth (en route elsewhere, perhaps even to Rome?) seems conceivable prior to Paul's writing in AD 55.

Like Ignatius before him, then, Dionysius here makes no attempt to introduce new information or to pull the wool over his readers' eyes. Instead, he can take for granted his readers' traditions and memories about the apostles' presence among them—speaking in part from the confidence of the Corinthian connection with both apostles, which indeed seems strongly implied both by Paul in 1 Corinthians and perhaps also by *1 Clement*. Although Dionysius is not himself a guarantor of these shared Roman and Corinthian memories, rhetorically his appeal presupposes them and depends on their existence for its effectiveness.

Marcion

No complete writings survive of Justin's famous contemporary Marcion (ca. AD 84–160), the affluent businessman from Sinope in Pontus who was born the son of a bishop. He arrived in Rome around AD 140 with a large gift to the church of 200,000 sesterces, but this money was returned to him after he was excommunicated not long afterward. What limited information we can extract from the writings of Tertullian and other opponents suggests that any opinions Marcion may have held about Peter were supported not by an appeal to memory but by his "dogmatic unorthodoxy." This sufficiently explains Marcion's preference of Paul over the Jewish Peter and the Twelve, exemplified perhaps in his (or his disciples') pioneering interpretation of the so-called Antioch incident of Gal. 2 in typically antinomian polarity as the definitive account of their relationship (Tertullian, *Marc.* 1.20;

4.3). Surviving fragments of Marcion's *Gospel of the Lord* follow the outline of Luke. They do, therefore, cover Gospel episodes involving Peter, but in every case these contain the Lukan version of events. Although certainty is elusive, we may wonder whether this Paulinist sympathy for Luke is strengthened by the fact that this evangelist's subject matter and biography, like Marcion's and Paul's, take in both Asia Minor and Rome.

What is more interesting is what Marcion's Gospel omitted. Epiphanius, writing in the fourth century, gives a detailed account of this. According to Epiphanius, the deletions included Jesus telling "Peter and the others" to prepare Passover (cf. Luke 22:8), and also (*Pan.* 42.11.6.67) Peter's severing of the high priest's servant's ear, as reported in Luke 22:50. In the former case, the omission is arguably driven by Marcion's ideological anti-Judaism; Epiphanius's refutation discusses especially the Passover issue in detail. The absence of the severed and restored ear is more difficult to explain. I am, however, intrigued by the suggestion that since Marcion did not like the sin-bearing Servant of Isaiah 53:12 in Luke 22:37, which he omitted, he would have wished for the same reason to thwart any thought of that same Servant as healer (Isa. 53:5, etc.) in 22:50–51.[10]

Nothing suggests that Marcion's project reflects or cares to reflect any Roman memory of Peter. Like Justin, he was not a native of Rome; and he belonged only very briefly to the Roman church, which traced its descent from the original Jewish apostles and evangelists (ca. AD 140–144). Predictably, but nonetheless intriguingly, Marcion's ideological preference for Paul evidently overrides any interest in the letter that Peter ostensibly sent from Rome to Christians in Marcion's home province (1 Pet. 1:1). Marcion ignores that letter, if indeed he ever knew of it, although it was apparently known in Rome since the later first century.[11] It is also worth remembering Marcion's special predilection for the dispute between Peter and Paul at Antioch, where, like subsequent Protestant interpreters, he takes an unabashedly pro-Pauline and anti-Petrine line.

Phlegon of Tralles

The relative silence of Roman Christian sources in the early second century continues to be an undeniable and unsolved puzzle. In relation to our subject, it has frequently been taken to imply that nothing much was known of Peter until such time as Roman bishops seized the assertion (or re-assertion) of Petrine traditions as an opportunity to consolidate their own position in the church, beginning perhaps with Anicetus (ca. AD 155–166), Stephen (AD 254–257), and

10. I am grateful to Christopher M. Hays for a related suggestion, as also for his study of the relationship between Marcion and Luke (see Hays 2008).

11. Second Peter is of uncertain location (cf. 3:1), but 1 Peter is apparently used in *1 Clement* (AD 96), in Polycarp (Pol. *Phil.*), and in Justin Martyr. The first explicit citations are in Irenaeus (*Haer.* 4.9.2; 4.16.5; 5.7.2), Tertullian (*Scorp.* 12), and Clement of Alexandria (*Strom.* 3.110).

Damasus (AD 366–384). However, a tight-lipped vagueness or anonymity about named individuals appears to be a consistent characteristic of Christian accounts associated with Rome until the mid-second century, and not merely in relation to Peter, as we will see in relation to *1 Clement*, Luke-Acts, Mark, and other sources. It is perhaps only after Hadrian that it becomes safe to speak frankly of Simon Peter in public. Only after this, for example, do explicit apostolic apocrypha thrive even in Rome; after this comes Marcion's assessment of the relative merits of Peter and Paul, and only then do we encounter the first public marker of Peter's tomb.

Here, however, I would like to draw attention to a neglected piece of evidence that may serve in a very small way as a missing link, inasmuch as it provides surprising awareness of a Roman memory of Peter, even among pagans, in the generation after his death. This evidence is found in a most unexpected source, and is perhaps for that reason usually neglected in the secondary literature. In a passage intended to refute the pagan philosopher Celsus's denial of Jesus's foreknowledge, Origen refers somewhat vaguely to a pagan text composed around AD 140 (*Cels.* 2.14; *FGH* 2B.257, F 16e):

> Now Phlegon, I think in the thirteenth or fourteenth book of his Chronicles, even granted to Christ a foreknowledge of certain future events—although he was confused in ascribing to Jesus some things that had to do with Peter; and he testified that the events turned out as Jesus predicted.

P. Aelius Phlegon (no relation to his Christian namesake in Rom. 16:14) was an educated freedman in the imperial household of Hadrian (AD 117–138), a native Greek speaker from Tralles in Caria, Asia Minor. Among his various literary activities is a *Book of Marvels*, composed in the sensationalist genre known to classicists as "paradoxography"—entertaining collections of weird and wonderful tales in the best tradition of tabloid journalism.

By far the most substantial and best known of Phlegon's works was a chronology of the Olympic Games from their beginning in 776 BC to the 229th Olympiad (AD 137–140), during which Hadrian died. Although this work survives only in fragments, it is clear that, in addition to a listing of the Olympic victors at each of the games, Phlegon discusses notable persons and events of the respective period, including various miracles and oracles. It is clearly this work, composed in sixteen books, that Origen cites here. Assuming that after the extant account of the founding of the games, the remainder of the 916-year history is evenly divided over the sixteen books, it is indeed book 13 that may plausibly be assumed to cover the lifetime of Jesus, and book 14 the apostolic period. Another popular patristic citation from book 13, known to Origen (*Cels.* 2.33, 59), Jerome, and others, concerns a solar eclipse associated with the darkness at the crucifixion of Jesus.

Quite what Phlegon says or knows, whether about Jesus's predictions or Peter's, is impossible to tell from Origen's fleeting comment. It seems nevertheless fair to assume that it must have been a sufficiently impressive tale for Phlegon to have heard of it and to comment on it—though it is impossible to be more precise than that.

In interpreting Origen's obscure citation, then, it is significant that he does *not* attribute to Phlegon any explicit knowledge of *Peter*. Rather, Origen says merely that, in speaking of Jesus, Phlegon erroneously introduces some facts that pertain instead to the apostle, attributing the lesser-known disciple's sayings to his master. What concerns us here is simply Phlegon's confirmation that, within a generation or two of Peter's death in Rome, certain local Christian memories of him had gained sufficient currency that an early second-century pagan resident of the city could come across them and mistake them for descriptions of Christianity's founder.

As a lover of tabloid sensationalism, Phlegon may have taken an interest in the memory of Peter, not just because of his supposed prophecies but also because of the stories of his miraculous exploits as a preacher and healer and possibly even the legend cycle of his encounters with Simon Magus. What could account for the confusion between Peter and Jesus is not clear, but among the chief similarities that might mislead outsiders are Peter's crucifixion and stories of his miracles. It is worth pondering that the famous (albeit now textually suspect)[12] *Quo Vadis* narrative in *Acts of Peter* 6 specifically links Peter's fate with that of Jesus in a Roman geographic setting. The prediction of Peter's martyrdom in John 21 also adds suggestively to that link.

Clement of Rome

A decade before Ignatius, we enter historical waters that are at once better charted and more treacherous. The conventional scholarly consensus regards the anonymously authored document known as *1 Clement* as a letter written around the year AD 96, although there are also arguments favoring an earlier date around AD 70 (others claim a date as late as Hadrian).[13] This is a treatise ostensibly written from the church at Rome in order to address a factious dispute in the church of Corinth. No individual author is ever identified, although the unity of style does point to a single writer. The superscript agrees with the consensus of subsequent ancient attestation in naming him as Clement, an *episkopos* of the Roman church during the 90s of the first century. Clement may have been a freedman of the consul T. Flavianus Clemens, from a family with possible Jewish and Christian links. Early Christian sources consistently regard him as a bishop of Rome, and he is also (perhaps somewhat too conveniently) identified by Origen and others as the Clement addressed by Paul in Phil. 4:3.

The main argument for a date around AD 96 is the statement in 1:1 that the letter has been delayed by "sudden and repeated misfortunes and calamities," which scholars have tended to associate very specifically with the end of Domitian's

---

12. Zwierlein (2009, 82–92) shows from a new MS that the original text read not "where are you going" but "why have you come" or "why are you here" (i.e., *quo venis* [*ti hōde*]).

13. Zwierlein (2009, 316–31) assumes that 1 Pet. 4:12–19 must refer to the persecution under Pliny (ca. 110–113) and would have required some time to become known in Rome.

reign. There is, however, nothing in the text to require that the church's setbacks are due to persecution that is both acute and recent. This does not necessarily require a date in the 60s or early 70s AD; even aside from the weight of the patristic consensus, internal evidence confirms that one generation has passed since apostolic times (*1 Clem.* 44.2–3; cf. 63.3). Fully aware of a certain tenuousness of the evidence, I accept the consensus view of a composition sometime in the 90s.

The passage of key interest to us here is the much-disputed chapter 5, in which Clement (like his Corinthian counterpart Dionysius, eighty years later) appeals to his readers' shared identification with the memory of apostles and their readiness to persevere in faith, even in the face of much enmity. In chapter 4, persecuted saints of the OT serve as the backdrop for Clement's own times and for his remarks about Rome's twin apostles in particular. He begins with Peter:

> Through resentment and envy the greatest and most righteous "pillars" were persecuted and contended unto death. Let us set before our eyes the good apostles— Peter, who because of unrighteous resentment experienced not one or two but many afflictions; and after giving his testimony in this fashion, he went to the place of glory that was his due.

This is followed by analogous remarks about Paul, who also demonstrated his endurance in adverse circumstances: "And when he had reached the limit of the West he gave his testimony before the rulers, and thus passed from the world and was taken up into the Holy Place." Chapter 6 adds that Peter and Paul were joined by a multitude of other martyrs in Rome "among us [*en hēmin*]," who perhaps likewise suffered the resentment of certain contemporaries.

As is well understood in the scholarly literature, Clement remains surprisingly ambiguous about the precise nature of both Peter's (and Paul's) ministry and his martyrdom. Was Peter killed for his faith at all? If so, was it really in Rome? Is it right to try to deduce genuine reminiscences from a text cast in the rhetorical garb of a philosophical *aretology* (praise of virtue)? Did Paul's travels to the "limits of the West" lead him to Spain? If so, is the implication that he was martyred there rather than in Rome?

We do not need to answer all these questions here. Several points, however, are reasonably clear: Peter and Paul are introduced as individuals, but jointly and in that order. At least for Christians in Rome and Corinth, it seems, these two apostles are, at this stage, the most obvious, uncontroversial recent examples of faithful endurance in the face of jealousy and persecution; indeed, they are the *only* two named individuals in a list of seven illustrations. (It is interesting to contrast this with the list of heroes in Heb. 11, where all are pre-Christian and several are named.) And the rhetorical emphasis on Peter and Paul as examples "nearest to us" and "in our own generation" is a clear appeal to living memory, linking the apostles with the host of other Roman Christians who were "joined to them" in persecution and martyrdom. Rhetorically, the writer seems able to assume that this is known and undisputed, not just in Rome but among his Corinthian readers too.

Both apostles are here included among the "pillars," a term that was applied to the original apostolic college in Jerusalem (Gal. 2:9) and, by extension, also to other apostolic defenders of the church.[14] The aorist participle, in both cases used of their "witness" (*martyrēsas*), is clearly understood to mean their martyrdom; it falls under the heading of persecution and struggle "unto death" (*1 Clem.* 5.2) and is the mode and means by which the apostles passed from this world to their place of glory.

At the same time, as many have noted, Clement is surprisingly taciturn about the actual details of the fate of Peter, with whom the consensus of later tradition personally associates Clement himself. No mention is made of any journey to Rome or of the mode of Peter's execution, although, as we have just seen, careful reading permits no doubt about the *fact* that he died for his faith. Far from supporting the idea that no martyrdom of Peter is in view at all (as, e.g., Goulder 2004 and others have argued), the rhetorical appeal here makes sense only if the author can assume a certain common knowledge of the events to be in place. In this sense, *1 Clement* parallels Ignatius's *Letter to the Romans*. What is more, in view of the continuing concern about recent and extensive persecution, it is most plausible to assume that we are dealing here with the sort of deliberate anonymity that might protect the author and readers from official presumption of their association with recently executed capital criminals. This is a point that has recently also been documented for the Gospel of Mark, a Roman document written at most three decades earlier than *1 Clement*.[15]

Nothing in the text suggests that Clement had personally witnessed Peter's fate, although its explicit placement in "our own generation" (5.1) does seem to imply that he was at least alive when it happened; and his first-person plural application of the tradition to the church at Corinth certainly implies that his readers there knew it too. No written sources are cited or even implied. In view of that, I would agree with Richard Bauckham (1992, 560) that Clement had learned of Peter's death "as a matter of common knowledge in the church at Rome when he wrote." Even the setting in Rome is not absolutely required, but it is made very likely by the rhetorical force that associates the "great multitude" of Roman Christians (6.1) with the two apostolic martyrs in 5.3–7: the former *as well as the latter* underwent their martyrdom "among us" (6.1).

A number of scholars have taken the rhetorical theme of resentment, cited above, to suggest that both apostles and the Roman martyrs died as a result of the jealousy of *fellow Jews* or even *fellow Christians*. That is an interesting and disturbing possibility, which would cast an interesting light on the role of lingering resentment about the significant disruptions of Jewish and Jewish Christian life since the riots of AD 48, leading to the expulsion under Claudius (and possibly

---

14. E.g., Eph. 3:10; Rev. 3:12; cf. 1 Tim. 3:15; etc.; in the second century, Hegesippus spoke of James the Just as "Bulwark of the People."

15. Bauckham 2006, 183–201; following a suggestion of Theissen 1992, 184–89.

his earlier suspension of assembly rights in 41). Its impact on the events of AD 64 may not be trivial, especially if members of Nero's household included his second wife, Poppaea Sabina, who, according to Josephus, intervened on behalf of the Jews (e.g., *Ant.* 20.195). On the other hand, gentile resentment remains a plausible reading too, not least in view of a recurrent theme in the apocryphal Acts.

Fuller accounts of these documents can be found in the extensive secondary literature.[16] Here, we may conclude in brief that in the letter to Corinth, composed most likely in the last decade of the first century, the Roman church appealed inter alia to the example of the apostles Peter and Paul, who had within living memory ministered and suffered martyrdom in Rome and who, it seems, were personally known and remembered in Corinth as well. The circumstances of their deaths did not need to be extensively discussed because they were well understood, and anonymity may have granted protection, as it does for any endangered community united around a rich but only minimally explicit discourse about the common experiences that most matter to it.[17] The rhetorical presumption is that shared memory allowed the readers to fill the gaps in the unspoken discourse.

By way of a postscript to the discussion of *1 Clement*, it is worth noting the question of an "apostolic succession," to which Rudolf Pesch (2001, 82) has suggestively drawn attention. *First Clement* notes repeatedly that "our apostles" not only appointed bishops and deacons in keeping with explicit OT precedent (citing Isa. 60:17 LXX) but also gave instruction that others should replace them when they died (42:4–5; 44:2). Pesch (2001, 111) also draws an interesting parallel with Acts 20:24, 28 as relating Paul's ministry (*diakonia*) received from Jesus to the task of shepherding the flock that Paul entrusts to the Ephesian elders. While all this does not, despite Pesch's implication, establish an exclusive chain of succession for the Petrine office, it does confirm an early expectation of a quite natural succession of episcopal leadership that appeals to biblical precedent.

Luke and Acts—Roman Memory?

We now return for a closer look at some of the NT evidence for the Western Peter, and we will include in this the Gospels of Mark and Luke. As we will see, while Mark arguably documents a lively Petrine memory, this is less clear for the Gospel of Luke (but perhaps a little more so for Acts). Nevertheless, it is with some hesitation that we begin with Luke as the latest—and thus our first—important Rome-related author. This hesitation is due to a number of major uncertainties surrounding the nature, date, and place of Luke's two volumes, his Gospel and Acts. Let me explain.

16. Cf. recently Lona 2011; also my discussion in Bockmuehl 2010a, 114–32.

17. A powerful illustration of this phenomenon is shown in the feature film *Valkyrie* (2008), about von Stauffenberg and others involved in the unsuccessful plot on Hitler's life.

First, Luke may well have written around the time of *1 Clement*, which is why I introduce him at this point. The dates of his Gospel and Acts are, however, highly contested, and even recent scholarly estimates continue to range widely from the early 60s until the 140s AD, with some going so far as to posit Luke's dependence on Marcion (ca. 85–160).[18] Especially in the case of Acts, to favor a date in the 80s or 90s AD is more of a compromise position than a conclusion based on solid evidence.

Next, a comprehensive analysis of Luke's treatment of Peter would need to come to grips with the thorny and, in recent years, increasingly contested problem of Gospel sources. Is Luke's knowledge of Peter dependent on Mark and Matthew, on Mark and Q (though Q is silent on Peter), possibly even on John's Gospel too? Or, instead, is Luke dependent only on Mark and other unknown sources? This question, to which the classic two-source hypothesis once seemed to provide assured answers, has again come in for considerable discussion among Synoptic critics and cannot be resolved here. That Luke knew Matthew, as recent critics of Q have argued,[19] seems possible and is, in some ways, attractive for its simplicity; but even then, it need not follow that the relationship is best seen as one of extensive literary dependence on that Gospel as we know it. Reversing the literary dependence[20] may seem to resolve some problems of the former view (e.g., Luke's apparent dismemberment of great Matthean discourses like the Sermon on the Mount), but it raises others of its own. For present purposes, we will simply proceed on the view that the literary evidence suggests Luke's use of something very like Mark and probably several other sources, one or more of which were also known to Matthew.

A further scholarly conundrum, less pressing here but still enough to give pause to any confident conclusions about the Lukan Peter, concerns the relationship of the Gospel to Acts. Where at one time students were confidently introduced to "Luke-Acts" as an integral work, the remarkably disparate second-century attestation and manuscript tradition of these volumes has generated a lively debate about that earlier certainty. I do not wish here to question common authorship of both volumes but want merely to recognize that ongoing wider discussion.[21]

Finally, not all readers may accept the geographic association of Luke's work with Rome; locations such as Syria, Asia Minor, or Greece continue to enjoy scholarly support. Nevertheless, and as I explained in chapter 2 above, here I wish to proceed cautiously on a reading of the structure of Acts that does point implicitly to a Roman conclusion to the stories of both Peter and Paul and thus of Luke's

---

18. E.g., Klinghardt 2006; 2008; cf. Tyson 2006; see also Hays 2008 in critique of Klinghardt.

19. Most notably Michael D. Goulder and Mark S. Goodacre, following Austin Farrer (e.g., Farrer 1955).

20. I.e., Matthew being dependent on Luke: this is argued, e.g., by Hengel 2000, 169–207.

21. See, e.g., Gregory and Rowe 2010 for the state of the debate. Too late for consideration in that volume, Walters (2009, 191) claimed to have established "beyond reasonable doubt" that Luke and Acts derive from different authors, though not all reviewers are convinced.

oeuvre as a whole. Acts sets in parallel the ministries of the two apostles as the two main human protagonists of Luke's narrative of the church. This is apparent in the sequential interlinking of the two (Peter: 1–12, 15; Paul: 7, 9, 13–28), done in such a way as to ensure, in the very structure of Acts, the conclusion that the story of the early church is incomprehensible without both Peter and Paul pioneering the mission to both Jews and gentiles.

Acts clearly, and at times explicitly, points forward to a Roman *terminus* that is finally reached by Paul (and by the narrator of the "we" sections in chapters 16–28) but never quite brought to a conclusion. By contrast, after Jerusalem, the last destination we hear about for Peter is the "other place" to which he goes in 12:17; Luke tells us nothing explicit even about a stay in Antioch (cf. Gal. 2). The author evidently depends on Mark but writes in a place where knowledge of a diverse range of other traditions is easily obtained. Uniquely among the evangelists, the nodal points in Luke's overall narrative perspective are clearly Jerusalem *and* Rome, with a seemingly inevitable direction leading from Jerusalem via Judea and Samaria to Rome (cf. Acts 1:8; 19:21; 23:11). This is highly specific to Luke: although Paul himself in Romans implies that the capital is a desired destination (1:10–15; 15:22–23), even there his goal is clearly Spain (15:24). Peter and Paul are Luke's greatest agents, yet the inference is that readers know something important about the climax of their fate in Rome, which he does not wish to discuss in detail (rather like *1 Clem.* 5–6, writing perhaps a little later and with a similar degree of reserve and anonymity about events that arguably continue to engender both searing memories and political peril for the Christian community).[22]

An origin in Rome, at least of Acts, has a measure of ancient support, such as in Jerome (*Vir. ill.* 7). Even Marcion's choice of Luke as his base text indicates that this Gospel was both available and regarded as authoritative in Rome by AD 140, with other sources, including Justin and possibly Hermas, offering modest but significant attestation (for fuller discussion, see Gregory 2003). Irenaeus, in fact, may be understood to represent a conventional Roman memory of the evangelists in the first half of the second century, according to which Luke composed his Gospel in that city; Irenaeus distinguishes Mark and Luke, who are simply linked with the twin apostles of Rome, from Matthew's earlier collection of logia "among the Hebrews," on the one hand, and John's composition "while he resided in Ephesus"—the implied geographical contrast evidently being with Rome. Irenaeus's source for this and related traditions (e.g., about episcopal succession) derives most plausibly from his own formative period in Rome, when he may also have had access to Christian archives.[23]

22. The circumstances may reasonably be expected to evoke unstated or covert engagement with current or recent oppression, what James C. Scott (1990) calls "hidden transcripts" of resistance. For the application of this insight to the period of Christian origins, see, e.g., Horsley 2004.

23. So, e.g., Thornton 1991, 48–55; also Schulz 1994, 17–18; although both may overstate the evidence.

Whether through personal memory or through a source indicated by the so-called "we" sections, Luke indeed claims local knowledge of the route Paul and his companions take through Southern Italy, landing at Puteoli (Pozzuoli), near Naples, following a perilous journey across the Mediterranean via Malta, Syracuse, and Rhegium (i.e., Reggio; Acts 28:13). Luke is aware, as well, of two way-stations on the Via Appia, the major road south of Rome, where Paul is met by advance parties of Christians: Forum Appii, among whose greedy innkeepers and mosquito-infested swamps Horace famously paused in 37 BC on his way to Brundisium (i.e., Brindisi; *Sat.* 1.5.3);[24] and then, thirteen kilometers farther toward the capital, Tres Tabernae.[25]

Luke's apologetic interest in Rome also comes into focus in relation to Roman institutions and authorities. From the start, Luke makes the most of Roman history (Luke 2:1; 3:1; etc.) and features specifically Roman figures, such as the centurion and public benefactor of Capernaum (Luke 7:2); Cornelius, the first gentile convert (Acts 10); and even the proconsul, Sergius Paulus (13:12). Acts makes the most of Paul's Roman citizenship and appeal to Roman authorities, and despite his pointed concern over Claudius's expulsions of Jewish Christians (18:2), Luke remains overall the most pro-Roman of all NT authors.

Scholars have also long mused about the question of whether certain parallels between Luke and Josephus suggest that the evangelist knew the writings of Josephus, perhaps especially the later volumes of the *Jewish Antiquities*. Such a Roman link between Luke and Josephus would shed interesting light on the possibility of common presuppositions and a shared intellectual climate. It is, however, of very limited consequence for our Petrine interest, and in any case, it seems wise to exercise caution.[26]

None of this, of course, proves that either the Gospel or Acts was *written* in Rome or Italy, even if that may be a good possibility. Nor does it deny Luke's awareness of other localities and other, especially Palestinian, traditions; on the contrary, it is significant that the presence of *both* Palestinian and Italian "local flavor" characterizes Mark and Luke in a way that is not the case for Matthew and John.[27] But the upshot of both the internal evidence of Acts and the external attestation of the Gospel arguably points to Luke's awareness of Christian memory in Rome.

24. Today the place is a hamlet known as Borgo Faiti, about 60 km southeast of Rome. Drainage of extensive swamps and the building of several new cities in the area changed the whole landscape dramatically during the twentieth century.

25. On the site of today's Cisterna di Latina, a busy modern town.

26. Luke's dependence on Josephus was classically proposed by Krenkel 1894; followed, e.g., by Burkitt 1925, 105–10; and Streeter 1936, 556–58. For discussion, see more recently Mason 1992, 185–229. Others (including Schreckenberg 1980; Sterling 1992, 365–66, 226–389, and passim) note the similarities but are more skeptical about any real influence. Mason (1995, 177) seems to allow that the overlap could be more in shared assumptions than in a direct link between them.

27. Riesner 1999 notes *both* Italian and Palestinian "local flavor" in Luke.

Peter in Luke's Gospel

The decision to treat Luke's Peter under the heading of Roman memory does not initially make a great deal of difference. Luke's Peter is largely Mark's. With very few possible (and marginal) exceptions, the Peter of Luke's special material has no distinctively Roman connections. And a good deal of what is distinctive about Luke's portrait of Peter appears to derive from his own redactional interests rather than from any recognizable appeal to memory.

Having said that, however, the very fact that Luke uses Mark so extensively is far more significant than the force of critical habit allows us to recognize. Whether or not Luke is dependent on Matthew or vice versa, and regardless of Luke's significant alterations and omissions of Markan material, the Petrine memory represented in Mark has already come to constitute a ready stock of the gospel tradition for all three Synoptic evangelists. That in itself suggests something of the influence of Roman memory of Peter for the Gospel of Luke. Luke's own claim does not appear to include any firsthand knowledge of Peter himself, but contrary to some commentators, he does claim at least proximate, and possibly direct, access to some of the "original eyewitnesses" (1:2), a point rightly stressed in Richard Bauckham's recent work (e.g., Bauckham 2006, 114–54, and passim).

□ *Peter's First Appearance (4:38–39)*

Despite his dependence on Mark, Luke's ambition for "certainty" (1:4) causes him to cast the whole beginning of Jesus's association with Peter in a narrative framework rather different from that found in Mark. In place of the latter's relatively logical narrative sequence of these events, Luke presents no fewer than *three* episodes that might seem to constitute the formal beginning of this teacher-disciple relationship.

First, and rather puzzlingly, Peter (here simply called "Simon") is mentioned in passing but plays no explicit role at all in the brief vignette of Jesus entering his house and healing his mother-in-law (4:38–39). It is as if this Markan story, which evidently occupies the tradition because of its link with Simon, is brought forward to slot into the reader's pre-existing framework of Petrine reference. Readers like Theophilus, in other words, are already aware of "the things about which you have been instructed" (1:4), and among those things may well be the identity and significance of Peter, who clearly needs no introduction. Redactionally, this first healing story fits well with the first teaching of 4:16–30 and the first exorcism of 4:31–37; together, this trio of characteristic vignettes provides the opening encapsulation of Jesus's ministry.[28]

□ *The Miraculous Catch of Fish (5:1–11)*

Next, Luke offers the unique story of the miraculous catch of fish, which here follows his summary of Jesus's initial ministry in Galilee (4:44). The story's main

---

28. I am grateful for comments on this passage from my colleague Christopher M. Hays.

NT links appear to be with the resurrection appearance in John 21, discussed above (chap. 3). While precise verbal agreements are few, and there are major differences in the narrative setting and details of the two stories, they do have a number of parallel motifs in common.

Luke	Motifs in Common	John
5:3, 10	Peter is joined by "the sons of Zebedee" (but not Andrew, unlike Mark 1:16//Matt. 4:18; cf. John 1:40–42)	21:1
5:5	The previous night's fishing has produced nothing	21:3
5:4	Jesus tells the disciples to let out the nets	21:6
5:6–7	They comply and catch an overwhelming quantity of fish	21:6
5:6	They have difficulty hauling in the catch, and their nets are close to breaking	21:6, 8, 11
5:7	Other disciples help take the fish to shore	21:8
5:8	Peter expresses contrition in the aftermath of this miracle	21:15–17
5:10	The miracle is interpreted symbolically	21:11
5:10	Jesus commissions Peter (as pastor or missionary)	21:15–19

One should not exaggerate the similarities at the expense of the differences, as if to see here simply a transposed resurrection experience, or John 21 as a recycled fishing story. Unless we consider either evangelist likely to engage in an inexplicable act of literary vandalism, we must assume that each of them encountered their narrative either as an independent tradition or in an already pre-formed narrative similar to the one in which they now appear. Nevertheless, both stories clearly serve a foundational ecclesiological significance for Luke and John, as many commentators point out. In both stories Peter is singled out, called, and commissioned in connection with his role as a fisher.

Scholarly debate about this question and about the apparently composite nature of Luke's narrative has been extensive; here we must focus on the text's significance for Petrine memory. Luke evidently received an individually transmitted tradition about a miraculous catch of fish involving Peter and may have supplemented this from other material, but to explain the story's literary origin beyond that is to enter the realm of speculation.

Only in 5:8 is the apostle first called "Simon *Peter*," which is a little awkward but hardly calls for the invocation of a separate source, as some have argued. Here again, Peter is apparently a known point of reference, so that no introductory explanation is needed. (His less familiar brother Andrew, by contrast, is not mentioned by Luke at all, unlike in Mark and Matthew.)

At the same time, Luke's picture of Peter in this call narrative differs significantly from that in Mark and Matthew. Only here does Peter fish from a boat that is evidently his own (5:3). And it may even be, as some commentators suggest, that the unexpected change in 5:4 from the singular (Peter being asked to "set out [*epanagage*] into the deep") to the plural ("let down [*chalasate*] your nets") denotes Peter and the men working for him or with him, rather like the hired men of Zebedee in Mark 1:20. On balance, it seems right to conclude with Pheme Perkins that Peter's call probably cannot be pinned down to a single event. Rather, his relationship with Jesus "involved several turning points" that, in all four Gospels, continue well past their initial encounter (Perkins 2004, 23). Luke's handling of his Markan source suggests that he conflates the story of Peter and Andrew with that of James and John in order to affirm a single vocation scene based around a remembered Petrine narrative about a miraculous catch of fish from a boat. Luke 5:10–11 returns to the themes of the Markan call narrative, including the note that "they left everything and followed [Jesus]," which, in Luke's account of Peter's fishing business, appears to have costlier implications for the apostle.

The spiritual symbolism of the story, whether in its Lukan or Johannine form, is not lost on the evangelists. Regardless of prior failures and disappointments, obedience to the call to "put out into the deep and let down your nets" is overwhelmingly rewarded—all the more in the missionary work of "fishing for people," a phrase found in all three Synoptics. This theme, with its fulfillment of Jeremiah's prophecy about God's messengers "fishing" and hunting for the exiles of Israel (Jer. 16:16), was well understood in the early church and is frequently reflected in the early patristic period.[29] The differences in Luke's account, then, appear to be due to Lukan editing rather than to any evident local memory.

□ Peter in the List of Apostles (6:14)

Few surprises surface in this next mention of Peter. Luke, like Matthew, is evidently dependent on Mark 3:16—although Luke's talk of apostles at this point (6:13) represents a minor agreement with Matt. 10:2, which may suggest either a common dependence on Q ("Mark-Q overlap") or else, perhaps quite plausibly in this case, Luke's use of both Mark and Matthew. The only small difference in the three Gospels' designation of Simon is whether Jesus "names" (Luke) or "surnames" (Mark) him "Peter" or whether he is already called by that name (so Matthew). The diversity may reflect some degree of early Christian uncertainty on this point, which evidently took different forms within the period of Christian memory. (And, as we have already seen elsewhere, there are good reasons for supposing that Matthew's Petrine account in this case may represent the most accurate version: Simon carried a Greek nickname from his youth, which Jesus interpreted and turned into the Aramaic "rock.")

Luke's list of the Twelve is unique in distinguishing the other Simon as "called the Zealot" (6:15; cf. Mark 3:18//Matt. 10:4: "Cananaean"). Neither this disciple

---

29. See esp. Tertullian, *Marc.* 4.9; cf. later Jerome, *Ep.* 71.1 to Lucinius (AD 398); Gregory of Nazianzus, *Or.* 16.2; 37.1; 41.14; etc.

nor Simon the Pharisee (7:40, 43–44) nor Simon of Cyrene (23:26) is ever confused with Simon Peter in the NT or early traditions.

▫ Peter, Jairus, and the Woman with the Flow of Blood (8:45, 51)

In all three Synoptics, Jesus is on the way to see the dying daughter of Jairus, a synagogue ruler, when out of the crowd emerges a woman with a hemorrhage, who touches his cloak from behind. Whereas Matthew's Jesus turns around to address her directly (Matt. 9:22), in Mark and Luke he asks, "Who touched me?"—and the disciples find the question unreasonable in the midst of such a crowd (see Mark 5:31). Only Luke ascribes the answer specifically to Peter: when everyone else shrinks back in denial, it is Peter who takes charge and replies on their behalf, addressing Jesus by the uniquely Lukan appellation "master" (*epistata*) and thereby toning down the potential note of scorn in the Markan reply. Taking 8:45 in isolation, it is impossible to tell whether Luke draws on a Petrine memory here or imaginatively extrapolates from 8:51 (only Peter, James, and John are with Jesus at the house of Jairus; cf. Mark 5:37) and Peter's role as spokesman elsewhere in the Gospel.

▫ Peter's Messianic Confession (9:20)

If Peter's role was enhanced vis-à-vis Mark in the previous passage, this is less obviously the case for the Caesarea Philippi episode. Luke follows the Markan outline of the dialogue but removes the specific geographical reference (although from 9:10 we may assume that Jesus is still in Transjordan rather than in Galilee) and adds that the dialogue happened "as he was praying alone" (9:18). As in all four Gospels (cf. Mark 8:29; Matt. 16:16; John 6:69), it is Peter who representatively confesses Jesus's identity. Where the Markan Peter confesses, "You are the Messiah," Luke simply adds "of God" (so also 23:35). As on several previous occasions, this addition offers useful qualification of a term that may not be intrinsically meaningful to gentile readers.

Luke retains Jesus's first passion prediction (9:22//Mark 8:31), although there is no sign here of Peter's rejection of it or of Jesus's consequent rebuke of Peter. The reasons for this have consumed much scholarly effort but are not immediately apparent. The most plausible explanation may be that Luke attempts to salvage a less "raw" and more "acceptable" Jesus. By contrast, cosmetic treatment of an embarrassing altercation appears to sit uneasily with Matthew, who enhances Peter's role in this context more than any other Gospel (16:17–19) yet offers the harshest version of Jesus's rebuke (16:23; cf. Mark 8:33).

Nothing here suggests the persistence of any distinct source of Petrine memory.

▫ The Transfiguration (9:28–36)

The most distinctive Petrine feature in Luke's narrative of the transfiguration is the statement that Peter (along with James and John) has at first been sound asleep but is then wide awake when he sees the glory of Jesus with Moses and Elijah (9:32) and suggests building three booths for them (9:33). Commentators generally recognize this as a Lukan formulation. On the narrative level, Luke may be relocating motifs from the Markan Gethsemane account (Mark 14:32–42) and anticipating motifs from the resurrection and ascension narratives in order to intimate a preliminary fulfillment of the promise of 9:27: some of those who heard Jesus would not taste death until they saw the kingdom of God. Additional implications for Petrine memory, if any, seem slight.

□ Peter's Two Interventions (12:41; 18:28)

Peter puts in two further brief appearances as spokesman for the disciples before the beginning of the Passion Narrative; one is unique to Luke, while the other derives from Mark. In 12:41 Peter responds to the parable of the unprepared householder leaving the house to be burgled by asking whether this parable is meant for the disciples or a wider audience: "Lord, are you telling this parable for us or for everyone?" Peter's question, oddly unexpected in its narrative context, prepares the ground for the answer in the form of the following parable about the faithful and wise steward (12:42–48//Matt. 24:45–51). Here, verses 47–48 conclude by pronouncing a special responsibility on those who know what their master requires.

In 18:28, Luke takes over the Markan Peter's implicit question about the reward for those who have left all in order to follow Jesus (Mark 10:28). Both Peter's question and Jesus's answer are considerably closer to Mark's version than to the Matthean parallel (Matt. 19:27–30). Luke does, however, add a wife among the relationships one might give up for the kingdom (18:29). This is probably inserted for the sake of completeness or possibly in keeping with a pattern of ascetic sympathies also found in 14:26 and 20:35. Given the persistent memory of Peter's married status even as a later missionary in the NT and early Christian tradition, not least in Rome, these passages are unlikely to harbor any Petrine allusion.

□ Peter and John Prepare the Last Supper (22:8)

It is interesting that both Luke and the Fourth Gospel appear to show knowledge of additional sources as we approach the Passion Narrative; and for Luke, this may well go hand in hand with his evident reliance on certain Jerusalem traditions in Acts 1–12. The Petrine passages from this point on are worth considering from that angle.

In the other Gospels, preparations for the Last Supper are made by an anonymous team of disciples, either two (Mark 14:12–13) or an unspecified number (Matt. 26:17–19). Luke, however, claims to know their identity: Peter and John (22:8). Luke showed Peter in John's company twice before, although on both occasions James is also present (8:51; 9:28). For our purpose it may be significant that Peter and John are similarly paired in the early chapters of Acts (1:13; 3:1, 3, 4; 4:13, 19; 8:14)—all before the death of James in Acts 12:2.

Since no other obvious Lukan theological agenda attaches to this pairing, we must consider the possibility that in this pairing Luke may reflect an independent tradition about Peter. It may or may not be relevant that the Beloved Disciple, traditionally identified with John the son of Zebedee, is likewise paired with Peter on several occasions in the Johannine Passion Narrative (e.g., 13:32–25; 18:15–16 [?]; 20:2–10; 21:7, 20–22). This has sometimes been thought to imply Luke's knowledge of the Fourth Gospel or vice versa.

□ Prediction of Peter's Denial (22:31–34)

This pericope is at once the most interesting and the most revealing of Luke's Petrine texts; its distinctive Jesus logion prefixed to the prediction of Peter's denial may well shed light on our understanding of Luke's Peter more generally.[30] We will return to the wider significance and impact of this text in chapter 5 below.

> Simon, Simon, listen! Satan has demanded to sift all of you [plural] like wheat, but I have prayed for you [singular] that your own faith may not fail; and you, when once you have turned back, strengthen your brothers. (Luke 22:31–32)

Dispute about the origin and meaning of these verses has been long and protracted, and we cannot here offer a definitive resolution. What matters for our purposes is that they are without parallel in the other Gospels; the first verse is also largely without obvious Lukan language or motifs.

Luke tends to refer to Peter as Simon until his calling in 6:14 and identifies him as Peter after that. "Simon, Simon" is unique in all the NT, although Luke likes to redouble vocatives.[31] Jesus addresses Peter by name only here (as Simon) and in 22:34, which is the only time in the Gospels that Jesus personally addresses (rather than describes) him as "Peter." In the conflict with Satan that marks not only Jesus's ministry of exorcism (note 10:18; 11:15–22) but also the events of the passion in particular (22:3), Peter too will come under attack. As in the case of Job, Satan can "demand" to test the faithful but cannot determine the outcome of the test: in this case he will be thwarted by the intervention of the "stronger man" (cf. 11:22), who will preserve Peter's faith. Here Satan's "sifting"[32] applies to the disciples as a whole (note pl. *hymas*), seeking to expose what is inedible roughage and what is the pure kernel of wheat.

Verse 32 is recognized in the commentaries as a more clearly Lukan development of this theme, with distinctive vocabulary. Jesus has already prayed that Simon's

---

30. A programmatic interpretation of this text is suggested by Schneider 1985; Ascough 1993 offers a similarly programmatic reading of this text

31. "Martha, Martha" (10:41); "Saul, Saul" (Acts 9:4; 22:7); cf. "Lord, Lord" (Luke 6:46// Matt. 7:21); "Master, Master" (8:24; cf. Matt. 8:25); "Jerusalem, Jerusalem" (13:34//Matt. 23:37).

32. For the image of the "sieve," see Amos 9:9; 11QtgJob 10.2.

faith will not "give out,"[33] and as a result, Simon will be the one empowered to "strengthen"[34] the others. Throughout the NT, this ministry of strengthening is seen as the work of Christ or of his apostle, a point that would appear to lend credence to a view of Peter as representative or "vicar" of Christ, although in the NT he is not unique in that respect.[35]

One of the more interesting questions is what is meant by Peter's envisaged "turning." It will apparently take place after the impending Satanic challenge of the faithful, from which, perhaps by his denial, even Peter will not emerge wholly unscathed. We will return to this question in chapter 5.

Peter's reply in 22:33 appears as a paraphrase of Mark 14:31, which is of interest for spelling out his preparedness to go even "to prison and to death." As many commentators note, Peter's rash promise now rings hollow but will become meaningful in due course. Since none of the Gospel passion predictions or narratives speak of Jesus in prison, this passage may well resonate with the memory of Peter's subsequent fate, both in Acts (5:19, 22, 25; 12:5, 6) and beyond it to the end of Peter's life. Paul, incidentally, makes a similar promise in Acts 21:13, which hints at the extent to which Luke views the two apostles' ministry and destiny as bound up together.

The closest parallel to Peter's declared readiness here is in John 13:37, "I will lay down my life for you"(Mark 14:31//Matt. 26:35 leaves this reply conditional). This possibility of a link with the Fourth Gospel is further strengthened in Luke 22:24, which resembles not only Mark 14:30 but also, and in some ways more closely, John 13:38.

The passion and resurrection narratives of Luke and John, in other words, share an analogous Petrine sequence of events:

Sequence	Event	Luke	John
1	Peter promises to die for Jesus	22:33	13:37
2	Jesus predicts Peter's denial	22:34	13:38
3	The denial comes to pass	22:54–61	18:15–27
4	Peter recovers from his fall	24:12, 34; Acts [?]	21:15–17
5	Peter receives a unique pastoral charge on behalf of his fellow believers	22:32; cf. Acts 1:15; 2:14, 38; 3:6; etc.	21:15–17

Of course, the last item is anticipatory for Luke and placed *before* the denial and restoration, but the resulting impression is that there again appear to be connections between the Petrine memory represented in the Johannine and the

33. *Hina mē eklipē hē pistis sou*: the verb is unique to Luke in the NT (16:9; 22:32; 23:45). See, e.g., Dietrich 1972, 130–33. But such statistics should not be overrated in assessing authenticity.

34. *Stērizō* too is unique to Luke (9:51; 16:26; 22:32).

35. Paul too understands his ministry to be one of "strengthening": see Rom. 1:11; 1 Thess. 3:2; in 1 Thess. 3:13, it is Christ who does this.

Lukan Passion Narratives. Given the variations in wording and sequence, a *literary* dependence is unlikely to account for this connection. More plausibly, Luke and the Johannine tradition (perhaps the Beloved Disciple himself) represent comparable expressions of a Petrine memory of commitment and commissioning, derived perhaps in both cases from Christian circles in Jerusalem or Judea.

This conclusion is by no means incompatible with the other Gospels: Matt. 16:17–19, in particular, represents the most explicit tradition of a broadly comparable dominical charge to serve the church, which Oscar Cullmann (1953, 180–81) believed Matthew had transposed from a passion or resurrection setting more akin to those envisaged in Luke or John. The overlap between Luke and John also serves to confirm the persistence of some such memory, however diversely expressed, of Peter as uniquely commissioned by the Lord to a ministry beyond Easter. Its vitality can be seen in that, especially in its Matthean and Johannine forms, this memory went on to enjoy an extensive afterlife throughout the first two centuries here in view.

□ Peter's Denials and Contrition (22:54–62)

Luke is the only Gospel in which Jesus's appearance before the Sanhedrin is not interwoven with Peter's three denials; instead, a single, uninterrupted episode brings into stark focus Peter's triple failure and ends with the haunting note of Jesus's long, convicting glance at Peter, causing him to break down in tears (22:61–62). Although Luke has significantly reshaped the Markan (or pre-Markan) narrative by concentrating it in this way, he remains reasonably close to Mark up to verse 60—close enough, at any rate, that it would be difficult to argue here for a distinctly Lukan shape of Petrine memory. In verses 61–62, however, a number of commentators have convincingly argued for additional source input:

> And the Lord turned and looked at Peter. And Peter remembered the saying of the Lord, how he had said to him, "Before the rooster crows today, you will deny me three times." And he went out and wept bitterly. (ESV)

Even if theoretically v. 61a might be just a literary flourish, as such it is not characteristically Lukan.[36] And the closest link with verse 62 is not Mark 14:72 but Matt. 26:75—both Matthew and Luke appear to follow a simpler version of Mark's complex prediction involving two cock-crows and three denials.

Whether a literary or oral derivation can be established, therefore, it seems right to affirm that Luke may represent an additional aspect of the early Christian memory of Peter's denial. On this account, what caused Peter's contrition and repentance was not only the predicted crowing of the rooster but also Jesus's silent, eloquent glance at his disciple in the high priest's courtyard.

---

36. Note that the "turning and looking" motif is used of Jesus in John 1:38, but in 21:20 it is used of Peter.

We cannot see here more than a possibility, since this theme appears not to be developed in later first- or second-century sources.[37] For Luke and his readers, however, it contributed a singularly poignant feature of Petrine memory. It was when the Lord "turned and looked" at Peter that Peter "remembered the word of the Lord" and was overcome by the contrition that proved the beginning of what Jesus had also predicted (22:31–34): his "turning back" to "strengthen" the others and, eventually, his going "to prison and death" for Jesus. "Remembering the Lord" also became a key theme in other Petrine texts, including 2 Peter (3:2), the *Acts of Peter*, and the *Pseudo-Clementine* literature. Clement of Alexandria cites a tradition of Peter encouraging his wife, on her way to martyrdom, with the words "Remember the Lord!" (*Strom.* 7.11.63; cf. Eusebius, *Eccl. hist.* 3.30.2).

□ *Resurrection (24:12, 34)*

Unlike Mark and Matthew, who merely imply it (Mark 16:7; Matt. 28:16), Luke agrees with John and the Palestinian tradition quoted by Paul in 1 Cor. 15:5 that Peter saw the risen Jesus. What sequence of events Luke has in mind, however, is not clear. On hearing of the women's discovery of the empty tomb, Peter runs to see it for himself and then returns home. Aside from the reference to the Beloved Disciple, there is a degree of verbal overlap, and probably a shared source, with John 20:3–10.

Somewhat surprisingly, however, Cleopas and his friend returning from Emmaus are told in 24:34 that "the Lord is risen indeed, and has appeared to Simon." Luke does not explain when or where this event happened. Some have suggested that its unexpected intrusion is simply Luke's way of safeguarding in narrative form the Petrine priority required not only by his inherited gospel tradition but perhaps also by the role of the Palestinian creedal formula of 1 Cor. 15:5 within the Pauline churches. The latter, however, would be difficult to strengthen by changing "Peter" to "Simon" (rather than "Cephas").

It need not be doubted that Luke wishes to give credence to a memory of a Petrine resurrection appearance or that it is important for him to situate this in Jerusalem rather than in Galilee, as the other three Gospels do (Luke 24:49). The evidence of 1 Cor. 15:5 and a number of other texts (e.g., Ign. *Smyrn.* 3.2) suggests that Luke was able to enlist among his sources existing memories attesting the fact of such an appearance to Peter. At the same time, the nature of those sources evidently did not leave him free to let their attestation generate a whole new narrative. What we witness here, in other words, may be the guiding and perhaps constraining influence of living memory inherited from Luke's "eyewitnesses" (1:2) in the formulation of his description of Peter.

---

37. In the fifth century, Augustine saw this convicting glance as inward and spiritual rather than literal—on the curious grounds that Peter could not have been within Jesus's line of sight (*Grat. Chr.* 48, citing book 9 of Ambrose, *Exp. Luc.*)!

All in all, then, the Gospel of Luke gives us only two or three pointers to an independent access to Petrine memory, concentrated in the Passion Narrative. For Luke's Gospel narrative, the evangelist appears to have neither firsthand knowledge of Peter nor extensive access to eyewitnesses. Matters are slightly different for Acts, however.

Peter in the Acts of the Apostles

Peter's image in Acts remains appreciably Lukan, but with a number of interesting changes vis-à-vis the Gospel. As soon as the ascension occurs and the disciples are instructed to await the Spirit's arrival in Jerusalem, Luke immediately foregrounds Peter as the leading apostle. It is Peter who proposes to appoint Matthias by lot as the successor of Judas (Acts 1:15–22). Throughout the first half of Acts, it appears that Peter is the main human protagonist—the pioneer missionary and chief public speaker, healer, and prophetic overseer of church discipline.

Peter's speeches sound, as scholars have long noted, somewhat "archaizing" and rather less theologically and christologically developed than we normally find in Luke.[38] This does not support easy assumptions about either historicity or Lukan sources, since analysis has also shown extensive overlap between the characterization of different apostolic figures. Nevertheless, we also need not assume that Luke is merely playing an elaborate game of literary charades. During the period of living memory, Luke presents us with a picture of Peter's teaching that would be recognizable and thus find resonance with a Roman church that remembered his ministry.

Peter, then, is indeed the prince of apostles during the first half of Acts. He acts as the public voice for the believers in his sermon on the day of Pentecost (2:14–41) and takes the lead in being the first to perform a miracle in the name of Jesus, with John playing an accompanying role (3:1–10). In fact, Peter remains the chief miracle worker among the Twelve, with the latecomer Paul a distant, almost derivative second; even Peter's shadow heals the sick (5:15; cf. the "handkerchiefs" brought to heal the sick after touching Paul's body at Ephesus [19:12]).

In the developing conflict with the authorities, Peter is again the leading speaker and defendant when he and John appear before the Sanhedrin (4:1–21). In terms of church discipline, it is also Peter who prophetically pronounces divine judgment on Ananias and Sapphira (5:1–11). Evangelism and apologetics in Jerusalem and well beyond, miracles, and prophetic speech and action are all predicated of Peter but not of James the Just, who exercises a vital but rather different leadership role in Jerusalem.

Interestingly, it is Peter, not Paul, who assumes early apostolic missionary leadership outside Jewish circles, becoming first the superintendent of an outreach to the

38. See, e.g., Johnson 2002; Ridderbos 1962; Scobie 1979; Soards 1994; Stroud 1994; Tannehill 1991; Zehnle 1971.

Samaritans (chap. 8) and then the pioneer of a mission to gentiles when he converts the household of Cornelius at Caesarea in response to a vision (10:1–11:18). This is an episode for which he has to defend himself before an initially skeptical Jewish Christian audience in chapter 11.

When Emperor Claudius grants Judea to Herod Agrippa after the death of Caligula in AD 41, Peter is immediately imprisoned at Passover, together with John's brother James, and nearly suffers the same fate of execution (chap. 12). But Peter makes a miraculous escape and abandons Jerusalem as his base; Acts 12:17 says cryptically only that he went "to another place [*eis heteron topon*]," and, like the prison guards of 12:18, we are left to wonder "what became of him." Peter appears once more in a position of some peripheral influence at the apostolic council of Jerusalem (15:7–11), but the deciding vote is cast by James rather than Peter, and this is the last we hear of him.

The subsequent silence of Acts has sometimes been assumed to constitute clear evidence that nothing much was known about what became of Peter, and certainly that no Roman ministry is likely to have occurred. The British scholar Michael Goulder is among a long series of keen critics who have suggested that this is because once Peter was deposed from Jerusalem, his story was effectively over. Goulder (2004) suggests that Peter returned after Agrippa's rule to die there in obscurity in the mid-50s AD. It is of course true that the NT is not very explicit about asserting a final ministry in Rome: in some ways the clearest statement is 1 Peter itself, to which we will turn below. Beyond that, we rely on what I have called the period of "living memory." But what we can also show is that none of the extracanonical witnesses of that period contradict a Roman martyrdom or narrate an alternative tradition—and several of those that explicitly affirm or strongly imply it predate the latest NT documents.

In literary terms, however, it seems significant that the narrative pattern of Acts parallels the public lives of Peter and Paul as Luke's twin *dramatis personae*, his two chief actors and witnesses. Without any significant overlap, their ministries are developed analogously.[39] From Acts 1:8 onward, the narrative points to the ends of the earth, and from 19:21 onward, we know that for Paul at least this means Rome (cf. 23:11; also 2:10). Luke does not, however, reveal what happens once he gets there—or indeed how it all ends, for either Peter or Paul. In other words, Luke's narrative vector points from Jerusalem all the way to Rome, and his twin narratives tell a tale that does end up there; and yet each of the twin stories ends not with a bang but a whimper. In both cases, a mysteriously anticlimactic exit makes it reasonable to suppose that Luke knows more than he tells, and (if he has any literary skill at all) that he knows his audience is aware of this too. This is certainly an impression that would follow well on the much-noted analogy of the martyrdoms of Jesus and Stephen. Moreover, it is possible that Luke may, like 1 *Clement* and the Gospel of Mark,

39. This "twin lives" emphasis in Acts has been widely noted; see, e.g., Clark 2001.

have good reasons for this somewhat taciturn narrative wink-and-nudge strategy (escaping "to another place" indeed!). Like any author of potentially dangerous underground (*samizdat*) literature, he seeks to protect both his sources and his readers from attracting official attention for what in the recent past has become a politically toxic cause.

Peter in 1 Peter?

Two canonical epistles claiming Petrine authorship date from the period of living memory, but the two documents differ strikingly in what they say, and were heard to say, about Peter. Unlike its opinion of 2 Peter (discussed in chap. 3), early Christian literature never doubts the apostolic and Roman pedigree of 1 Peter. And from the earliest period, the words of this letter were heard as unambiguously authoritative and speaking in the voice of Peter.[40]

Somewhat contrary to the drift of modern scholarship, I wish here to argue that while there are indeed weighty reasons to doubt Peter's sole literary authorship of this letter, the conventional arguments for a fully pseudonymous composition (after his death, unconnected with his ministry or even with the envisaged readership) do not merit the wide acceptance they have received and should be shelved. To be sure, the origin of 1 Peter is now often supposed to be similar to that of 2 Peter: a posthumous attempt by someone possibly belonging to a "Petrine circle" in Rome. However, as soon as one tries to locate and animate such a scenario with more specific ecclesiological, sociological, or religio-historical considerations, imaginative projection and circular argumentation inescapably set in (rightly noted by Söding 2009a, 7; Feldmeier 2005, 23; and others).

First, the problems. It is often taken as self-evident that the Greek in 1 Peter is too refined to have originated from the pen of a backwater fisherman from Bethsaida (cf. Acts 4:13, where Peter is described as *agrammatos* and *idiōtēs*). Tied to the fluency in Greek is the fact that the OT is cited from the LXX exclusively. Beyond the issues of language, a number of other problems emerge in trying to situate the letter historically. The discussion of the "fiery ordeal" in 4:12–19 and the notion of a consistent conflict between Christians and society (5:9) are difficult to envisage before the time of Nero (AD 54–68). An even better fit might seem to be the period of Trajan (AD 98–117): he corresponded about the persecution of Christians with Pliny the Younger as governor of the troubled province of Bithynia-Pontus, whose Christians are among the addressees of 1 Peter (1:1; cf. Pliny the Younger, *Ep.* 10.96).

---

40. Indeed, in the face of 1 Peter's effective de-canonization in much recent NT scholarship, it is worth recalling that the apostolicity of 1 Peter was one of the first to be attested in antiquity and one of the last to be widely discounted in the heyday of historical criticism. It is peculiar how much slower the discipline has been to question the received certitudes of nineteenth-century German Protestants than the unwavering consensus of the early church.

Similarly, "Babylon" as a stand-in for Rome (5:13) is often supposed to be a post-70 phenomenon in Jewish apocalyptic thought. What is more, the content of the letter displays none of the first-century concerns over non-Christian Jews, law observance, or the gentile mission: Jewish traditions appear happily transferred to gentiles without remainder (e.g., 1:4, 15–16; 2:9–10). Also, the structure of the church pictured in 1 Peter has been deemed too developed for a date within or near the lifetime of Peter and as better attributed to a time when charismatic gifts have been suitably routinized and replaced by presbyterial governance. Finally, rather than using explicit links with Jesus of Nazareth, the author seems to make use of tradition, even quasi-Pauline tradition, while addressing churches within the Pauline orbit in a catechetical style. (This last position, on the other hand, has come to be increasingly questioned by those scholars who note that "the differences between 1 Peter and the Pauline writings are numerous and striking.")[41]

While any attempt to address these justifiable concerns involves a certain amount of speculation, the objections to a genuinely Petrine connection are weaker than is often admitted. First, the notion that Peter himself could not have been a competent Greek speaker is simply unfounded. His childhood in Bethsaida, a village with little Jewish presence, in which his brother Andrew and close friend Philip were known exclusively by their Greek names, would have ensured his ability to speak tolerable Greek from a young age, even if not perhaps to read or write it.[42] Signs of a wider literary sensitivity in 1 Peter may indeed imply more than a basic competence in writing, a point readily accounted for by the reference to writing "through" (rather than "with"!) Silvanus in 5:12.[43] If this Silvanus is to be identified with the companion of Paul (2 Cor. 1:19; 1 Thess. 1:1) and the Silas of Acts, Acts 15:22–40 suggests that he was a person with linguistic and hermeneutical competency in Greek and that he neither experienced nor imagined an unbridgeable gap between the missions of Peter and Paul.[44] Indeed, such help or influence could also account for the apparently exclusive reference to the LXX throughout the letter.[45] On this point, it is also pertinent that the LXX was most likely the Bible with which the Christians in Rome and Asia Minor were familiar.

41. Elliott 2000, 40. Cf., e.g., Brox 1993, 47–51; Herzer 1998; and Söding 2009c, 30–36.

42. See further chapter 6 below; note also the seemingly self-evident assumption that Peter's brother Andrew and friend Philip, both known by their Hellenistic names, are the most appropriate point of contact for the "Greeks" (Greek-speaking Jewish Passover pilgrims?) who ask to see Jesus in John 12:20.

43. Karen Jobes (2005, 325–38) has argued that the Semitic "bilingual interferences" "indicate an author whose first language was not Greek" (337). On the other hand, her suggestion that the "exiles" were actually Jewish Christian colonists settled in Asia Minor by Claudius has little evidence to support it (cf. Elliott 2006, 2).

44. Silvanus as the author of 1 Peter has been discussed from time to time. See Dschulnigg 1996, 174–75; Stuhlmacher 1992–99, 2:71–72; Wilckens 2005, 1.3:366–67; Söding 2009b, 16.

45. We must note, however, that the textual traditions of the LXX were still so fluid in this period that it is very difficult be sure if variant citations are a result of a given author's hand,

The issue of gentile persecution and the "fiery ordeal" is only historically problematic if the envisaged persecution is officially state-sponsored. But that is not clear from the references in the letter itself. *Gentile* opposition—concerted, even if not yet officially sanctioned and organized—is attested as early as 1 Thess. 2:14–16.[46] Indeed, the statement in 4:16 about suffering "as Christians" requires no formal denouncement before government officials such as occurred later under Trajan (Pliny the Younger, *Ep.* 10.96). It need refer only to endemic social prejudice arising from the Christians' failure to participate in pagan cultural and religious practice, prejudice that might well be manifest in violent actions already noted in 4:4.[47] At the same time, 1 Pet. 5:9 also should not be pressed too far in the direction of constant, universal tensions with society; the author attributes this suffering to the work of the devil rather than to society or culture and suggests only that the readers' experience is typical rather than exceptional. On another note, the marked absence of any references to an all-pervasive imperial cult also seems consonant with a Western origin and a date well before Pliny's letter.

Finally, the use of Babylon as a cipher for Rome does in fact pre-date the year AD 70. Jewish reapplication to the second temple of prophecies about Babylon's destruction of the first temple is well attested since at least Dan. 9 and appears to feature in Jesus's predictions of the temple's destruction (e.g. Mark 13:14). Josephus likewise believed Jeremiah to be speaking about the year 70 (*Ant.* 10.79), while Yohanan ben Zakkai was said to have attributed the prophecy of Jerusalem's fall to Isa. 10:34.[48] As early as Dan. 11:30 one encounters the identification of the "Kittim" with the Romans (explicitly so in the case of the Septuagint and several other ancient versions), an interpretation that is also common in the Dead Sea Scrolls, where additional links with Assyria/Babylonia are also found (cf. 4Q163 [Isaiah pesher] frag. 4 7.ii.1–4, frag. 8 10.1; 4Q385a; 4Q554 frag. 3 iii.14–22). In the first century AD, the *Sibylline Oracles* lump together "Babylon and the land of Italy" (5.159–60; cf. 168–70).[49]

The allegedly decisive evidence against some sort of Petrine connection with 1 Peter turns out, therefore, to be rather inconclusive. Conversely, as a fully pseudepigraphal document (i.e., composed by an anonymous person unconnected with the apostle), 1 Peter would require an almost impossibly rapid process of acceptance as authentic by the group to whom it was sent. As Friedrich Neugebauer (1980, 67–68) notes, such a pseudepigraphon—in which the author and addressees are identified, as in 1 Peter—would presumably need to be written after the death of *both* the implied author and the implied recipients. Assuming the ostensible recipients would have left some memory, at least with the next generation, regarding

---

textual variation in the LXX, or translation from a Hebrew text. In any case, the citations in 1 Peter conform largely to known LXX versions.

46. Cf. my discussion of this pericope in Bockmuehl 2001b.

47. This point is well argued by Holloway 2009.

48. *'Abot de Rabbi Nathan* A 4.41ff. (cited according to Schechter 1887, p. 11b); par. *b. Giṭ.* 56a.

49. Cf. also the Christian text *4 Ezra* [= 2 Esdras/6 *Ezra*] 15.46–48.

the religious texts at their disposal, this pushes the window of opportunity even later, and yet that window must close before the earliest mention of the letter in early sources.

On that note, however, one of the strongest arguments for an early date and at least broadly Petrine origin of 1 Peter lies in its wide and early attestation. In Rome, *1 Clement*, dating perhaps from the 90s AD, makes abundant (if unattributed) use of 1 Peter.[50] The pseudonymous author of 2 Peter, who wrote perhaps around AD 100–120, has no question that the first letter of Peter is of apostolic authorship (2 Pet. 3:1); indeed, there is a sense in which this author bases his own authority on that earlier document's authenticity. While the usual arguments from language, style, and erudition clearly do make it seem unlikely that Peter himself put pen to paper, 1 Peter does not actually claim that he did, leaving plenty of scope for a mediated or "authorized" authorship in whatever form.

What light, then, does 1 Peter shed on Peter's remembered profile in the West? First, the link with Pontus and northern Asia Minor is interesting (1:1). It has been observed that while some of these areas do potentially overlap with the Pauline mission in Acts, most do not; and in the case of Bithynia at least, there may be considerable interest in Luke's otherwise curious statement that the Spirit of Jesus "did not allow" a Pauline mission in that territory (Acts 16:7). Later tradition consistently affirms Peter's ministry there, though we cannot be sure whether this is asserted independently or is based on 1 Pet. 1:1. It is intriguing too that Trajan later finds his governor in Pontus/Bithynia (AD 110–112) dealing with a substantial Christian community, large enough to incur the concern of the governor. Pliny came across those who had been *Christiani* for twenty years or more (*Ep.* 10.96)—that is, quite plausibly within a generation's memory of 1 Peter and potentially among the addressees of 2 Peter, who are concerned about the Lord's delay. Significantly, 1 Peter considers the specter of persecution specifically for the name of being *Christiani* (cf. 1 Pet. 4:14, 16), a neologism still relatively uncommon until Trajan's time. Additionally, 1 Peter's address to Christians in Pontus as *included* in the Israel of God raises a provocative note of dissonance for the subsequent views of Marcion, traditionally said to hail from the port of Sinope and profoundly opposed to an Israel-centered understanding of Christian faith.

Throughout the letter, the author emphasizes the fact that Peter is a witness or guarantor (*martys*, 5:1) to the passion and resurrection of Jesus. While this is not an emphasis unique to Petrine tradition, it is nevertheless very fitting for the apostle who was remembered as the key witness to this material in early Christianity (cf. Elliott 2000, 818–19). Some scholars have suggested, with varying degrees of confidence, that the term *martys* is a subtle reference to Peter's own martyrdom in Rome provided by the anonymous author.[51] However, this is unlikely for a number

---

50. So even Zwierlein (2009, 278–87), who dates 1 Peter to the time of Pliny and believes it uses the Pastoral Epistles.

51. See Meade 1986, 177; Achtemeier 1996, 324.

of reasons. First, the term *martys* appears to have acquired the technical sense of "blood-witness" only around the very end of the first century; before that, it tended straightforwardly to denote a witness.[52] Second, the witness is given quite specific syntactical content, namely, the sufferings of Christ (so, rightly, Söding 2009b, 22). Rather than referring to his own death, Peter is presented as the witness and bearer of the memory of the passion events, somewhat as he also appears in John or Luke.[53] It is in this position as witness that he, in turn, continually "reminds" the recipients of the "new birth . . . through the resurrection of Jesus Christ" (1:3) and that "Christ suffered for sins . . . was put to death in the flesh and made alive in the spirit" (3:18–19) and "suffered in the flesh" (4:1).

The portrayal of Peter in this letter is particularly striking in that no special Petrine privilege is either assumed or asserted. Rather than having a tone of authority and distinction, Peter is "born anew" alongside the readers "into a living hope" (1:3), and yet this is an affirmation that seems strikingly to reverse the death of hope expressed by the two disciples on the road to Emmaus (Luke 24:21).[54] Peter is a "fellow-elder" *among* the elders to whom he speaks in 5:1–5, in marked contrast with the succession theme in 1 *Clement* and later texts (Söding 2009b, 30). And just as the call to "watch" in 5:8 employs the same verb with which Jesus unsuccessfully exhorted Peter and the others in the garden of Gethsemane (note esp. Mark 14:37 and pars.), so also the shepherding metaphor in these verses is inclusive and reminiscent of Jesus's own commissioning of Peter in John 21. However, whereas Jesus commands Peter to be the shepherd of the sheep in John 21:15–18, 1 Peter extends the shepherding metaphor to the "elders among you" (5:1–2) and claims that the chief shepherd (*archipoimenos*) is none other than Christ himself (5:4). It may even be argued that 1 Pet. 2:4–8 indicates a similar diffusion of Peter's authority as the "rock" when Jesus is portrayed as the "living stone [*lithon zōnta*]." It is Christ who is set in Zion as the precious foundation stone, and *all* believers who "come to him" are "built up into a spiritual house like living stones [*hōs lithoi zōntes*]."[55]

All in all, it seems clear that 1 Peter cannot be seen as a repository of historical Petrine memory or theology. In some ways, Thomas Söding (2009b, 43–44) captures the point well in suggesting that what marks 1 Peter is its basic *compatibility* and catholicity rather than its distinctiveness within early Christian literature. The letter shows a subtle but identifiable awareness of aspects of Petrine memory relating to the Gospel narratives, and it is a mark of its catholicity that it also

52. See Marxsen and Steck 1979, 393; Elliott 2000, 819–20.

53. Indeed, the injunction to "keep alert" (*grēgorein*) in 1 Pet. 5:8 recalls Mark's account of Jesus's final prayer in the garden (Mark 14:34–38), thus providing another possible link with the passion of Jesus.

54. This passage is addressed more fully in chapter 5 below.

55. It is striking that Origen (*Comm. Matt.* 12.14) interpreted the "rock" pericope in Matt. 16:13–20 to mean that all church leaders who live a worthy life become the rock upon which the church is built. See also Cyprian, *Ep.* 73.7.

manifests a number of substantive links with the Petrine profile in the Acts of the Apostles and with aspects of the theology of the gentile mission that also come to articulation in the letters of Paul.

Mark: Peter's Evangelist

The Gospel of Mark's connection with our subject has long been highly controversial. Mark is widely regarded as the earliest of the canonical Gospels and the one on which Matthew, Luke, and possibly John are dependent.

For this study, the inclusion of Mark at this point immediately raises enormous historical and methodological problems. Was the author of the Second Gospel a man called Mark? If so, is he the Mark associated with Peter in the consensus of patristic tradition? And what place does that traditional image of Mark have in the NT, which seems to know one, two, or possibly even three persons called Mark? Only a single passage, after all, appears to associate Peter in Rome with a man called Mark (1 Pet. 5:13), and that in a letter regarded by many critics as a pseudonymous product of the late first century.

In order to clarify the place of Mark's Gospel in our study, it seems appropriate to rehearse in a few paragraphs some of the features of the Markan tradition in the NT and the church fathers. This in turn will help us to see some of the diverse ways in which Mark's Gospel might be said to serve as a source of Petrine memory in Rome.

For present purposes, we will take for granted the relatively mainstream (if occasionally contested) position that Mark was written in Rome, perhaps in the late 60s AD, but with plenty of Palestinian influence on the language and content.

Realistic Memory of Peter?

In the case of Peter, the interpretative fashion in Markan scholarship has been to understand him as prominently representative of the problematic light in which the disciples as a group appear: he and they alike are not merely fickle and unseeing in their faith, but at crucial moments they signally oppose the work of Jesus. This theme, which does find a degree of support in the text, is, on this reading, interpreted as Mark's deliberate literary creation, serving as a backdrop to accentuate the sovereign action of Jesus. An alternative, or sometimes complementary, view is to suggest that the disciples, and Peter in particular, are specifically singled out for attack as representing a Christian group or viewpoint that Mark sought to undermine. While this reading trend attracted a good deal of attention in the later twentieth century, it has declined in popularity in recent years.

Ancient readers, however, did not as a rule, and never in the first instance, see the Gospel characters as ciphers. They did allegorize narrative, but this applied above all to the stories of the OT and, to a lesser extent, the parables, which seem to invite such a reading. For the early Christian readers, as indeed for most subsequent Christians, the Gospel of Mark is not written in code. Its *dramatis personae*, however paradigmatic in homiletical application, were of interest for them above all as real persons, and only thus as personal examples. Mark's concern too is for "Peter as Peter," as one helpful corrective puts it (Wiarda 1999). Peter is no mere literary cipher for inadequate discipleship, as has sometimes been suggested, but is presented instead with an evident desire for realistic verisimilitude and extra-textual *reference*. To the extent that Mark offers access to the *remembered* Peter, this point seems particularly self-evident.

In an important and usefully controversial book, Richard Bauckham (2006; following Byrskog 2000 and other Scandinavian scholars) appeals to the conventions of ancient historiography to argue that the named characters in the Gospel narratives point to the authors' recourse to eyewitnesses: for him, the texts are warranted or even written by such eyewitnesses. Although the argument may lend itself to overstated or maximalist conclusions, in principle the assertion of personal guarantors of the gospel tradition is long overdue and well rooted in ancient historiographical tradition. (See also Bockmuehl 2010b in conversation with Dunn 2003b.)

Mark's Peter as Peter

Mark's *positive* interest in Peter is rather more significant than scholars often assert. Peter is the first to be called (1:16) and remains from the start the most prominent member of the Twelve, typically taking the initiative. Indeed, that first episode simply introduces "Simon and his brother Andrew" in 1:16, as if Mark, like the evangelists that follow him, expects the readers to need no further introduction to Peter (cf. Luke 4:38; John 1:42; contrast Matt. 4:18). Similarly, the first reference to the disciples as a group is "Simon and those with him" (1:36). Mark's Peter is always included in references to the inner circle of Jesus's confidants, usually alongside James and John (e.g., 5:37; 9:2; 13:3; 14:33). Peter is virtually the only member of the Twelve with whom Jesus converses individually, and he is the only one addressed by name (14:37). The evangelist also, and quite pointedly, makes Peter the Gospel's *last*-named individual, awkwardly singling him out at the conclusion *in addition* to "the disciples" (16:7; cf. 1 Cor. 15:5; Luke 24:34). This is possibly a deliberate bracket (*inclusio*) around the Gospel with 1:16 and 3:16, sure to impress itself on readers who already had other reasons to affirm Peter's rehabilitation and to regard him as linked with Mark's Gospel.

Quite apart from such general observations about Peter's importance in Mark, however, a number of more detailed narrative features contribute to the shape and prominence of Petrine memory in Rome. These perspectival features have the effect, and almost certainly the intent, of accentuating the remembered Peter as the guarantor of Mark's Palestinian story of Jesus for a Roman readership. By following where Mark's narrative goes, one discovers a striking sense of proximity to Peter.

In the call narrative of Mark 1:16–20, Simon and Andrew are engaged in their profession as fishermen, casting nets from the shore into (lit. "in") the sea. The redundant repetition in "Simon and Andrew, Simon's brother" is striking and immediately draws attention to the more important figure. The narrative contains a famous play on the brothers' profession, which anticipates their future missionary activity as "fishers for people," a connection rooted in OT prophecy of restoration and judgment (Jer. 16:15–16) and also exploited by patristic interpreters. There may be a significant reminiscence in the fact that Peter and his brother are fishing solely with cast-nets: unlike the sons of Zebedee in 1:19 (and unlike Luke 5:3), Peter evidently does not have a boat, let alone hired hands, to leave behind—a claim that resonates with patristic assertions about Peter's impoverished youth. Be that as it may, however, "Peter's" Gospel displays vivid and considerable knowledge about such professional details as cast-net fishing (1:16), the acoustics of a fishing boat on water (4:1), and even the cushion kept in its stern (4:38).

In 1:22, Jesus is described as teaching "with authority and not as the scribes," a tradition clearly suited to reinforce the impression that its bearer was not a man of letters but rather an *agrammatos* (cf. Acts 4:13), a person to whom scholars might well seem remote, irrelevant, and dithering.

A more explicit, personal Petrine touch is introduced in 1:30–31, where Jesus enters Simon and Andrew's house and heals Peter's mother-in-law. As a matter of historical plausibility, the source of such an intimate vignette of domestic life must be sought in the family of Peter himself. Leaving aside the question of its historical origin, though, this story resonates particularly well with other Roman traditions about Peter's wife and daughter, including the former's martyrdom in the city. Together with Paul's testimony in 1 Cor. 9:5, which circulated in Rome before the end of the first century, the healing of Peter's mother-in-law reinforced both Palestinian and Roman memories of Peter as a family man who had hosted the ministry of Jesus in his home. To an audience familiar with it, this image of Peter might be thought to color the understanding of related texts about marriage and children, including the tradition of Peter's handicapped daughter (e.g., in the *Acts of Peter* 1a), later said to have been buried in the catacomb of Domitilla.

The Markan Peter's personal involvement in the inner circle of disciples, mentioned earlier, also raises a number of interesting issues relevant to the profile of a Petrine memory. One of the narrative corollaries of this role is Peter's explicit and implied access to conversations or events conducted in private. On the one hand, it obviously places him in a privileged position to be the spokesman for the disciples of Jesus. As such, he single-handedly brings to a point the confession of their faith in Jesus, only to incur Jesus's caustic rebuke for their incomprehension of his calling (8:27–33). This is followed later by the physical and spiritual desertion of the Teacher at Gethsemane and in the high priest's court. Scholars have sometimes taken the severity of Jesus's and, implicitly, the narrator's criticism of Peter as indicative of a sustained anti-Petrine bias in the Gospel. This interpretation, however, is hardly required and would militate against the grain of Peter's cumulative profile in the Gospel, a profile that does not conceal the volatility of a flawed and fallible character but that nonetheless assigns him immense importance as both confidant of Jesus and authentic point of access to his tradition. We may speculate whether some such image of the apostle is also assumed, despite subsequent sharp words of criticism, in Paul's early contact with Peter reported in Gal. 1:18.

Be that as it may, privileged access to private episodes of Jesus's life and ministry recurs elsewhere in the Gospel. Peter witnesses the raising of Jairus's daughter (5:37) and Jesus's Aramaic instruction, *talitha cum*, in private. Together with the other disciples, Peter overhears Jesus's cursing of the fig tree in 11:14, and then he draws the withered tree to Jesus's attention in 11:21. Jesus's private apocalyptic instruction is in Mark restricted to the four disciples who were the first to be called (13:3).

The Markan Peter's private access to Jesus is perhaps most striking in relation to the transfiguration (9:2–13), as well as the arrest and trial narratives (14:29–42, 54–72). The former story had a special (if indirect) impact on subsequent Petrine memory, as we saw when discussing 2 Pet. 1:16–18 (chap. 3 above). Peter is represented not only as having been present but also as the disciple who articulated the believer's awestruck response to Jesus as the equal of Moses and Elijah and who heard the divine voice confirming Jesus as Son of God.

What is more, the transfiguration's narrative link with the eschatological logion about the kingdom's coming in 9:1 may, however remotely, reflect a memory of Peter's preaching: that same dominical prophecy appears in the later first century to have occasioned a degree of concern in Petrine and other circles (see 2 Pet. 3:4, 9–10; cf. John 21:21–23). Mark's placement of this isolated saying immediately before 9:2–8 may have sought to forestall such anxiety: commentators since the patristic period have suggested that these three disciples on the mountain were precisely the ones who did not "taste" (violent) death before they saw in this episode "the kingdom of God coming with power." Some deliberate redactional connection of this sort seems likely. As I suggested in a previous chapter, it is instructive too to compare the promise that some would see the kingdom coming "with power [*en dynamei*]" with 2 Peter's assertion that the transfiguration *actually* (if proleptically) disclosed Christ's "power and coming [*dynamin kai parousian*]" (1:16), exemplified in the heavenly voice "on the holy mountain." Mark's redaction here may subtly counteract any idea that Peter assumed he would live to see the Lord's return (see also 1 Pet. 4:7).

A number of features in Mark 14 have, from time to time, been thought reminiscent of eyewitness memory. Peter plays no special role in the Last Supper, although David Daube (1990, 367–68) has suggested, perhaps somewhat optimistically, that the Passover *seder*-like features of that meal would be consistent with the traditional idea of Mark's dependence on a Petrine source and with the possibility that Mark 14 could derive largely from Peter. But nothing demands a unique link with Peter here. Even the narrative stance of Mark's singling out Peter in the immediately following prediction of his denial (14:27–31, closely paralleled by Matt. 26:31–35) does not necessitate a Petrine point of view, although it does not preclude it.

But in the arrest and trial narratives, Peter, James, and John are singled out to accompany Jesus in prayer at Gethsemane (14:33), while only Peter is personally reproached for his failure to stay awake (14:37). Mark is silent regarding the Fourth Gospel's assertion that it was Peter who severed the ear of a named servant of the high priest (14:47; cf. John 18:10–11) and regarding the Johannine claim that Peter's access to the high priest's court was procured by the Beloved Disciple, who was a household acquaintance.

The Markan Peter, finally, is the only disciple said to accompany Jesus after his arrest, where Peter is shown sitting in the high priest's courtyard warming himself by the fire (14:54), another extraordinary narrative detail implying a vivid eyewitness claim. That ringside seat not only grounds Mark's narrative stance but, at a canonical level, seems to echo claims about Peter as an eyewitness of the passion and the majesty of Jesus in 1 Pet. 5:1 (cf. 2 Pet. 1:16). A Petrine echo also links the assertion that "Jesus was silent and did not answer" (14:61) with Jesus refusing to return threats and abuse in 1 Pet. 2:23.

In this way, Peter becomes the only one actually confronted with the challenge that results in the unflattering threefold denial of Jesus in the space of one hour (14:66–72). Peter is "*below* in the courtyard" (v. 66) and, after the first denial, exits immediately into the *outer courtyard* (v. 68), an interesting architectural touch that allows Peter to remove himself gradually from the proceedings. Then, after a further denial is made fruitless by Peter's unmistakable Galilean accent, he hears the rooster crow. At that moment, Peter remembers Jesus's words, words that have an awkward but memorable ring in Greek syntax. *Dis tris* ("twice thrice")—"before the rooster crows twice, thrice you will deny me." That same emphasis on Peter's remembering of Jesus echoes through all subsequent Petrine literature, including the sermons in Acts, the Petrine letters, the Roman legends of the apocryphal acts with their famous *Quo Vadis* episode (*Acts of Peter* 6), and Peter's reminder to his wife on the way to execution to "remember the Lord" (cited by Clement and Eusebius; see above). Mark's is merely the earliest and most influential account in a whole tradition of Peter as the chief witness to the memory of Jesus.

It suits Mark's theme of Petrine memory that the apostle's departure from the scene marks the point at which the narrative camera's zoom in on the proceedings suddenly pans out into more stereotyped generalities, both for the rest of the night and before Pilate the next day. No further implicit claim of privileged Petrine reminiscence is made for the remainder of the Gospel. Significantly, we are told that it was the women who saw where the body was laid. Peter evidently did not, and there is no attempt to claim that he did, however convenient that might have been. Later readers closer to Rome might conceivably know, or at least wonder, whether the Rufus whose father carried the cross in 15:21 could have represented something of this memory in Rome (along with his mother, who was well know to Paul; cf. Rom. 16:13). The women at the cross also became, to Peter and the others, the first witnesses of Easter Sunday. Peter is, however, evidently rehabilitated as the last named person of the Gospel's original text, the only individual identified as a recipient of the women's resurrection message that Jesus would go before them to Galilee as he had promised (16:7). That promise, of course, reiterates a pre-Easter conversation with none other than Simon Peter, who swears undying loyalty (14:28–31).

Finally, with respect to this realistic Markan narrative posture, it is also interesting to note that no such Petrine perspective is in evidence in the longer ending, Mark 16:9–20. Although composed in the mid-second century, it does not mention Peter and appears not to assign Petrine tradition a privileged role.[56]

Mark on Peter's Palestinian Context

Certain other elements in Mark's narrative are more elusive and tenuous in their bearing on the Roman memory of Peter. Among these is the substantial evidence of the Gospel's linguistic and geographic connections with Galilee and Palestine. We must bear in mind once again that the historical or geographic accuracy of these aspects is not our primary concern, even if the evangelist himself had a better understanding of these matters than has sometimes been supposed.[57]

It seems reasonable to assume, moreover, that most of this exotic material would be largely meaningless to a gentile Roman audience. Even for Greek speakers in Rome, of course, the very clumsiness of outlandish places, phrases, and expressions intruding into the narrative would reinforce the impression of verisimilitude: like the other evangelists, Mark underscores the sense that these "memoirs" record real events and are not mere literary playthings. Herein lies an important difference between Christian and pagan belief: the remembered Peter roots the Gospel episodes in actual experiences and not in stereotyped timeless myths that "always are" (as pagan apologists liked to put it).

The introduction into the narrative of individuals such as Zebedee, Alphaeus, Bartimaeus, and the like illustrates the surprising lack of embarrassment with which the Gospel employs such exotic-sounding (and consistently translated) Semitic names and patronyms. It suggests a confidence about sources that lends a colorful plausibility to the oriental setting of Peter's memoirs and preaching. This

56. In this respect, it differs from the variant "shorter ending" inserted after Mark 16:8 in a number of early medieval Greek, Coptic, and Ethiopic manuscripts: "Now they briefly reported everything they had been told to Peter and those with him. And after this Jesus sent out through them, from East to West, the sacred and incorruptible message of eternal salvation."

57. The Gospel's numerous Palestinian linguistic and geographic features raise problems that have been expansively pursued in the commentary literature. Here it will suffice to single out a few items that seem relevant to the image of Peter as the remembered source of gospel tradition, specifically in Mark. No explicit connection with Peter is made; nor does the redactional shaping of many of these passages make it likely that such a connection was foremost in the writer's mind. But the implied and remembered Petrine influence behind the Gospel, suggested by the narrative features cited here and reinforced by the unanimous consensus of early Christian tradition, would inevitably gain in shape and color from the striking particularity of the features noted here.

understanding of Mark's Gospel encouraged a memory of Peter as a foreigner, an uneducated man whose preaching was sprinkled with remembered phrases, names, and places in a foreign tongue. The same goes for the narrative of the passion, with prayers to "Abba" and an incomprehensible cry of dereliction on the cross. The narrative effect, especially when we bear in mind its oral performance, is strikingly evocative of eyewitness testimony.

Numerous other references root the narrative in a deep and, for Roman readers, unassailable local knowledge of the times and places of Jesus's ministry. Jesus's activities in synagogues and homes, his relationships with different indigenous groups, the names of people and places around the Sea of Galilee—all this would serve to underline the narrator's representation of the memory.

Memory's Echoes and Lacunae

Other Petrine associations in Mark are decidedly more tenuous but still may be of interest in lending a degree of color and definition to this Gospel's representation of the apostle's memory. In a number of cases, what Mark's source implicitly knows or does not know dovetails suggestively with what Roman Christians remembered of Peter, even if none of them can be treated as evidence of such memory. We will look briefly at two or three examples.

To the astonishment of his disciples, Jesus likens rich people's access to the kingdom of God to that of a camel passing through the eye of a needle (Mark 10:23–25). When Peter responds by stressing the sacrifices the disciples have made in order to follow Jesus, Jesus responds with the promise (10:28–29)

> Truly I tell you, there is no one who has left house or brothers or sisters or mother or father or children or fields, for my sake and for the sake of the good news, who will not receive a hundredfold now in this age—houses, brothers and sisters, mothers and children, and fields—with persecutions, and in the age to come eternal life.

Commentators generally allow for a degree of redactional development in these verses, including especially the qualifying reference to "persecutions" (though it is unnecessary to find here an allusion to a specific situation either in Palestine or in Rome). Mark, like Matthew, who follows him (19:29; contrast Luke 18:29), omits "wives" from the otherwise comprehensive catalog of closest relatives forsaken in the service of the kingdom. This omission was striking enough that copyists, from early on, attempted to rectify it in both Mark and Matthew based on the Majority Text's inclusion of "or his wife"; some early commentators even took its presence in the text for granted. Mark's original version of Jesus's answer, however, resonates intriguingly with the fact that Peter, like other apostles, was remembered in Rome and elsewhere as conducting his ministry in the company of his wife. Our passage, though, is probably too general to permit specific conclusions.

A similarly tenuous and tantalizing possibility arises in the eschatological discourse of chapter 13. Mark's famous aside addressing "the reader" (13:14) has occasioned a great deal of comment, not least because it appears to invite the reader to correlate Jesus's prophecy with contemporary events. Since Matthew also adopts this aside, it is at least worth considering that he regarded it not as his predecessor's redactional license but as already a part of the tradition.

Gerd Theissen (1992, 125–65, esp. 128–29) argues plausibly that the most appropriate historical episode with which to associate the fear of an imminent "abomination of desolation" in the sanctuary is not the temple's destruction but rather Caligula's disastrous and narrowly averted attempt to erect in it his own pagan statue; the events of AD 40 rather than those of AD 70, then, are what hang over the original composition of the eschatological discourse. Although not without its own difficulties, this intriguing thesis, if correct, suggests something about the stages of "sedimentation" that Mark's tradition will have undergone. In particular, the intriguing possibility of an initial written form of this part of the discourse around AD 40 might shed light on Peter's departure from Jerusalem in AD 41 or 42. After this time, the attestation of Jesus tradition would presumably have ceased fully to reflect the further developments in the apostolic mother church. Thus, while I do not wish in any way to prejudge or detract from the extent of either Mark's own or his source's redactional freedom, the compositional layering of Mark 13 may lend support to an interesting scenario. It seems arguable that at least the eschatological discourse Mark inherits underwent a degree of initial, and possibly *literary*, sedimentation shortly before Peter's escape from Jerusalem. In other words, whether or not Mark's readers know it, the type of eschatological Jesus tradition that Mark's implied Petrine source represents is formulated prior to the apostle's departure in AD 42. This could, of course, be mere happenstance and is unlikely to have been evident to many Roman readers of Mark. Nonetheless, its compatibility with the story of Peter known in Rome remains an interesting feature of Mark's role in shaping the Petrine message of Jesus—both internally, in terms of its narrative posture, and externally, in terms of its public place in Christian Rome.

One other aspect of the eschatological discourse offers a fascinating correlation with teachings widely remembered as Petrine. On the most general level, it is striking to see Peter so closely associated with the somewhat unexpected appearance of this strictly private block of intensely apocalyptic material in Mark. He places particular stress on Peter's role, underlined by the grammatically awkward choice of a *singular* verb in the disciples' question that sparks Jesus's extended eschatological reply (Mark 13:3). In other words, Peter is the one who asks the question, with James, John, and Andrew in parenthetical supporting attendance. All this links Jesus's concluding discourse not only with his first disciples in Galilee but also with extensive apocalyptic motifs in the Petrine material in Acts, 1–2 Peter, and several apocryphal documents.

The exhortation to watchfulness (Mark 13:23, 32–37), addressed to the first four Galilean disciples, may be recalled in 1 Pet. 5:8 (and also in 1 Thess. 5:6, using the same two verbs as 1 Peter). It also raises the question of who is meant to be the doorkeeper of Mark 13:34, an individual specially commanded to be on the watch. This role appears to share certain similarities with the Petrine keeper of the keys in the Gospel of Matthew, even if subsequent interpretation apparently did not pick up on this for several centuries (see Leo III, *Sermon* 12). In Mark, the exhortation to the watchman and doorkeeper is uniquely associated with Peter in the garden of Gethsemane, where he is the only one specifically upbraided for failing to keep watch (14:37–38): "Simon, are you asleep? Could you not keep awake one hour? Keep awake and pray that you may not come into the time of trial."

The Exception to Prove the Rule

For all the evidence just discussed, however, it is also difficult to miss the fact that Mark repeatedly and uncompromisingly singles Peter out for criticism. This is most obvious in relation to the passion of Jesus: thus, immediately after Peter voices the disciples' faith in Jesus as the Messiah (8:29), his rebuke of Jesus for the first passion prediction is famously swept aside by the searing reprimand "Get behind me, Satan!" (8:33). Peter's slowness to comprehend the nature of Jesus's messiahship is memorably symbolized in the immediately preceding pericope (8:22–26), in the difficult, two-stage healing of another, unnamed man from recalcitrant Bethsaida, who is afterward warned "not to go back into the village." In 14:29–31, Peter swears undying loyalty to Jesus, promising not to desert or deny him but rather to die with him if necessary. Before long, of course, this promise rings hollow: in 14:37, Peter is again singled out for failing to keep awake with Jesus in prayer, a reprimand whose aural dimension is heightened by the fact that it is the only time Mark's Peter is addressed as "Simon." And if, as we pondered earlier, the appointed doorkeeper of 13:38 resembles Peter, here that "watchman" patently fails in his most basic duty. Most tragically, of course, Peter breaks his promise of 14:31 in 14:54–72, denying his master three times in the space of less than an hour.

All this and more has often been alleged to document the evangelist's relative *lack* of interest in the apostle or even a desire to denigrate his profile in the Roman church. To be sure, Peter's stunning downfall in the high priest's courtyard does seem to constitute the climax of an entire counterpoint drama in which this most prominent of disciples is repeatedly singled out as the one who also most spectacularly fails his master and incurs his rebuke (8:32–33; 14:29–31, 37). Even to many moderate scholars, this strikingly harsh treatment of Peter in Mark, as compared to Matthew, seems pretty clearly to militate *against* any close link between the apostle and the evangelist.

Hostility to Peter is, however, far less pronounced than commentators have often assumed. As Joel Marcus (2000–2009, 1:77) puts it, Mark's disciples (Peter included)

are confused bumblers, not traitors; whatever their failings, they do for the most part follow Jesus, even in spite of their fear (10:32–34), and their desertion of him at the end seems to be overruled by his promise of renewed fellowship after the resurrection (14:28; 16:7).

In several cases, though, Peter seems to be *less* exposed to criticism than one would expect in the case of a systematic anti-Petrine sentiment, and such criticism is diluted by his association with other disciples. Even the significance of the denial episode, for example, needs to be seen in relation to the fact that it is both preceded (14:28) and followed (16:7) by the promise of a reunion with Jesus, a promise that transcends Peter's failure and that evidently presupposes his rehabilitation. On any reckoning, it remains strikingly indicative of Peter's importance for Mark that the denial represents the only episode in the entire Gospel in which the main protagonist is a disciple.

The theory of Mark's supposed anti-Petrine intent, moreover, adopts a far more circular logic than its advocates tend to appreciate. It presupposes both that Peter *himself* would naturally have painted a more flattering picture of his past and that his hearers would similarly insist on an uncritical reading. The possibility that the influence or recent memory of Peter might instead *underscore* such critical elements is rarely considered.

For a powerful counterexample to both suppositions, however, we need turn only to the apostle Paul. Far from either glossing or passing over his former life in silence, he explicitly highlights and disowns his previous enmity to Christ and the church in order to accentuate the nature of his new life. It is a point also amply documented in Acts and the Pastoral Epistles that Paul's earliest followers understood and embraced his rehearsal of pre-Christian errors as theologically vital to his practice of evangelism and catechesis: Jesus came to save even the chief of sinners (e.g., 1 Tim. 1:15).

It is admittedly more difficult to trace this self-critical theme explicitly in the Petrine tradition, because of the dearth of authentic early documents. The evidence is quite thin in the Petrine Epistles, although hints of it may surface in 1 Peter, as we saw above. The second-century *Acts of Peter* does seem to convey the impression of Peter as someone who tends to show moral courage only on second thought. As Nero's persecution breaks out in Rome, Peter flees for his own safety and returns only after a visionary encounter with Christ, who enters the city "to be crucified again." Given the dramatic development of Peter's turning back, the original story may have involved a deliberate change of heart on his part. In the extant *Acts of Peter*, this theme is blunted in that Peter escapes at the urging of his friends and does this only after objecting that he does not want to be a deserter (*Acts of Peter* 9.35.6).

Be that as it may, the narrative force of this later Roman episode does constitute a striking counterpoint to the Markan memory of Peter's denial. There Peter protested that he would not desert or deny Jesus but was prepared to die with him (14:29, 31, 50); instead, he did the former and failed to do the latter. It is Jesus who confesses (see esp. 14:62), Peter who denies; indeed, the whole passage of Mark 14:54–72 can be read as a masterful interlocking narrative offsetting the story of Peter's failure with that of Jesus's trust and steadfastness in affliction (a theme that, incidentally, recurs in 1 Peter). In the *Acts of Peter*, although initially resolving (or at least consenting) to escape, at the critical moment Peter turns back to confess his Lord and follow him to the cross (35–39). Even allowing for an undoubtedly edifying element, this correspondence lends an interesting hue to other first- and second-century traditions surrounding Peter's subsequent preaching about the passion and his own crucifixion.

What can we conclude from all this? For all its complexity and critical candor, Mark's Gospel implies a degree of narrative proximity to Peter that would mutually reinforce rather than undermine Roman memories of their actual association in the city. To some extent, this is an argument about the intertextuality of Petrine and other early Christian writings, which no doubt reciprocally confirmed and shaped the nature of Petrine memory in the first two centuries. In other words, the reading of Mark's narrative in the Roman churches both reflected and contributed to their memory of Peter. At the same time, it is of great interest to note the extent to which Mark's account resonates with a Roman living memory that would lend color and definition to its account of Peter and of Jesus.

Western Memory of Peter before Mark's Gospel

Mark was read in Rome in the 60s AD and reflects a living Petrine memory tied not only implicitly to the author but perhaps also to other figures, including the sons of Simon of Cyrene (15:21). It is not clear whether Mark knows Peter to be dead. Is there evidence, though, that the readers had a Petrine memory, direct or indirect, prior to Mark? Two Pauline letters with a particular connection to Rome may help us in our quest.

Romans

Paul's letter to Rome, composed from Corinth, most likely in the winter of the year AD 56 or 57, might seem the obvious location for a brief acknowledgment of Simon Peter, especially if, as more than a few scholars have from time to time suggested, this elder statesman of the Jesus movement was either in the capital at the time of writing or had been there on a previous occasion (see below). Yet Peter is never mentioned by name, even though this could have assisted Paul's rhetorical stance in addressing the place of Israel in chapters 9 to 11—at the very least including Peter in his example of saved Israelites (11:1)—or Jewish-gentile tensions in chapters 14 and 15. Although the question of the audience of Romans remains debated, it has long been argued that Paul wrote Romans to an audience with a high proportion of gentiles, addressing the reintegration of Jewish believers who returned to Rome after the death of Claudius (AD 54), when his expulsion of riotous (Christian) Jews in AD 48 was rescinded. Indeed, if Peter really were the unifying centrist force that he is in subsequent memory, why does Paul not draw on the work and testimony of his "coworker"? Is this not evidence that nothing was known about Peter in the Roman church for at least the first six decades of the first century, let alone any tradition that he himself had a ministry there?

In considering this question, it should be kept in view that, as noted in chapter 2, Paul writes this letter as an outsider to a church he has yet to visit (Rom. 1:13). He thus proceeds diplomatically, opening and closing the main section of the letter with positive descriptions of the Roman Christians (1:8, 12; 15:14). Omission of any reference to the addressees as the "church" or even "churches" at Rome is also telling: the diffuse organizational structure of multiple house churches without central cohesion in a very large city made generalizations of any sort rather difficult. Throughout the letter, Paul is extremely careful about what he can assume, as seen in the surprisingly ecumenical treatment of issues surrounding food and sacred days (Rom. 14; cf. 1 Cor. 8–10; Gal. 4:10–11). Paul's desire to secure the support of the Roman churches necessitates careful diplomacy: compared to letters he sent to some of the churches he himself founded, it repeatedly seems as if Paul pulls his punches.

At the same time, Paul does explicitly assume that the Romans have been catechized according to a standard form of instruction (*typos didachēs*, Rom. 6:17), and he also confesses that he does not wish to build on "another man's foundation [*ep' allotrion themelion*]" (15:20). Paul uses the term *themelios* elsewhere of the *apostolic* foundation of the church, including Paul's own at Corinth (1 Cor. 3:10–12; also Eph. 2:20). It seems conceivable, then, that Paul knows or at least suspects a little more about the apostolic birth of the Roman church than he lets on. That beginning need not have involved Peter, of course, and on balance it seems unlikely that it did. But on the other hand, Paul's language leaves more room than is sometimes supposed for his awareness that another apostolic figure—or more than one—preceded him to Rome.

In the previous chapter, we looked briefly at one of Paul's Eastern letters, Galatians. Nothing explicitly suggests that it *circulated* in the West in the first century, and, conversely, nothing in Romans reveals similar Pauline passions about Peter. Nevertheless, there are subtle links between Galatians and the memory of Peter in second-century Rome. Most famously, perhaps, the great controversial Pauline interpreter Marcion, discussed above, arrived in Rome around 140 from Pontus, one of the regions associated with a Petrine mission in Christian tradition (cf. 1 Pet. 1:1). Far from being a pro-Petrine interpreter, however, Marcion advanced an interpretation of Galatians that cast Paul's dispute with Peter at Antioch as the fundamental divide of the apostolic era (e.g., Tertullian, *Marc.* 1.20; 4.3; 5.1). Such presumed animosity against Peter is present neither in Romans nor, as we will see in a moment, in 1 Corinthians.

1 Corinthians

Paul's Corinthian correspondence could in theory be discussed under either an Eastern or a Western heading. For several reasons, however, it is appropriate to link it here more closely with Rome than with Asia Minor. First, after the ancient city of Corinth was razed by the Romans in 146 BC, it was refounded as an emphatically Roman colony by Julius Caesar in 44 BC.[58] The close communicative ties between Corinth and Rome were not only political but also pertinent in Christian terms. This is evidenced, for example, by early Christian figures like Aquila and Prisca (Acts 18:2, "a native of Pontus"; Rom. 16:3) and in the fact that Paul writes his important letter to Rome from Corinth. As the "Macedonian vision" of Acts 16 implies, for a Jew from Syria and Cilicia to "come over to Macedonia" and Greece was to cross a more significant boundary than any since Antioch, a point rightly noted by scholars of Pauline geography.[59] Just as important for our purposes, the Petrine references in 1 Corinthians have a palpable bearing on Peter's memory in Corinth and Rome. Later in the same century, Peter's ministry is cited in the Roman church's letter to Corinth known as *1 Clement*, highlighting the martyrdom of Peter and Paul in Rome as apparently agreed upon between the author and his readers (*1 Clem.* 5.1–6). In the later second century, Dionysius of Corinth reminds the Roman church, in his letter to them around AD 175 (in Eusebius, *Eccl. Hist.* 2.25.8), of the ministry of Peter and Paul in both Corinth and Rome. Petrine memory of the first two centuries does not link Corinth in comparable fashion with any eastern Mediterranean localities.

If one turns from the rather heated conflict of Galatians to the evidence of 1 Corinthians, written from Ephesus in AD 54–55, it is striking to note that here, within five to seven years of Galatians (and possibly the Antioch incident itself), Paul is remarkably *positive* about Peter's role. Although scholars have long considered the so-called Cephas party another example of the deep factionalism that existed between Pauline groups and other (esp. Petrine) groups, a closer examination of the language and rhetoric of 1 Corinthians reveals a Paul who seeks to unite groups rather than to defeat opponents (see esp. Mitchell 1991). In the midst of his exhortation toward unity, Paul deliberately speaks of Peter and Apollos as his fellow "servants of Christ and stewards of the mysteries of Christ" (4:1–2; cf. 3:5). Interestingly, Peter is the only person listed by name in 9:5 as a traveling missionary accompanied by his wife: "Do we not have the right to bring along a believing wife like the rest of the apostles and the brothers of the Lord and Cephas"?

In another important passage (15:1–11), Paul's discussion of the "gospel which we preached" (15:1) again suggests greater confessional commonality with the original disciples, especially Peter, than has often been assumed on the basis of Gal. 2. First, Paul singles out Peter as the first witness to the resurrection of Christ (15:5). This separation of Peter from the other apostles is strikingly similar to Mark 16:7 and Luke 24:34, which also highlight Peter as the key witness among

---

58. Pausanias, *Descr.* 2.2. See 7.16 for an account of the destruction of Corinth; cf. Polybius, *Hist.* 39.12–14.

59. See, e.g., Riesner 1998, 293 and n80.

the Twelve. Whatever *chronological* difficulties this raises with alternative accounts (cf. Matt. 28:9–10; Luke 24:15–31; John 20:14–18), Paul evidently regards Peter as the foremost apostolic figure in this regard.[60] Moreover, Paul explicitly claims that his preaching is fully consonant with the other apostles, including Peter: "whether I or they, thus we preach and thus you believed" (15:11). This stresses the theological commonalities between Paul and Peter already noted even in Paul's Galatian polemic (Gal. 2:15–21).

A more speculative argument has occasionally been made linking Paul's statement in 1 Cor. 11:23 about the Last Supper narrative tradition "from the Lord" to his two-week stay with Peter (Gal. 1:18). Philologically, as commentators tend to recognize, the Greek phrase "from the Lord [*apo tou kyriou*]" here does not denote some sort of ecstatic or visionary communication transmitted by the celestial Christ[61] but identifies instead the tradition's originating authority: this narrative praxis is rooted "in the explicit command of Jesus as the Lord."[62] Even so, the positive appraisal of Peter and his ministry in 1 Corinthians fits Paul's own narrative in Gal. 1:18. The complex evidence of Galatians and 1 Corinthians taken together indicates that the rift at Antioch, though emotional and sharp, was a temporary disruption in an otherwise positive working relationship, if not friendship.

Local Memory in Rome?

At this point, we may remind ourselves of the first chapter, in which I mentioned the importance of particular people and places for the understanding of how living memory works. It has often been noted that places, objects, sights, and sounds can serve as pegs by which to support both individual and collective memory—a phenomenon that can be documented for ancient and medieval times too. Whether or not they read Proust, most people will recognize the sensation that even the smell or touch of particular places or persons may linger vividly and powerfully reinforce their memory long after they are gone. The importance specifically of places for collective memory was stressed in the mid-twentieth century by the sociologist Maurice Halbwachs (1941; 1992). More recently, Pierre Nora (1984; 1996) has made a great deal of the importance of place in the broadest sense as focusing individual and communal memory. (The literature of collective memory has also been applied to NT study in the work of Anthony Le Donne [2009; 2011], a student of James D. G. Dunn.)

60. On the question of Peter as the first witness of the resurrection, see also Kessler 1998.

61. As Watson 2007 envisages. Philologically, one might expect reception *para tou kyriou*, as at Acts 20:24 (cf., e.g., Gal. 1:12; 1 Thess. 2:13; 4:1; also Eph. 6:8; Phil. 4:18).

62. Rightly, Thiselton 2000, 867; quoting Marshall 1980, 112. A specific link with the visit to Peter in Gal. 1:18 is explicitly endorsed, e.g., by Donfried 2002, 15; Skarsaune 2002, 168; Tomson 2001, 399; cf. previously, e.g., Cullmann 1956, 65, 72–73; Hunter 1961, 118; Roloff 1965, 86, 88.

Previously, we noted the relative dearth of local memory of Peter in Palestine and Syria, including Antioch; a similar point could be made about Corinth. In Rome, by contrast, we have a profusion of claims about both Peter and Paul. The modern-day pilgrim can visit places where Peter received hospitality, see the chair on which he sat to teach and the table at which he celebrated the Eucharist (in two different places), and even observe his imprint on the paving stone where he fell on his knees to bring his opponent Simon Magus to a crashing fall from the sky. Popular imagination was not slow to identify the place where he dropped a bandage while fleeing the city or where, according to the *Acts of Peter*, he met Jesus on his flight from Rome before turning back to face the persecution. There at Rome are the chains that bound him while on trial, his prison, and his place of execution and burial; his skeleton is pointed out in one location and his skull in another. There seems to be no end to these traditions, most of them first attested several centuries after the window of living memory in which we are interested here. Others, however, were clearly very popular and well established as early as the second and third centuries, as can be seen by the frequency with which Peter and Paul appear in catacomb paintings and on sarcophagi of the third and later centuries.

Christian Geography of Rome: Where Christians Lived

One useful exercise to orient ourselves to the places of Petrine memory in Rome is to create a map showing where the majority of Christians actually lived. Peter Lampe's important study of Rome (Lampe 2003) does this by comparing the locations of the earliest Christian churches (the so-called titular churches) and seeing in which city quarters they are concentrated. This is followed by looking at the locations of the earliest known Christian cemeteries, which were placed along the roads radiating out of town from the nearest city quarter in which their occupants lived. And, finally, this is correlated with known areas of Jewish settlement in Rome. Only where two or three of these criteria overlap does Lampe see the strongest evidence for Christian settlement; where only one of them is present, he considers significant Christian presence unlikely. In my view, this method is reliable for what it affirms, but probably less so for what it denies or downplays. The key results point to a strong Christian presence in Trastevere on the west bank of the Tiber and in the lowlands along the Via Appia in the south; rather less certainty is affirmed for the Via Flaminia in the north, the Aventine Hill, and the area surrounding the Viminal Hill. This is not a decisive conclusion, but it sheds light on why certain areas of town have a stronger claim to early Christian traditions than others.

Whether as an instantiation or as a consequence of these clusters of Christian inhabitation, a few of the diverse localizable Petrine traditions do tend to be associated with some of Lampe's key areas. These include the Via Appia, the area relating to the so-called *Quo Vadis* episode of the *Acts of Peter* and the catacomb of Domitilla, with its supposed tomb of Peter's daughter Petronilla; the Viminal Hill, with the church of St. Pudenziana, where Peter was believed to have lodged in the house of her father Pudens, a senator's son (cf. 2 Tim. 4:21); and several other catacombs elsewhere, including St. Priscilla, with the reputed chair of Peter and near the place where he baptized. Trastevere, on the other hand, is strikingly absent.

Gaius

We alluded earlier to this famous figure around the end of our period, a Roman presbyter Gaius, who, in the time of Pope Zephyrinus (AD 198–217), was engaged in controversy with the Montanist leader Proclus and apparently also with Hippolytus. Although the evidence may date from the early third rather than the late second century, the importance of Gaius for our purposes is in voicing an apparently well-established local memory of the apostles' tombs. His well-known but much-debated statement in argument with Proclus asserts, "But I can point out the trophies of the apostles, for if you will go to the Vatican or to the Ostian Way you will find the trophies of those who founded this Church" (Eusebius, *Eccl. Hist.* 2.25.7). The contrastive "but" suggests the polemical use to which the tradition is evidently being put. Countering the Montanist's appeal to new revelation (and perhaps, like others in the second century, to the ancient apostolic heritage of Asia Minor), Gaius presses the familiar catholic point that the gospel is to be rooted in the authentic apostolic testimony. To his own day, local memory retained the most eloquent attestation of that testimony in the two apostles' *tropaia* (the "trophies" or "victory monuments" that presumably marked the site where their bodies were "deposited").

Needless to say, a great deal of debate has concerned the precise meaning of Gaius's assertion, which is crucial to the claim that Peter's tomb is situated under the present-day basilica in the Vatican. Gaius's knowledge of the two sites is unmatched by other Roman writers (e.g., Justin Martyr). On the other hand, it is presumably in response to Roman claims like these that Polycrates wrote to Pope Victor in the year AD 195, insisting that "we in Asia *too* have a claim to apostolic pedigree, as many of the tombs of the early Christian heroes document" (Eusebius, *Eccl. Hist.* 3.31.3). The phrase "we too" could be said to concede the Roman claim, even if, in Polycrates's mind, it does not justify Rome's arrogance about the date of Easter.

At first sight, Gaius's Roman assertion seems compromised by the alternative tradition of a *joint* memorial of Peter and Paul in the catacombs of San Sebastiano on the Via Appia Antica. There a tradition attested by profuse amounts of graffiti and a famous inscription of the fourth-century Pope Damasus points to a period when the remains of Peter and Paul were *jointly* honored at this third location, of which Gaius knows nothing. Regular Christian gatherings were held here in the presence of the twin apostles' remains, which we know from Damasus's inscription and the graffiti found in the catacombs below. The most plausible solution to this particular problem draws on an early Christian calendar and suggests the creation of a joint apostolic memorial at San Sebastiano around AD 258, possibly during the persecution under Emperor Valerian, when Christians were forbidden to assemble or visit their cemeteries. San Sebastiano had the benefit that it was a pagan cemetery, which would not be closed. The relics of the apostles, or at least some of them, were taken outside the city for safekeeping and graveside occasions, perhaps mingled in with a lot of other burial traffic. The very idea that these bones were buried in the same place at the same time suggests that this was a secondary burial. They were then eventually resettled seventy-five years or so later at the respective basilicas built by Constantine—St. Peter's at the Vatican and St. Paul's on the Ostian Way, both outside the walls of Rome.

Our main point here is that, in a context of public controversy around AD 200, Gaius felt able to invoke a local memorial of Peter's martyrdom and/or burial at the Vatican Hill to the west of the city. The existence of such a memorial is evidently open to verification, and Gaius implies that he himself knows the site well. Such claims do not amount to personal memory of Peter himself or even of an apostolic eyewitness, but they do point to Gaius's personal identification with the Roman church's communal memory of the place in which the apostle was martyred.

There are at most half a dozen localities with Petrine associations that are even, in principle, discussable as dating back to the second century. Some claims, although relatively early, seem impossible to extract from the realm of legend, including the dispute between Peter and Simon Magus on the Via Sacra (*Acts of Peter* 32). One or two others bear thinking about a little more, including the supposed place of Peter's baptism along the Via Nomentana and possibly the ancient church of St. Pudenziana, whose family allegedly hosted Peter. There is even one place known as Forum Novum, in the country twenty miles north of Rome, for which some ancient sources claim a visit by Peter—though for our purposes no second-century tradition can be demonstrated.

Aside from this, it does seem intriguing, from the perspective of memory, that one can go to the Vatican museum and see the statue to the Sabine god Semo Sanco, which second-century Greek-speaking Christians saw on the island in the Tiber and associated (erroneously) with Simon Magus, Peter's legendary archenemy. Certainty about the origin of the Simon Magus legend eludes us. The likeliest explanation seems to be that migrant Christians like Justin, who had encountered (or brought with them) traditions of Simon's presence in Rome and Christian memories of Peter's fatal struggles against enemies of the church, found on the Tiber Island a way to connect these local memories, seemingly supported by Luke's narration of just such a conflict with Simon in Palestine.

In the interest of space we will need to concentrate on the Vatican excavations, which provide the earliest clear evidence of a Petrine memory being asserted in the second century.

The Tomb of Peter at the Vatican?

It has long been known that the area around the Vatican Hill contained pagan graves. In the first century, this was the area of Nero's gardens, where he built a circus for entertainments, including staged naval battles, and planted an obelisk in the middle of it. (This obelisk was moved only when the new St. Peter's was built in the sixteenth century, and it now stands in the middle of the square.) According to Tacitus (*Ann.* 15.44.4–5), it was in Nero's circus, with the nearby gardens, that Christians who had been singled out for causing the fire of Rome on July 19, AD 64, were executed by crucifixion and wild animals and were even turned into torches as night fell. This places the location adjacent to the Vatican Hill. It is not clear, though, whether Peter was killed in this first wave of mass executions or died later, but there is a strong likelihood that this was the place.

The story of the excavations under the crypt of St. Peter's is once again reminiscent of the serendipity and messiness of the graffiti in Peter's house at Capernaum. Exploration began in the 1930s with a chance rediscovery of the cavities Constantine had vaulted and filled in under his basilica to compensate for the rising Vatican Hill. It is an extraordinary feature of St. Peter's that it is built into the side of that hill. What was uncovered was initially an enormous and opulent necropolis of intricate house-like structures and alleyways, four hundred yards in length, dating mainly from about AD 120 to 150. One tomb inscription specifically quotes the occupant's last will and testament, requesting to be buried by Nero's circus at the Vatican. Near the western end, some earlier tombs came to light that were mainly of poorer people, who were simply buried in the earth (without being cremated) and covered with tiles (one of which bears a stamp dating from Vespasian's time, AD 69–79). These burial sites densely surrounded an apparently venerated tomb that was eventually marked in the mid-second century by the *tropaion* of which Gaius speaks, a little classical edifice set into a wall. In the floor of this edicule was inserted a covering slab set at an angle, which evidently covered a tomb. Around AD 150, the large adjacent necropolis required the construction of a red wall, which ran at an oblique angle to the Christian grave and cut across it. Christians were evidently not in a position to resist the encroachment of this red wall from the pagan necropolis, although the builders altered their foundations at this point and permitted two niches. The *tropaion* memorial was erected at the same time, backing against one of the niches in the red wall, to protect the tomb from further encroachment. It is built of local travertine limestone in two levels, of which the lower level rises to 1.34 meters and the upper level ends at about 2.35 meters. All in all, the memorial and its surrounding tombs strongly indicate members of the lower classes. A fragmentary graffito on the red wall reads PETROS ENI. ENI either means "inside" (e.g., in Guarducci 2000, 94–95, and passim) or, perhaps more likely, is short for *en [e]irēnē*, "in peace."

A great deal more could be said about this monument and also about the tricky question of whether it contained the bones of Peter. The history of the discovery of the supposed bones is strange and does not inspire confidence regarding the archaeological procedures in place: the tomb itself was empty, but parts of the skeleton of a sixty- to seventy-year-old man, about 5 feet 5 inches (1.65 meters) in height, were indeed discovered in a cavity of the graffiti wall. Interestingly, only part of the skull was present, with no sign of the feet. Some have suggested this is what one would expect if someone had been crucified, possibly upside down, and perhaps burned as well. Are these the bones of Peter? It is possible. Further discussion would be interesting but fruitless without more evidence. One suggestion has been that when Constantine returned the bones of Peter, they were reburied not under the *tropaion* but in the wall. Given the circuitous discovery and haphazard preservation of these remains, it seems right to join the majority of scholars in being cautious about Pope Paul VI's claim in 1968 that these are indeed the bones of Peter.

Nevertheless, there appears to be a substantial and growing body of scholarly opinion holding that we almost certainly have under the Vatican the site identified by Gaius and still known in the time of Constantine as the tomb of Peter. Both its early attestation and the reported circumstances of the Neronian persecution render this at least plausible, though of course that still leaves us some way from *probability*. If Peter's body was available to be buried at all, this patriarch and ring leader of the Christian agitators, executed as a capital criminal in the gardens of Nero, would need a quiet and quick funeral carried out in the vicinity by surviving associates, who may have known their own lives to be in danger.

The *tropaion* marks the site remembered by second-century Christians as the tomb of Peter, near the place of his martyrdom. Unlike what is the case for John and Mary and indeed for John the Baptist, no other place ever claimed to have Peter's tomb. The absence of rival sites is striking and attests, if not necessarily to historicity, then certainly to an early and universal consensus. Even if the tomb is plausibly Peter's, we can say much less about his bones. Exactly what happened to them—even those supposedly discovered in the twentieth century, let alone those buried in the first—remains impossible to verify.

In a claim of this magnitude, the scope for self-deception is clearly enormous, and it is not only Protestants who feel that discretion is the better part of valor. But it is worth considering that a properly Christian approach to such claims ought to be reluctant in practice but sympathetic in principle. Early Christian reverence for the memory and the tombs of important saints testifies to the persistence of the faithful in their belief in the power of the incarnation of the Word of God and the continued manifestation of his Spirit among the apostles. In the case of Simon Peter, arguably, Rome houses both authentic artifacts and a great deal else besides, combining important grains of truth with much frothing superstition.

Conclusion: Peter in Eastern and Western Memory

What I have tried to show in this and the previous chapter is that the living memory of the first two centuries allows modest access to a period when eyewitnesses of Peter, and those who remembered them, were still alive. There is not enough here to write a history, yet there is more than just a late fiction invented out of whole cloth after AD 150 in order to combat Gnostics.[63] Paying special attention to this privileged period of memory and faith requires careful critical discernment but can in a few cases yield unique and unexpected insights.

We find the prince of apostles as a man who reached out to conflicting factions of the church and who was converted from a fisherman to a fisher of people, who worked from Galilee to Rome. Far from polarizing or vacillating, as has sometimes been claimed, the remembered profile of Peter appears to hold the capacity to bridge the tensions between Paul's radical mission and Jerusalem Christianity's mission to Israel.

The apostle's remembered connection with particular places and people—*lieux de mémoire*—is always tenuous and ranges from the occasionally probable to the frequently implausible, but it weaves a fascinating tissue of reception in which Peter emerges as a person of strong but fascinatingly ambivalent characteristics. It is a difficult but rewarding task to explore the relationship between that reception and its historical development, as we have tried to do. Two key features of Peter's remembered profile, his conversion and his place of origin, will occupy the final two chapters of this book.

63. As argued, e.g., by Zwierlein (2009, 332, and passim), who takes only the most patchy cognizance of non-German scholarship on this matter.

PART 3

History and Memory—Two Case Studies

5

How Peter Became a Disciple

The bulk of this book has presented a back-to-front approach to Simon Peter. We began by introducing the study of apostolic persons from the perspective of their living memory in the immediately following generations. After a brief survey of Peter's formative canonical impress in the NT, we turned to examine the astonishingly diverse but nevertheless frequently illuminating ways in which Petrine memory developed in the East and the West, tracing selected sources in both regions from the end of the second century back to their NT antecedents.

For the concluding chapters of this book, I turn from this geographical tracing of memory to its application in two specific case studies—one *exegetical*, the other *archaeological*. The former applies features of Petrine memory to the exegesis of the NT back to front; the latter—proceeding, conversely, front to back, as it were—finds the shape of that remembered footprint suggestively tethered to the historical-critical "brute facts" of Peter's background and place of origin. Through these two studies, I hope to illustrate how this early Christian *anamnetic*, or remembered, reception may help us understand the relationship between the historical Peter of critical reconstruction and the historic Peter of memory and story, whose complex life gave rise to such richly interwoven strands of tradition and memory. Both, of course, pertain to history in the proper sense of the word.

Our first case study, then, is exegetical. It takes its point of departure from a puzzling lacuna in the development of the theme of conversion in Peter's Lukan profile in the Gospel and Acts. We will then attend to early Christian reflection on the surrounding Gospel narrative (normally not in specific Lukan garb) to see how the NT author draws to his readers' attention a theme that is filled in and illuminated by the wider context of Petrine memory.

For readers acquainted with the study of Paul, the problem of his conversion is familiar territory, which has long since been foundational to historical, theological, and artistic accounts of Christianity's origins. Peter's conversion, however, is quite another matter. Where popular or artistic renderings may have accentuated, in picturesque fashion, the implications of Peter's call to discipleship by the Sea of Galilee, critical NT scholarship has paid very little attention to the question of this apostle's conversion, even allowing for the much smaller number of books on Simon Peter.

Preliminaries

Given the prominence of the topic of conversion in Pauline study, a small amount of methodological throat-clearing is inevitable. In the past, scholars sometimes advocated rather romantic and psychologizing ideas of what conversion might mean (W. James 1902; Nock 1933). In NT scholarship, a long tradition of Protestant dominance also encouraged, and in some circles still encourages, a notion of conversion in somewhat clunky, modernist categories as a change from one "religion" to another.[1] This led to the view, for example, that since Paul seems to speak of his Damascus Road experience in terms of a vocation rather than an abandonment of Judaism, one cannot really speak of his "conversion" at all.[2] More recently, however, such anachronistic and somewhat opaque conceptions have tended to give way to categories drawn from social-scientific studies of conversion phenomena. Scholars began to speak in terms of an individual's "cognitive shift" (Gaventa 1986), a radically reconstructed identity (Segal 1990, 29, and passim; cf. Bockmuehl 1992), a socially recognized transformation of the self in newly structured relationships (Chester 2003, 13, 41, and passim), or even a change of patronage, clientele, and loyalty to a patron deity (Crook 2004). Others have pointed out that Paul seems to speak of "calling" in contexts where we might employ the language of "conversion."[3] All in all, socially or communally construed ideas of conversion are clearly in the ascendancy, and as long as this is not at the expense of theological analysis, there is much to be gained.[4] Throughout much of Europe and North America, inherited Christian social and cultural structures are in serious decline, while, conversely, Islam and some other religious traditions are enjoying unprecedented growth and attention. This seems a good time to consider whether collective, cultural, and "tribal" dimensions of conversion could benefit

1. For the conceptual problems of the notion of "religion," see especially Lash 1996.
2. Most influentially, Stendahl 1976, 7–8, and passim.
3. Esp. Chester 2003, 153–59 (and cf. others cited there).
4. See further the seminal analysis of Rambo 1993, whose categories are usefully applied to ancient Judaism and early Christianity by Sterling 2008.

from urgent reconsideration. Certainly historical precedent in ancient cities like Edessa, or even ancient nations like Armenia, holds considerable interest for contemporary Christian missiologies reflecting on the reality of strongly socialized people groups, including in the Islamic world.

In one sense, neglect of Peter's conversion is hardly surprising. Though Peter is called to follow Jesus along a path of unpredictable challenge, change, and adversity, the NT narrative of Peter's life does not, in most people's minds, evoke images of dramatic conversion. Peter is affiliated with the Jesus movement for the rest of his life, despite his patent failures at times like the trial of Jesus. New Testament narrative evidence about any dramatic change is remarkably limited: two letters attributed to Peter remain implicit on the subject, while Paul does not hint at Peter's conversion. The NT does not explicitly affirm the tradition of Peter's death in Rome, although that outcome is certainly compatible with it. None of this, however, gives us a conversion remotely like that of Paul, whether one understands that primarily as a religious or a social and cultural phenomenon.

Is this all that can be said? In the absence of adequate historical-critical evidence, I would like now to apply the reception and memory-based approach advocated in this book to the question of how the biblical and early Christian sources *themselves* describe Peter in the language of conversion or calling, of turning or repentance. We shall see that they fill the historical-critical lacuna with a set of highly suggestive and historically plausible narrative reflections on certain episodes in Peter's life. Contrary to what we might expect, in early Christian theology and art Simon Peter's paradigmatic role in repentance and conversion in no way lags behind that of Paul.

An Eloquent Silence in Luke's Passion Narrative

Luke 22 raises a striking narrative expectation whose fulfillment is left strangely obscure. Following the Last Supper on the eve of Passover, Jesus first bestows on the Twelve the kingdom he has received from his Father; on that day, they will sit on thrones judging the twelve tribes of Israel (22:29–30). Then, Jesus says to Peter in particular,

> Simon, Simon, behold, Satan demanded to have you [pl.], that he might sift you like wheat, but I have prayed for you [sg.] that your faith may not fail. And when once you [sg.] have turned back, strengthen your brothers. (22:31–32 ESV)

This unexpected saying has generated much debate. We are not helped by the fact that it has no parallel anywhere in the gospel tradition.[5] There is clearly a reference here to Peter's impending struggle against Satan, in which he will be severely tested and will not be immune from serious mistakes, hence the talk of "turning back."

5. Over forty years ago, Prete (1969) published a whole book on this passage.

(It is worth stressing here that "when you have turned *again*," though favored by many translations, has no support in the Greek.)

A brief glance through a concordance shows that Luke is particularly fond of the verb *epistrephō*, "to turn" or "convert" (7x in Luke, 11x in Acts; 4x in Matthew and in Mark, with just 3x in all of Paul).[6] Although it is sometimes used of a literal return to a geographic point of origin,[7] Luke has already used the word *epistrephō* twice to denote a moral and spiritual conversion: early in this Gospel, John the Baptist was prophesied to be one who would "*turn* many of the children of Israel to the Lord their God," and more specifically "*turn* the hearts of the fathers to the children, and the disobedient to the wisdom of the just" (1:16–17 ESV).[8] It is not hard to see that John set out to do precisely that, in keeping with those OT prophets who sought the same sort of "turning" (*epistrephō*) in the people of Israel: God "sent prophets among them to *bring them back* to the LORD. These testified against them, but they would not pay attention" (2 Chron. 24:19 LXX).[9] Here in Luke 22, we are told that only Peter's turning can enable him to strengthen the disciples.[10]

But when, where, or how does Peter's turning occur? It is here that we come to the nub of the problem. Even on this last night of his ministry, Luke's Jesus evidently still anticipates Peter's conversion as in the *future*. How can that be? Peter is already a disciple, he has "left everything" (5:11; cf. 18:28) and stood by Jesus in his trials, and he will sit on a throne judging one of the twelve tribes of Israel (22:28–30). Even in the present saying, he clearly has faith (*pistis*), no matter how imperfect that may be. Yet the talk of turning, conversion, or even repentance is at no point in the Gospel associated with Peter.

This is despite the fact that Luke 5 features a quite distinctive narrative of Peter's call, which might be thought to lend itself to a closer analogy with Paul's Damascus Road experience as both call and conversion. Whereas Mark and Matthew have Jesus call Peter as a disciple at their first encounter, Luke's Jesus has by this point already met Simon and in fact healed his mother-in-law (4:38–39). Luke's Peter receives his call to discipleship following a miraculous catch of fish, which causes him to fall at Jesus's feet and leave everything to become a fisher of people. One might have thought this a plausible experience of something like conversion, not least in view of parallels with OT prophetic call narratives (e.g., with Isa. 6:5; Exod. 10:4, 13), but even in Luke 21:32, the *conversion* of Peter appears still to lie in the future.

6. The fullest study of *epistrephō* in Luke 22:32 remains Prete 1969, 103–35; cf. Prete 1967; and more generally, Nave 2002.

7. Luke 2:39; 8:55; 17:4, 31 (although repentance might be implied in 17:4).

8. Interestingly, Luke here introduces the verb *epistrephō* into a Septuagintal passage (Mal. 3:23) that does not use it.

9. The Septuagint has over one hundred pertinent uses of this terminology in the Latter Prophets and uses it similarly of repentance or conversion elsewhere.

10. A point rightly stressed by Dietrich 1972, 133–34.

Nowhere in the NT is Peter said to have been baptized, whether by Jesus or by John the Baptist. In 1 Pet. 3:21, the author discusses the readers' baptism but does not mention Peter's own: "Baptism . . . now saves you, not as a removal of dirt from the body, but as an appeal to God for a good conscience, through the resurrection of Jesus Christ."

Moving on through the Gospel of Luke, even Peter's identification of Jesus as "the Christ of God" (9:18–20) does not generate reference to his repentance and conversion. Unlike Matthew or Mark, Luke does not localize this episode at Caesarea Philippi and gives it a markedly less Petrine emphasis. Shortly afterward, Jesus's encounter with Moses and Elijah leads to a correction of Peter's misunderstanding of Jesus's significance at the transfiguration, an episode that comes to prominent focus when it is cited in 2 Pet. 1 as undergirding the apostle's definitive access to the revelation of the gospel in the person of Jesus.

As we pass Luke 22 on our journey through the Gospel, we encounter one plausible later point of reference for the conversion: Luke's story of Peter's denial. This is an episode familiar from all four Gospels. Peter flees and weeps bitterly when the rooster crows after his denial of Jesus. This is an undeniable act of shame and remorse, which must relate in some fashion to the earlier talk of possible mistakes and failure. Yet nowhere does Luke describe it as repentance or conversion, even though 22:33 might lead us to expect that. Strikingly, the only person who "turns" in this context of denial is not Peter but "the Lord [*kyrios*]," who hauntingly turns (*strapheis*) and convicts the apostle with a wordless gaze (22:61).

On Easter Sunday, Peter runs to see the empty tomb before going home (Luke 24:12; cf. John 20:6, 10). We are given a report, but no narrative, of the risen Lord's appearance to Simon (Luke 24:34). Luke's Gospel thus ends without any further reference to Peter's conversion.

When we turn to Luke's sequel volume, the Acts of the Apostles, almost from the start we find Peter, like Paul later on, preaching repentance and conversion, but now Peter himself appears *already* to have turned and to be busy strengthening the others, as instructed in Luke 22. Beginning in Acts 2, we find Peter confessing Christ publicly rather than denying, even before Caiaphas's council that marked the scene of the earlier denial (4:1–21). Whereas Peter previously fled from his promise to follow Christ to arrest and death, Acts 12 has him in prison awaiting execution before his miraculous delivery.

As for the language of "turning," the word *epistrephō* often features in Peter's preaching as he calls his audience to repentance and conversion.[11] The hearers at Pentecost are "cut to the heart" and moved to action. Peter's sermon in the next chapter concludes by calling his audience to "repent therefore and turn [*metanoēsate oun kai epistrepsate*]" (3:19), because God has sent Christ "to bless you by turning [*apostrephein*] every one of you from your wickedness" (3:26).

11. The only examples of more straightforward spatial usage are at 9:40; 15:36; 16:18.

Similarly, the people of Lydda "turn to the Lord" in response to Peter's preaching (9:35; cf. 11:21). Gentiles turning to God (15:19) is the phenomenon that perhaps above all impels the apostolic council of Jerusalem to action.

It is not difficult to find plenty of additional evidence in Luke's Pauline narrative. At Lydda, Paul preaches "that you should turn from these vain things to a living God who made the heaven and the earth and the sea and all that is in them" (14:15 ESV; cf. 1 Thess. 1:9). In his defense before King Agrippa, Paul describes his mission to the gentiles as being sent "to open their eyes, so that they may turn [*epistrepsai*] from darkness to light and from the power of Satan to God" (26:18; cf. 26:20). In the concluding verses of Acts, Paul's warning to the Jewish community at Rome cites Isa. 6:9–10 (using the same word, *epistrephō*) to underline the possibility of Jewish repentance (28:27).

But where is Peter himself converted in Acts? Many regard as definitive Peter's vision at Joppa before the visit to the house of Cornelius in Acts 10. But contrary to a certain contemporary hermeneutical fashion to see Peter embracing a fundamental religious shift or conversion away from his own practice of the law, the text itself merely describes a vision whose application is that Peter should not call any human beings common or unclean. The change is a gain in *understanding* (e.g., 10:34). It is interesting that conversion language here applies only to Cornelius and his household; indeed, the Jerusalem Christians conclude from Peter's report that "*to the Gentiles* God has granted the repentance [*metanoian*] that leads to life" (11:18).

It seems clear that Luke himself offers no clear answer to our opening question. Since the Lukan Jesus evidently looks *forward* to Peter's conversion as something still in the future at the Last Supper, where might this have taken place? Though Luke raises expectations, the evangelist himself does not answer this question. This amounts to an encouragement to his readers to answer the question in terms of things they already know about Peter, whether or not these are an explicit part of Luke's story in the Gospel and Acts.

There are many other examples of Luke involving the reader in supplying knowledge gained from other sources. Perhaps chief among these are the questions of what happens to Paul at the end of Acts or during his three years at Ephesus. In relation to Peter, there is much room for additional information—or, of course, speculation!—in the apostle's departure "to another place" (Acts 12:17).

What Luke had in mind with these tantalizing hints is not in our grasp, as authorial intention rarely is. What is a little more accessible to us is an answer to the question of what Luke's earliest audiences heard in this text or, in other words, what its footprint was in the first two or three centuries of Christian reflection and appropriation. The key principle here is simple but important and draws on an insight widely encountered and illustrated in earlier chapters of this book: if Luke here implicitly invites his readers to draw certain conclusions, one of our best available exegetical guides is to ask what those earliest readers themselves concluded.

Here we will once again tackle this question back to front, taking three snapshots as we travel in reverse historical order from third- and fourth-century visual interpretations to second- and then back to first-century texts. What emerges from this way of approaching the text is the realization that early Christian readers of the Passion Narratives saw the question of Peter's conversion as inextricably linked with his experiences on both Good Friday and Easter Sunday, which in turn set a pattern for the whole course of a subsequent mission and eventual martyrdom. In other words, the effective footprint of our passage from Luke 22 offers important clues to its range of meaning.

Peter and the Good Friday Rooster in Early Christian Art

The striking motif of Jesus facing or pointing at Peter in ways that appear to heighten and accentuate certain themes in the biblical narrative emerges as a feature in early Christian art around the third century. Our first extant painting of Peter appears around AD 230 among the relatively simple third-century wall frescoes of the small Christian chapel at Dura Europos in Syria, near the more opulently decorated and better-known Jewish synagogue. The painting of Peter shows him with Jesus in the context of what may be the story of Jesus walking on the water.[12] By the later third and fourth centuries, we encounter the very popular motif of Peter and Christ accompanied by a rooster, which may be on the ground or on top of a pillar but always occupies a position of great artistic and symbolic prominence. Well over 120 sarcophagi, ivories, and frescoes featuring this motif have been cataloged and discussed (cf. Post 1984, 24–42).

We cannot here enter into a detailed discussion of these images,[13] which appear to relate to their texts somewhat as classic orthodox icons do: the image invites the viewer to participate in the reality identified in the word, and the word disambiguates the meaning of the image. In this case, that image encapsulates a particular vignette of the trial scene. Although the distinctively Lukan focus is not exclusively developed, it is nevertheless present in features like Peter's repentance and in the Lord, who turns to Peter, beckoning him with his gaze (22:61).

What is present here must be more than simply a cartoon-like narrative encapsulation of the denial scene punctuated and bounded by the rooster's crow.[14] If that were all that these images seek to convey, they might merely substitute for the written text in a setting of widespread illiteracy but would have no real explanatory force beyond that. The very popularity of this motif, however, together with the graphic prominence and position regularly assigned to the rooster,

12. A full discussion of this fresco can be found in Nicholls 2008.
13. More detailed argumentation is offered in Bockmuehl 2010a, 188–205. See also Canetri 2006; Dresken-Weiland 2011.
14. Somewhat as envisaged by Wilpert 1903, 1:329–31.

guarantees that something more must be afoot: this bird is displayed far larger than life, almost turkey-sized, and often on top of a pillar or with a finger pointing at it—the point can hardly be missed! Scholarly studies have not found it difficult to pinpoint the significance: Greco-Roman antiquity saw the rooster as symbolizing the arrival of light, of victory, and occasionally of immortality. For Christians, on the other hand, that same motif proved highly conducive to a link with the resurrection of Christ.

By the fourth century, the rooster as symbolic herald of spiritual daylight surfaces quite explicitly in Christian poetry, including influential hymns. In *Aeterne rerum conditor* ("Framer of the Earth and Sky"), Ambrose of Milan connects the cock's crow of the Passion Narrative to the heralding of health, hope, and faith that allowed both Peter and ourselves to wash our sins away as Jesus turns to look at us. Prudentius, whose Christmas carol "Of the Father's Love Begotten" is still widely sung to this day, similarly develops the theme of the rooster as symbolizing redemption and new life in *Ales diei nuntius* ("The Winged Herald of the Day"), a traditional early morning hymn for Lauds on Tuesdays.[15]

Denial and remorse, repentance, and the hope of resurrection and renewal are prominently developed here. By reading the Passion Narrative in a way that appears to superimpose the threefold restoration of John 21 onto the threefold denial of Luke 22, the image of the cock's crow rolls into one the three stages of Peter's fall, repentance, and renewal. In that sense, the very depth of Peter's failure is redeemed as the point of his conversion: the cock's crow projects into the dark night of Maundy Thursday the bright daylight of Easter Sunday.

Peter's Conversion and Crucifixion: The *Acts of Peter*

Back in the second century, we first encounter a puzzling and fanciful literary document known as the *Acts of Peter*, conventionally dated in its earliest literary form to around AD 190. Given the extreme textual fluidity of the material, there is little point in seeking to pin down the document's date and setting with any degree of precision; yet the relationship with other late second-century documents, such as the *Acts of Paul* and the *Acts of Andrew*, clearly shows that the story of Peter's upside-down crucifixion at the hands of Nero was known in Rome by the mid-second century and was sometimes linked with legendary accounts of his struggles against real or symbolic enemies of the church, such as Simon Magus.

In this puzzling and largely legendary apocryphal document, however, the theme of conversion occupies a surprisingly strong place throughout. Peter

15. Ambrose's text and translation are available online at http://medieval.ucdavis.edu/20A/Music.html (accessed June 19, 2009). Prudentius's text with translation by J. M. Neale is at http://www.preces-latinae.org/thesaurus/Hymni/AlesDiei.html (accessed June 19, 2009).

concedes that he denied Jesus three times due to an attack of Satan but employs his personal example to urge his Roman audience to "change your hearts" and be strong in "the Father of our Lord Jesus Christ" (*Acts of Peter* 3.3.7). We must pass over the subsequent chapters that relate a series of highly peculiar and exotic miracles accompanying the conflict with Simon Magus, which, in their very subversion of the enemy's attempt to hijack the created order, seem emblematic of the "upside down" theme on which the story also ends. When Peter's life is in danger and fellow believers urge him to leave the city, Peter rejects this suggestion at first, saying, "Shall we act like deserters, brothers?" (9.35.6, ed. Vouaux, 1922)—as if reflecting on what the disciples did when Jesus was arrested. Peter then agrees to his friends' request and leaves the city in disguise, but as he leaves the gate, he sees Jesus entering Rome. On seeing Jesus, Peter says, "Lord, where are you going?" When Jesus replies, "I am coming to Rome to be crucified," Peter turns (*hypestrepsen*) back to the city, where he is soon afterward crucified upside down at his own request (9.37.8–38.9). The author clearly assigns great symbolic importance to this upside-down crucifixion as subverting all secular human values by the cross of the new Adam, placing a long speech on this subject on the dying Peter's lips. The hearers are exhorted to "leave your former error and turn back" to the cross of Christ (9.38), whose central nail symbolizes the point of humankind's conversion (*epistrophē*) and repentance (*metanoia*).

By means of this extraordinary narrative, the author of the *Acts of Peter* presents the figure of the apostle as a graphic embodiment of his own message of repentance and conversion. Above all, the story of Peter's return to Rome to face martyrdom is developed here as the redemptive reversal of that earlier episode. Previously a denier and deserter, Peter now turns back to face the challenge of this vocation as soon as he encounters Christ on the way to the cross, in fulfillment of Jesus's prediction in the Gospel of John (13:36; 21:18–19). Here at the end of his life, Peter has become the second-chance disciple, the apostle of conversion who turns around to love and follow Jesus the second time around. In doing so, he shares upside down in his Master's fate and in his subversion of all worldly values. The cross becomes a parable of faith's conversion—but above all of Peter's own—from the powers of the world to the God and Father of Jesus Christ.

Making Sense of Peter's Conversion in the New Testament

With this early Christian exegetical footprint in mind, we may return now to the question of Peter's conversion in the remainder of the NT. A number of passages might usefully be explored, but given the tradition's evident interest in connecting the challenge of conversion to the death and resurrection of Jesus, I would like here to highlight just two such passages as suggesting a particularly clear correlation of these themes within the NT itself.

1 Peter on New Birth

In an explicitly Petrine context, the prologue of 1 Peter identifies the first person plural "us" as the beneficiaries of "new birth" to living hope through Christ's resurrection (1:3):

> Blessed be the God and Father of our Lord Jesus Christ! By his great mercy he has given us new birth into a living hope through the resurrection of Jesus Christ from the dead.

Although "born-again" language is known from the Gospel of John, biblical Greek attests the transitive verb "to give renewed birth [*anagennaō*]" only here and in 1 Pet. 1:23, where again it denotes the gift of spiritual new life where previously there was none: "You have been re-born not of perishable but of imperishable seed, through the living and enduring word of God" (1:23). In other words, we are talking about an experience of moral and spiritual conversion. The author includes himself in that experience at 1:3, while in verse 22, he describes the transforming purification of his readers (second-person plural) through obedience to truth and love. At the same time, the context makes very clear that this divine transformation has been achieved through the death and resurrection of Jesus Christ (e.g., 1:2, 11, 19). Peter himself is here presented as a beneficiary of that gift, having participated on Good Friday and Easter in penitent turning from fear and false hopes to a true hope and obedient love.

We see, then, that the first letter of Peter offers a remarkable resemblance to the progression in Luke's narrative, from Jesus's passiontide prediction of denial and turning (Luke 22:31–34) through Easter Saturday despondency (cf. 24:21) to seeing the risen Lord (esp. 24:34) and being launched by the gift of the Spirit (24:49) on the adventure of mission that takes hold in the book of Acts.

Peter's Threefold Restoration in the Gospel of John

Another powerful NT perspective on what might be meant by Peter's conversion is offered by the concluding chapter of John's Gospel. Just as the Lukan passion account seems to some scholars to show links with that of John, so also echoes of John 21:2–14 have been seen in the largely unparalleled narrative of Peter's call in Luke 5:1–11 (discussed in chapter 4).

At the beginning of John 21, Peter makes the somewhat "pre-converted" suggestion to go fishing, but he and the other disciples catch nothing after fishing all night. They then hear Jesus advising them from the shore to cast the net on the other side, and they immediately capture a large number of fish that can only be pulled back to shore (21:6, 8, 11).

Unlike Matthew, the Fourth Gospel has no previous commission of Peter as the community's foundation or keyholder. Here we find Peter not so much restored but rather newly appointed to a unique pastoral role, his threefold declaration of love corresponding to the gravity of his threefold denial. Countless Christian homilies have been preached on that correspondence, and careful readers have noted that the only two coal fires in John's Gospel mark the scenes of Peter's betrayal in the high priest's courtyard (18:18) and his post-Easter commissioning at the Sea of Galilee (21:9). After three denials, followed by three expressions of affirmation, Peter is commissioned and equipped to follow in the footsteps of Jesus as his deputy and pastoral representative, tasked with strengthening and shepherding his fellow believers. Indeed, Jesus goes so far as to predict that Peter too will lay down his life for the flock on a cross (21:19, 22; cf. 13:36–37 with 10:11).

The application of this narrative to the exegetical footprint we examined above seems very clear: here too it is the crucifixion-resurrection sequence that marks the moment of Peter's conversion.

Conclusion

Luke 22:31–34 presents an intriguing and convenient peg for investigating the puzzling silence in the NT, especially in Luke, concerning the conversion of Simon Peter. The third evangelist leads us to expect that at some point following Peter's denial of Jesus at the rooster's crow, he will turn back and assume the pastoral task of strengthening the church. Nevertheless, that expectation is nowhere explicitly fulfilled in either of Luke's two volumes.

Three vignettes of this narrative's early exegetical footprint help us to articulate an approach to the problem of Peter's conversion and Luke. We have seen the rooster's crow intimately linked in early Christian art and hymnody with Jesus's cross and resurrection to new life. Peter's own upside-down imitation of that death was already the subject of sustained narrative and homiletical reflection earlier, in the *Acts of Peter*. Finally, light can be shed on the NT's own elaboration of this theme in the motifs of repentance and rebirth to resurrection life in 1 Pet. 1 and John 21.

Although Luke never makes it explicit, he may hint at this answer in the almost gratuitously oblique and unvoiced resurrection appearance to Peter (24:34): "The Lord is risen, and has appeared [*ōphthē*] to Simon." Jesus turns and *gazes* at Peter to convict him of his guilt (22:61), and Peter's Easter morning seeing of Jesus (24:34) turns him from darkness to light. The rooster comes to symbolize the whole movement, marking the beginning of the end of darkness and heralding instead the beginning of dawn. That is the insight of the text's exegetical footprint, and it lends a fresh insight into Jesus's statement that the rooster cannot crow *until* (*ou . . . heōs*) Peter has denied him three times.

6

From Unlikely Birthplace
to a Global Mission

In the course of our East-to-West and back-to-front examination of Peter, we turn finally in this chapter to the second of our two case studies, returning from the remembered to the historical-critical *background and setting* of Peter in order to demonstrate how the latter shapes the former. Peter's hometown might shed light on the complex personal background and shaping of a man remembered as an apostle for a church of both Jews and gentiles. I wish to suggest that the case of Bethsaida may bring together the memory of the missionary with the archaeology of his ancestry in a particularly fruitful correlation.

Chapter 3, on the Eastern Peter, began with an illustration of the so-called house of Peter in Capernaum, suggesting that the effective history of Petrine memory resembles the serendipitous fate of the generations of pilgrims' graffiti scrawled on the walls of that house. In the present chapter, I want to suggest that the same process may sometimes be illuminated from the opposite end of that timescale: just as a person's remembered profile may (however tenuously and dialectically) reveal vital insight about their identity, so there may be similar organic links between that prosopography of memory and what historical critics used to call the "background" that originally shaped the person remembered. We have no access to the sorts of causal or predictive links once confidently assigned to such backgrounds by NT scholarship. Conversely, *some* sort of reciprocal and potentially illuminating, if rarely traceable, relationship between what is remembered of a person and what shaped that person may reasonably be expected. What I suggest here is that just as Capernaum's graffiti attends a memory of Peter's home, so Peter's Bethsaida hints at the symbolic worlds that came to shape the missionary. This relationship, somewhat romantically mooted over half a century ago by Oscar Cullmann (1953, 22), is in fact more complex than the connection between smoke and fire. Nevertheless, this latter clichéd image does turn out to capture something of the circumstantial connectedness of history and memory that we can observe in Peter's case.

Peter's Origin: The Gospel Traditions

John 1:44 is the single verse in the NT that tells us that Peter and his brother Andrew came from the village of Bethsaida on the Sea of Galilee. Can that passing and prosaic observation really offer anything of interest to an understanding of Peter's apostolic profile? Even if it is historically true, some scholars have deemed it trivial and irrelevant.[1]

After reminding ourselves briefly of the gospel traditions about Peter's origin and his background in Bethsaida, we will examine some recent archaeological work on Bethsaida before considering some possible conclusions for its relevance to the remembered Peter.

Bethsaida in Jesus's Ministry

Bethsaida is mentioned five times in Matthew, Mark, and Luke, but nowhere do they suggest that any of Jesus's disciples originated there.[2] Matthew and Luke claim that at Bethsaida and Chorazin Jesus performed "works of power [*dynameis*]" (Luke 10:13//Matt. 11:21). Even so, both villages evidently gave Jesus's ministry the cold shoulder, and he curses both:

> Woe to you, Chorazin! Woe to you, Bethsaida! For if the deeds of power done in you had been done in Tyre and Sidon, they would have repented long ago, sitting in sackcloth and ashes. But at the judgment it will be more tolerable for Tyre and Sidon than for you. (Luke 10:13)

But what are these deeds of power? Even Matthew, with his explicit emphasis on Peter, blots out almost any reference to Bethsaida: the only mention comes in this word of judgment. Perhaps even in Matthew's day this locality continued to prove particularly resistant to the gospel mission.

The church fathers, however, do cite one tradition from the Jewish Christian *Gospel of the Nazarenes*, which reiterates the city's importance to the ministry of

1. De Burgos (1991, 239) calls it "an insignificant tradition."
2. For fuller documentation and discussion of the following material, see also Bockmuehl 2010a, 158–87.

Jesus. This source affirms that Jesus performed no fewer than *fifty-three* miracles at Bethsaida and Chorazin!

Bethsaida was a highlight of Pope John Paul II's tour of Galilee in March 2000, when he was presented with a copy of what was claimed to be the key to Peter's house in the city (see Freund 2004, xvii). The NT Gospels, in stark contrast, engage in a virtual conspiracy of silence on Bethsaida. In fact, the entire gospel tradition situates only *two* miracles at or near Bethsaida: the second feeding of the multitude, in Luke 9, and, more significantly, the two-stage healing of the blind man, in Mark 8. Even in Luke 9, though, there are reasons to think that what is meant is not the village itself but rather the hillside wilderness in the district of Bethsaida.

Only Mark has the second Bethsaida narrative, about the blind man who first sees "people walking like trees" before he is healed at the second attempt. This is perhaps the only story that is set in the town of Bethsaida itself (8:22–26), and because of its unusual two-stage healing it makes for an exciting, if relatively unfamiliar, narrative.[3] But even here in Mark, it is surely significant that Jesus takes the man *out of the village* before healing him and then tells him not to go back! If the traditional link of this Gospel with Petrine tradition has any merit, one wonders if Mark's failure to comment on Jesus's judgment on Bethsaida may itself be in deference to the home of Peter. There is something profoundly symbolic—dare one say almost Petrine—about the story of Jesus reaching out to the blind man from the faithless, unwelcoming town of Bethsaida. The only way to heal the blind man is to take him physically away from Bethsaida, and even then it takes a second healing touch, as also for Mark's Peter, to move from blindness, via dulled and partial sight, to full apperception of Jesus. And like Peter, the formerly blind man is *not* to return to his place of birth.

Although one or two other stories could conceivably be linked with Bethsaida, no such suggestions are entirely compelling, and none of them shed any obvious light on Peter. Reading only the Synoptics, we would have guessed that Peter had always lived in Capernaum. There is "the house of Simon and Andrew," and there he lives with his wife and mother-in-law.[4] Only John suggests any link with Bethsaida.

Peter's Origins

Despite or precisely because of its apparently deliberate obscuring, Peter's connection with Bethsaida is questioned rarely in scholarship and never in antiquity (although some manuscripts and literary sources appear to confuse it with the site of Bethesda in Jerusalem). Can we know anything more about Peter's background there and about why he moved to Capernaum? The church fathers like to depict

---

3. Remarkably, the fabled country singer Johnny Cash (1932–2003) produced a song about it in the 1970s, "I See Men as Trees Walking."

4. Mark 1:29–31; cf. Matt. 8:14–15//Luke 4:38–39 ("Peter's house"). Peter's wife is also mentioned in 1 Cor. 9:5.

Peter as having grown up in poverty and possibly as an orphan.[5] It is true that the living standard of those in the fishing industry would have been a little more stable than the experience of the many casual and unskilled day laborers, who faced the daily threat of unemployment and imperiled subsistence. Nevertheless, the Gospel narratives seem to concur that Peter was less prosperous than some other disciples. Zebedee, the father of James and John, evidently ran a business that could rely on its own boat, supplies, and hired staff (Mark 1:19–20). Jesus first meets Peter and Andrew while they are fishing from the shore, rather than from a boat. Indeed, only a single, somewhat problematic passage in the Gospels implies that Peter even owns a boat (Luke 5:3), and in that case, many scholars suspect a conflation or dislocation of several different traditions.

Very little can be said with confidence about Peter's education. Acts has his adversaries in Jerusalem call him an uneducated, common man—an *agrammatos* (Acts 4:13). An elementary family upbringing in marginal conditions of Jewish life might well extend only to the most basic rudiments of literacy. Since Bethsaida soon came to bear a Greco-Roman name (Julias), and only Greek names are known for Peter's brother Andrew and their friend Philip, it seems quite reasonable to suppose that Peter spoke passable Greek ever since childhood; but it is much more difficult to say how well he could read or (especially) write.

John's Peter and Bethsaida

It is only the Fourth Gospel that places Peter's origin in Bethsaida (1:44; 12:21): Peter, Andrew, and Philip are from "Bethsaida of Galilee" (so 12:21). But the limited evidence does not mean that it is unimportant or unreliable. The shoe may well be on the other foot: it is precisely the Synoptic Gospels' *silence* about this place that calls for explanation.

All three disciples' names in John 1:40–44 are Greek. The Fourth Evangelist develops that Hellenistic character in a number of ways. Philip and Andrew are portrayed throughout John's Gospel as the disciples who are most comfortable in a Greek-speaking context. Thus Philip is the first port of call for pilgrim "Greeks" (probably Greek-speaking Jews) who have "come up to worship at the feast" and now want to see Jesus, and Philip naturally calls on Andrew to act on this request (John 12:21–22).

At the same time, the Fourth Gospel explicitly suggests that Andrew had a close connection with the ministry of John the Baptist even before meeting Jesus. A certain plausibility of memory in this otherwise surprising claim may be sought in that this evangelist links Andrew with John specifically in "Bethany across the Jordan" (1:18). This has long been recognized as more likely denoting a location not in Judea[6]

---

5. So John Chrysostom: "he of Bethsaida, the uncouth rustic" (*Hom. Act.* 4 on Acts 2:1–2; cf. *Hom. Jo.* 2 on John 1:1; also *Ps.-Clem. Hom.* 12.6).

6. Origen and some MSS "correct" to *Bēthabara*, and a few other MSS more accurately *Bētharaba* (i.e., "Beth Arabah," the place just north of the Dead Sea where Israel traditionally

but rather in *Batanea*, the designation commonly given to the tetrarchy of Herod's son Philip to which Bethsaida also belonged. If John was for a time active in this region, it could more easily explain his connection with members of Peter's family and eventually with Jesus himself.

Interestingly, Andrew appears together with Philip, also from Bethsaida—and separately from Peter—in Mark's list of disciples (Mark 3:18), although this is "corrected" in Matthew and Luke. Both of them (and not Peter) are approached for local information in John's story of the feeding of the five thousand. John may or may not know the Lukan tradition that this took place at (more likely near) Bethsaida (9:10), but he does indeed place it on the eastern side of the lake (6:1). Andrew and Philip evidently serve as "local experts." Philip will know where to buy bread for the crowds (6:5), and it is Andrew who locates the boy with the five loaves and two small pickled fish (John 6:8–9). Here, then, it is again Andrew and Philip who seem to have the stronger link with the vicinity of Bethsaida, perhaps reflecting Peter's move to Capernaum many years earlier.

Bethsaida: Status, Place, and Context

The Jesus tradition contains several other hints about Bethsaida's socio-political and linguistic setting, some of which, like the notion of Peter's poverty, bear interestingly on his remembered profile.

Geography

We begin with several passing remarks of relevance to Bethsaida's geographical and political location on the Sea of Galilee.

□ From Village to City and Back

Luke and John call Bethsaida a "city" (Luke 9:10; John 1:44), but Mark describes it as a "village" (8:23, 26). Mark's usage here reflects the vocabulary of Jesus's lifetime; its elevation from a village to a Roman *polis*, renamed Julias, took place around AD 30. Bethsaida's new Greco-Roman name interestingly never seems to stick in early Christian or rabbinic literature. Greco-Roman writers, by contrast, consistently call it Julias. Jewish and Christian memory was untroubled by Philip the Tetrarch's relatively short-lived political *fiat*: after his death, Bethsaida rapidly returned to its previous obscurity.

---

crossed the Jordan). *Bēthania* has by far the best textual support, but it does not fit a Judean location. The arguments are persuasively presented in Riesner 1986; 1992, who follows Bargil Pixner (ET, 2010, 177–91). See also, most fully, Riesner 2002, who points out (129–31) as well the story of the ravens feeding the prophet Elijah at "the brook Cherith east of the Jordan" (1 Kings 17:3, 5). This brook is sometimes identified with the Yarmuk River, which flows into the Jordan from Batanea just south of the Sea of Galilee.

□ *Bethsaida of Galilee?*

Another geographical puzzle is why John calls Peter's hometown "Bethsaida *of Galilee*" (12:21) even though it is not actually in Galilee but east of the Jordan in the Golan (Gaulanitis/Batanea). Various explanations have been tried, but it is now more widely agreed that Jewish settlements in the Jordan Valley and around the lake were indeed sometimes loosely described as part of Galilee. The evangelists, after all, speak of the "Sea of *Galilee*."[7] Several ancient writers follow this practice of a somewhat inflated "Galilee" surrounding the lake.

Peter's Language

The Gospels offer insight into two different features of Peter's native language. One of these has to do with Peter's linguistic accent and the other with a wordplay on the name of Bethsaida.

In Judea and elsewhere, Galileans were notorious and mocked for their careless pronunciation, especially of gutturals.[8] As can be the case with cultural jokes to this day, perceived linguistic sloppiness is assumed to translate into the moral or cultural realm. Thus Galilean linguistic carelessness was sometimes associated with ignorance and imprecision in other areas of life, including religious matters.

In this vein, Peter's Galilean accent gets him into trouble in Jerusalem. In the story of his denial of Jesus in Jerusalem (Mark 14:70; cf. Matt. 26:73), Peter's accent is recognizable as unmistakably *Galilean*—not, for example, Greek. Despite periodic scholarly assumptions to the contrary, Peter's origin in Bethsaida will have made him bilingual. Rudolf Pesch rightly points out that even subsequent traditions of Mark as Peter's "interpreter" (*hermeneutēs*; Eusebius, *Eccl. Hist.* 3.39.15) do not necessarily signify that the latter needed a *translator*. Whether or not the role is partly linguistic, it may just as easily cover functions of a spokesman and a transmitter of tradition.[9] In Judea, therefore, the Galilean Peter stands out as socially marked by his accent and its inevitable cultural connotations.

Bethsaida Fishing Themes

It is worth considering the extent to which Bethsaida and motifs of fishing are interwoven thematically in the ministry of Jesus. The name of the village means "place of fishing" (or "place of hunting"). Even after its decline in the third century, the rabbis remembered it precisely for the rich variety of its fish. The Gospels also highlight the importance of stories and teachings about fishing, "fishermen," "fishing nets," or the fishing "catch"—all of which may be assumed

7. Heinz-Wolfgang Kuhn (2004, 124) concludes that Mark does know the location of Bethsaida.
8. Cf. Dalman 1905, 56–68, noting specific reference, e.g., to the inhabitants of Beth She'an.
9. Pesch 1980, 11–12. Cf. Hengel 2010, 12, 37, but contrast 13 (Peter knew "exotic" Greek).

to use cognate Aramaic words (as in the later Syriac Peshitta translation). Most importantly, Peter and Andrew are called as "fishermen" who are to become eschatological "fishers of people." Many of these are puns on Peter's profession and on the place of his birth.

The Gospels also offer some intriguing insights into Peter's connection with the north shore of the Sea of Galilee near Bethsaida. In their call narrative, Mark and Matthew show Peter and Andrew engaged in cast-net fishing, throwing their circular nets from the shore or while standing in shallow waters. Until even a hundred years ago, indigenous fishers frequently stood on the shore or in the shallows of the lake to take advantage of large shoals of the local *musht* fish (now called "St. Peter fish") that tend to congregate around the northern part of the lake in the winter months. Favorite locations were Capernaum's fishing outpost of Tabgha (*Heptapegon*), with its warm lakebed springs, and also the mouth of the Jordan near Bethsaida, where fish entered or left the lake and could more easily be caught even without the benefit of a boat.

The Archaeology of Bethsaida-Julias

The identification of the site of Bethsaida has long been controversial. In recent years, two sites near the northern end of the Sea of Galilee have been particularly debated: a large ancient mound that Israeli maps now identify as Tell Bethsaida and a smaller site known as el-Araj nearer the lakeshore. Let's look at each in turn.

Et-Tell (Tell Bethsaida)

Since 1988 an international team has carried out annual excavations on a large rocky mound about 25 meters high, known as et-Tell when it was part of Syrian Golan. The site, which is the largest tell around the Sea of Galilee, is today located a little over 500 meters east of the Jordan and 2.5 kilometers north of the lake.[10] Aside from particularly impressive Iron Age finds, the site has yielded evidence primarily from the Hellenistic and Early Roman periods. The place apparently never recovered its former glory after its destruction by the Assyrians in 732 BC. Between the third centuries BC and AD, the tell hosted a small town with primarily private houses, until it declined in the third century AD and was eventually abandoned a hundred years later, perhaps after a major earthquake (Arav 1999b, 81–83). Although the site is large enough for a population of several thousand, the archaeologists have identified a small village with a population of only "several hundred people during the time of Jesus" (Arav 1999b, 83; cf. Strickert 1998, 68–74).

10. So, e.g., Google's satellite map. The precise distance from the shore varies with seasonal water levels.

□ *Architecture*

In the first century AD, despite some larger courtyard-style buildings, most of the houses were fairly modest. Based on associated artifacts, one has been dubbed a "fisherman's house" and the other a "winemaker's house." One of the more puzzling issues is the virtual absence of public architecture from the Greek and Roman period, even after Bethsaida was turned into the city of Julias, and even though Josephus speaks of settlers and fortifications. Virtually no material evidence for this has come to light: we seem to have nothing of the usual Hellenistic city structures like a theater or amphitheater, a hippodrome, gymnasium, palaces, temples, pools, pillars and porticoes, statues. There are no inscriptions, no aqueduct or public baths, and no signs of concerted fortification. Only a handful of first-century AD coins have come to light, very few of them minted by Philip the Tetrarch. The silence of the archaeological record does seem peculiar. Can this really be one of the four main cities of Galilee named by Ptolemy in the second century AD or one of the four "lovely" cities on the Sea of Galilee described by the Roman geographer Pliny the Elder in AD 77?[11]

Several things must be said in reply. First, the site experienced a long history of looting and re-use of building stones, facilitated by the fact that its abandonment in antiquity left the Roman remains close to the surface (Arav 1995, 5). The tell also suffered significant damage under the impact of Syrian army trenches and other military installations deployed in the 1950s and 1960s (Arav 1999a, 6).

The excavators do claim to have found a Roman temple of the goddess Julia Livia, also badly damaged by a twentieth-century Syrian trench. This east-facing building measures six-by-twenty meters and contained a single column base. A bronze incense shovel was found nearby and has also been related to this building, and subsequent excavation reports note several other vessels recovered from an adjacent pit.[12] Of possible further relevance is a small Greco-Roman figurine, said to be of Julia Livia; additional pagan figurines have subsequently surfaced in the residential quarter. The identification of this proposed temple, however, remains somewhat tentative, and other critics have expressed considerable doubt.[13]

Finally, if Julias was turned into a city only in the year AD 30, Herod's son Philip had barely four years to implement his project before he died in AD 34. Philip apparently visited often and is reported to have died there. On his own orders, he was formally buried in a previously commissioned mausoleum, although this has not yet come to light. But the area then reverted to direct rule

11. Ptolemy, *Geogr.* 5.15.3; Pliny the Elder, *Nat. Hist.* 5.15.71.

12. See Arav 1999a, 18–24, 32–44. For the possible additional temple vessels, see the 2007 excavation report in Arav 2008.

13. Chancey (2002, 108) concludes that no cultic use of either the building or the figurine has been established; and Josephus's uncharacteristic silence about a Herodian temple at Bethsaida seems to him "strong evidence that none existed."

by the Roman governor of Syria, who had no sentimental attachment to Philip's unfinished pet project.[14]

□ The Social Life of Bethsaida

If the buildings are rather plain, the evidence for Bethsaida's material culture turns out to be much more interesting. There is some evidence of fishing but not of a major fishing industry, as elsewhere on the lake; fishing was more likely recreational or for private use.

The tell's animal remains cast some doubt on the notion that Bethsaida was primarily a Jewish fishing village. Only a small percentage of extant animal bones are of fish, many of which are non-kosher catfish unlikely to be eaten by Jews (Arav 1999a, 84).[15] Other animal bones confirm that the inhabitants raised cattle, horses, donkeys, and mules, as well as sheep and goats—but also, more significantly for our purposes, pigs (Arav 1999a, 84).

Archaeologists have also found barley flour mills and implements for winemaking, a tannery, and the manufacture of textiles (pollen analysis has suggested an active commercial flax-growing industry).[16] A brief period of prosperity in the second and first centuries BC is attested by considerable evidence of imported Hellenistic fineware, but the village's fortunes appear to have declined again before the time of Peter's birth.[17]

The faunal evidence agrees with the archaeological fact that there is as yet no concrete evidence of a Jewish presence at Bethsaida: no synagogue, no immersion pools, and no Jewish writings or inscriptions. There are a few Jewish coins, though these cannot by themselves suffice to attest Jewish habitation. The only epigraphic evidence is in Greek.

A Second Site?

An alternative location of Bethsaida has sometimes been proposed. It looks at first more promising, but on balance it has less to commend it. The site of el-Araj lies at the end of an unmarked dirt track down to the lakeside. The main evidence of ancient remains are miscellaneous rough and cut stones scattered around the site and along the embankment on a narrow strip of the floodplain that recedes toward the shore. Based on a limited ground-penetrating radar survey, the Bethsaida Excavation Project believes that the settlement of el-Araj was built in the late Roman or early Byzantine period, perhaps after the destruction of Bethsaida itself, in order to move nearer the water's edge, which had moved dramatically in the aftermath of an earthquake.

14. Josephus, *Ant.* 18.108. It was briefly under the rule of Agrippa I (AD 41–44), and from AD 53, intermittently under Agrippa II.
15. Might these be among the "bad fish" of Matt. 13:48?
16. For the suggestion of flax industry, see, e.g., Schoenwetter and Geyer 2000; Geyer 2001.
17. See Fortner 1995; also several subsequent excavation reports.

Much of the argument rests on supposed geological changes. Others, from the nineteenth century to the early 1990s, repeatedly claimed Greco-Roman remains at el-Araj, including traces of a large mosaic, an aqueduct, assorted architectural fragments, and a Roman road linking the site with the tell. As is the case for Tell Bethsaida, the situation has not been helped by twentieth-century politics: in 1956 the Israeli air force bombarded a Syrian ammunitions store on the site, inflicting unspecified damage.

Josephus offers what at first seems contradictory information about the location of Bethsaida. He describes the Jordan River entering the lake *after* passing the city of Julias (suggesting a city at some distance from the shoreline, as today), and yet he also claims that the erstwhile village of Bethsaida is directly "*on* the shore of the lake of Gennesaret." Can Bethsaida be in both places at once? Debate has tended to favor one site or the other exclusively, but some kind of significant relationship between the two sites has long been seen as plausible. Regardless of whether we can confidently document a Roman road linking them,[18] the idea of Julias as a kind of acropolis that had its own small fishing suburb on the lake should not be dismissed. Ancient cities quite often afforded their most secure and temperate accommodation on a hillside, protected from the dangers of flooding or bandits and, important in a setting like this, away from the humidity and the malaria of the lakeside swamps. Nevertheless, a harbor outpost would ensure more immediate access to vital trade connections and the region's best fishing.

Something like this has been shown to be the pattern for several other cities around the lake: Hippos (Susita), with its harbor near today's En Gev, for example, and Gadara with Tell Samra.[19] Capernaum was directly on the lake but nevertheless had fishing outposts at Tabgha to the south and, perhaps, at Aish to the north (e.g., Nun 1999, 27; cf. Dalman 1935, 136–37). Some such twinning of town and harbor may explain the situation quite well.

Conclusion

The evidence suggests that Tell Bethsaida is relevant to the NT Bethsaida and therefore to Simon Peter. As a youth in Bethsaida, Peter would have had economic and social links with the small and unimpressive village on the hill, which probably had very few observant Jews living in it. Peter became a fisherman perhaps only after moving to the more prosperous village of Capernaum, or else he may have practiced it from a site closer to the lake.

Archaeology suggests that Bethsaida's culture in the first century was under strongly Hellenistic influence, and in the Petrine context this is also confirmed by the Greek names of the three Bethsaida disciples as well as in the stories told

18. So, e.g., Schumacher 1888, 94, 246; and, more recently, Strange 1992.
19. Cf. Nun 1992; 1999, 30–31, 64; Dalman 1935, 171; so also Baudoz 1985, 30.

about them. If there were any Jews at Tell Bethsaida, then unlike in other parts of Transjordan, they may not have followed a way of life that distinguished them clearly from their gentile neighbors.

What might this mean for Peter's formation? Bethsaida Jews were probably very few in number. They did have easy professional and social links with the thriving Jewish community of Capernaum in which there was much less Hellenistic influence. Clearly, Jewish culture and religion across the river from Capernaum were more marginal, existing among a gentile majority, and it is surely significant that by the second and third centuries AD, the rabbis had ceased to consider these regions part of the Jewish land of Israel.[20]

Peter, then, almost certainly grew up fully bilingual in a Jewish minority setting. Although they were Aramaic speakers, his parents and their friends were at ease with their Greek-speaking environment, and their children were known by Greek names—Andrew, Simon Peter, Philip. The political context of Bethsaida would have afforded the young Peter a strong awareness of larger imperial realities, given the periodic visits by the entourage of its pro-Jewish but fully Hellenized local puppet king.

So why did Peter move to Capernaum? Another way of asking this might be: what would Peter and his friends have made of the primarily pagan flavor of life in Bethsaida? What would they have thought of their ruler's increasing devotion to the Roman emperor cult? This is a difficult question, but in a family who named one son Simeon (a patriarchal Jewish name revived only since Maccabean times)[21] and whose other son was evidently linked with the renewal movement of John the Baptist, it certainly seems plausible that marriage into a culturally and perhaps religiously Jewish family—and therefore most likely away from Bethsaida—was desirable. So it may be indicative that Peter had transferred his social and personal connections to Capernaum well before meeting Jesus. Galilee, although resettled only in the Maccabean period, was by the first century AD far less gentile than Batanea.[22]

By all accounts, Bethsaida was fairly impervious to Jewish faith and to the gospel of Jesus. The NT suggests that Jesus and his disciples expended considerable energy on Bethsaida, which was part of his mission to "the lost sheep of the house of Israel" (Matt. 10:6; 15:24), but we also hear that this village was strikingly unresponsive to his ministry and message, a point that seems imprinted on the gospel tradition and Christian memory in silent and explicit condemnation. The difficult two-stage healing of the blind man in Mark 8 is, in this respect, clearly iconic, although Mark himself does not comment on this.

There are also certain hints of Jewish cultural resistance in the Gospel accounts. Andrew, Peter's brother, joined the Jewish renewal movement of John the Baptist (John 1:40–42). We cannot tell if Peter joined this too, but he seems

20. See also Bockmuehl 2003, 67–69, and passim.
21. See on this subject Bockmuehl 2010a, 137–40.
22. See, e.g., Reed 2000; Chancey 2002; 2005.

to have married into the more clearly Jewish environment at Capernaum in the Galilean heartland. One assumes that this was encouraged primarily by familial and cultural or religious considerations rather than, as has been suggested, by the attraction of a "tax break" (so Murphy-O'Connor 1999, 27, 48). The Gospels give occasional hints of Peter's militant sympathies and concern for national renewal, and in Acts he protests his faithful observance of the kosher laws, a point that is confirmed (not always approvingly) in patristic tradition.[23]

Life in a minority context frequently either dilutes or heightens religious zeal. The young Peter's Judaism in marginal circumstances would have left him precariously balanced between two very different, if equally religious, construals of his identity and vocation—nationalist zeal, on the one hand, and a global and multicultural articulation of faithful Jewishness, on the other. The Gospels, Acts, and early Christian tradition suggest that the remembered Peter did show signs of both sympathies. Just as clearly, of course, Peter is remembered as coming to embrace God's outreach to Jews in the homeland and the Diaspora, to gentiles among Jews, and eventually to Jews and gentiles everywhere, "not wanting any to perish, but all to come to repentance" (2 Pet. 3:9 NRSV). What matters for our purposes here is that once Peter was persuaded of that call, his upbringing would have left him culturally and perhaps linguistically better equipped than James to envisage the gospel's outreach from Jerusalem to Antioch and Rome. In that sense, there is a kind of *symbolic* link between the menagerie of animals that the Peter of Acts 10 sees coming down from heaven in a square fisherman's sail[24] and the indiscriminate assortment of clean and unclean fish and animals that archaeology tells us his gentile neighbors used to eat in Bethsaida. In Acts, in 1 Corinthians, and in 1 Peter, we encounter a Peter who, after Joppa, was remembered as gladly proclaiming a multicultural and international gospel. On that point, the memory of his end can learn appreciably from the history of his beginning.

23. Mark 8:32; 14:29, 31 and pars.; John 18:10 pars. Peter is also associated with the saying about the Twelve judging the renewed twelve tribes of Israel (Matt. 19:27–28 par.), and the Lukan Peter's speeches similarly contain elements of a concern for national restoration (e.g., Acts 2:36, 39; 3:19, 22–25; 5:31). Peter claims that he has "never eaten anything that is profane or unclean" (Acts 10:14; 11:8).

24. Acts 10:11; 11:5: an *othonē* with "four points." The meaning "sail" is attested in *T. Zeb.* 6.2; *Mart. Pol.* 15.2; and a number of classical sources. That fishing boats had rectangular sails can be seen on a first-century Magdala floor mosaic now on display at Capernaum, on coinage issued by Tiberius, and on a later fifth-century mosaic at Scythopolis (Beth She'an). Cf. Nun 1989, 58–59.

Concluding Observations

Our journey has led through a bewildering set of mazes and byways. The more we attend to Peter's history and memory, discovering each as a function of the other, inherited myths and certainties give way to a fresher, more unstable, and yet more engaging picture of the man whose prominent but evanescent appearance on the pages of the NT generated such a strong and diverse profile in Christian memory. To conclude, let us first consider what our investigation has shown.

Taking Stock

Peter the uneducated fisherman. Peter the irascible disciple. Peter the miracle worker. Peter the eyewitness, the pillar, the repositor and guarantor of tradition. Even within the relatively narrow constraints of this book, the variety of images, evidence, and texts can be disorientating, whether we begin with Paul's polemical early testimony in Galatians or work backward from much-later hagiographies like that of the *Pseudo-Clementine* literature. Despite the occasional sense of intellectual whiplash, however, we have seen that there are several areas of striking continuity between the memories of Peter from different historical and geographical locations.

The overview of the NT Peter in chapter 2, though incomplete in biographical details, revealed a complex personality. The Gospels present Peter as an uneducated fisherman who lived in Capernaum and whose house functioned as a center for Jesus's ministry. His profile is that of the leading disciple in the privileged group of three, present with James and John at key moments in Jesus's ministry such as the transfiguration. The first half of Acts continued that picture of Peter, while portraying him as something of a missionary pioneer, a powerful miracle worker, and one who played a role in every major event in Jerusalem Christianity until around AD 49. Paul's notorious comments in Gal. 2 confirm Peter's importance, as well, even if Peter was in the wrong at Antioch, as Paul thought. Paul himself soon afterward, in 1 Corinthians, sounds much more eirenic about this pioneer witness of the resurrection and "fellow steward of the mysteries of God." For all their striking differences in theology, language, and evidently authorship, the Petrine Letters show an apostle who is at least implicitly presented as an eyewitness of Jesus (of his passion and transfiguration, respectively) and as a shepherd of his flock, as already in the Fourth Gospel.

In chapter 3, we turned to the remembered profile of Peter in the East. It is immediately striking that although Peter lived most of his life in Eastern regions, so few local traditions about Peter survived. To gain some sense of Peter's memory in the East, this chapter worked back to front—from Serapion of Antioch at the end of the second century through Justin Martyr to Ignatius at the beginning of the second century and then into the NT for a closer look. In the case of the three second-century writers, certain types of tradition about Peter were evidently taken for granted. Even in the 190s AD, Serapion still appealed to a tradition that "we" had received about Peter, deploying this as a criterion to cast doubt on the value of the *Gospel of Peter*. Justin, in his much-earlier *Dialogue with Trypho*, found it wholly uncontroversial to link the Gospel of Mark with Peter's "memoirs." Ignatius of Antioch, as well, used memories of Peter as an apparently uncontroversial foundation for his catholic appeals to Smyrna and Rome. For Ignatius, Peter shares with Paul the distinction of being a martyred apostle, while Peter appears as the central witness for Jesus traditions (Ign. *Smyrn.* 3.1–3), much as in Paul's earlier account (1 Cor. 15:3–5).

Peter appears in a wide range of other Syrian texts, from orthodox and Gnostic apocalypses under his name to several Gospels from various theological points of view. These texts demonstrate a surprising degree of continuity in their Petrine memory, though they also evidence what might be considered a collective forgetting of narrative particulars outside the Gospels. Notably, whether these texts produce a positive or a negative view of Peter, he remains a spokesman for the disciples. In the appreciative sources, Peter's importance in the ministry of Jesus and his position of authority and eminence are supported (as in the *Apocalypse of Peter* and the *Gospel of Peter*), while a handful of others implicitly accept his importance for the orthodox position yet also seek to subvert his authority by appeals to other figures such as Mary (as in the *Gospel of Thomas* and the *Gospel of Mary*). It is interesting to note the extent to which many of these Eastern texts take for granted Peter's work in Rome. The *Pseudo-Clementine* literature is among the most pro-Petrine Syrian texts and portrays his leadership, his power, his miracles, and his resistance against heresy in fantastical detail.

This view of Peter as foremost among the disciples occurs also in the NT documents from the East, though with some ambivalence. The Gospel of John is well known for an apparently intentional displacement of Peter from the leading role among the disciples, replacing him with that Gospel's uniquely characterized

Beloved Disciple. Peter is eager to act but slow to understand. Yet even here, Peter ultimately retains his exemplary role, leadership function, and indeed his unique commission in John 21.

Matthew presents Peter as the Palestinian Jew that he was, painting a complex portrait of Peter's successes and failures. However, as in the later sources, Peter occupies the center of Matthew's Jesus tradition as an eyewitness of the Messiah.

Despite undeniable tension, Galatians and 1 Corinthians, straddling our divide of Eastern versus Western memory, show Paul consistently affirming the unique importance of Peter. Similarly, the author or authors (perhaps one in the West and one in the East?) of 1–2 Peter present the apostle as a prominent figure whose role centrally comprises the transmission of Jesus tradition and apocalyptic wisdom.

Despite these key instantiations of Petrine memory, however, there are few localized traditions from the East, aside perhaps from the apostle's house in Capernaum. Eastern traditions agree in placing Peter in Rome, at least in his defining witness at the end of his life. The memory of Peter as the "rock" appears less as personal memory or polemical tradition than as a consensual principle held in common among many different communities.

In chapter 4 we saw that the lack of local traditions in the East stands in stark contrast to the situation in the West, especially Rome. Despite periodic scholarly doubts that Peter was ever in Rome, we noted the wholly uncontested traditions that Peter ministered in Rome and was killed there by Nero. In time, this univocal memory gave rise to numerous additional accretions (one can visit his prison, his grave, the place where he opposed Simon Magus, the place where he partook of the Eucharist, etc.). Irenaeus, Justin Martyr, Dionysius of Corinth, and Clement of Rome, among others East and West, place Peter in Rome at the end of his life, and the latter two mention his martyrdom. Further, it seems that Peter's memory had grown so popular in Rome that a second-century pagan author like Phlegon of Tralles was able to mistake stories about Peter as stories about Christ. Peter again appears as a pillar apostle, a transmitter of orthodoxy, and a faithful witness.

Western NT documents that mention Peter also share a strikingly common picture of him, despite being remarkably taciturn about the details of much of his ministry. Luke presents a largely Markan Peter, one who struggles to understand Jesus and his purposes but who will ultimately turn and support his fellow disciples (22:31–34). He is foremost among the disciples, both before Jesus's death, when much of Jesus's Galilean ministry is based out of Peter's house, and after his resurrection. (Mark, of course, omits any sustained post-resurrection narrative.) Peter is impetuous and brave at Gethsemane yet cowardly at the high priest's house. In Acts, this portrayal of Peter continues: he is the chief spokesman for the apostles at Pentecost yet slow to understand in the rooftop vision. The narrative ends with Peter's enigmatic departure to "another place" (Acts 12:17), leaving Peter with only a supporting role at the apostolic conference in Acts 15.

First Peter presents the apostle as present in Rome and suggests missionary ties with northern Asia Minor. Peter is a witness and guarantor of the passion and resurrection of Jesus and an elder of the church, though not *the* elder. The Gospel of Mark, like Luke who followed him, sees Peter as the central disciple of Jesus. However, Mark also demonstrates suggestive ties with Petrine memory noted by later writers such as Justin Martyr. Like the end of Peter's narrative in Acts, Mark's narrative ends on something of a whimper, omitting any discussion of what happened to Peter after the resurrection.

In Paul's correspondence with his key European parish of Corinth, he again notes Peter's central role as a witness to the resurrected Christ (a tradition later used by Ignatius in his letter to Smyrna) and may hint at Peter's missionary work in Corinth (as Dionysius of Corinth firmly believed in the 170s AD).

Twin case studies of this NT reception appear in chapters 5 and 6. The exemplary nature of Peter's discipleship and leadership can be seen from the start to be embedded in a cycle of stories that show his journey to faith as gradual, stumbling, and challenged—a person who gets things right the second time around and for whom conversion is not an initiation so much as a way of discipleship. We retraced memory's steps to ask what images of Peter's birthplace and conversion to discipleship shaped the apostle's remembered profile. In looking at his birth in Bethsaida, we found that Peter's astonishing progression to the role of an international missionary pastor can be rendered historically and culturally comprehensible. He grew up in a consciously, perhaps even devoutly, Jewish family that eked out a living in the largely pagan, gentile, Greek-speaking context of Bethsaida before moving to the Aramaic-speaking Galilean Jewish heartland at Capernaum. Across the spectrum of these texts from different theological, historical, and geographical locations, a complex but not necessarily contradictory portrait of Peter emerges. Peter is the rock, an eyewitness to the passion and resurrection of Jesus, and he is a witness, healer, miracle worker, and martyr. Beginning as a fisherman from Capernaum, the apostle became a centrist, bridge-building, and uniting figure in the early church, often pictured with Paul as the twin pillars of the Roman church. A sincere, if flawed, disciple of Jesus.

Implications for the New Testament Peter

We began our investigation of the biblical Peter with reference to Oscar Cullmann's path-breaking study from half a century ago (Cullmann 1952). Employing the lens of a remembered profile in the early church has shown that the question of Peter's centrality for the Jesus movement and its subsequent development retains considerable historical interest and ecclesiological vibrancy. Cullmann first reopened ecumenical dialogue about Simon Peter, and his irenic approach to old contentions continues to find support, whether explicit or implicit, in careful study of this pivotal apostle of Jesus Christ. Some of Cullmann's conclusions and assumptions have not won the day or remain highly contested, such as the authenticity of Jesus's naming of Peter as the rock of the church in Matt. 16 or his notion that a Petrine "suffering servant" Christology can be clearly discerned. Nevertheless, the Eastern and Western churches' uncontested memory of Peter and Paul's martyrdom in Rome robustly confirms Cullmann's more tentative conclusions to that effect. Indeed, they would tend to give a little more credence to the presence of an early memorial marking the apostle's death and his burial at the Vatican. We also saw that archaeological and reception-historical evidence bears out certain other, more speculative aspects of Cullmann's interpretation: for example, the extent to which Peter's youth in Bethsaida may have laid meaningful cultural groundwork for the apostle's subsequent ability to reach out to the Greek-speaking world within and well beyond the boundaries of Palestine.

In these and other key questions, scholarship on Peter has tended to vindicate Cullmann's basic approach, despite notable exceptions and differences in perspective. It has become far less common for the NT Peter to be presented as either a vacillating irrelevance, a polarizing opponent of the true (read "Pauline") gospel, or the primarily mythical figment of authoritarian "early catholic" ecclesiastics.

Part of the argument of this book has been that attending to the footprint of the apostle's living memory can provide insights that, although historically tenuous and theologically diverse, nevertheless help us understand the canonical images and the interstitial spaces between them. The second-century researches of Christian Grappe (1995) and Terence V. Smith (1985) continue to give valuable access to the sources; as Anthony Casurella (1997) rightly has said about Grappe's work, we now do not need to cover this ground again. In my book, I hope additionally to have shown that the ambivalence of early Christian prosopographical tradition need not render it historically irrelevant or reducible to a kaleidoscopic collection of topical "axes."

In this respect, it may be pertinent to recall a key methodological emphasis in my earlier study *Seeing the Word* (Bockmuehl 2006). There I commended the connection between the NT's historical criticism and its early effective history as holding promise both for exegetical insight and for the health of NT study more generally. The biblical Peter's footprint, I suggest, constitutes a case in point.

And after That? The Question of Continuity

There is one final question that, for historical reasons, looms disproportionately large in the study of Simon Peter and that I have deliberately sidestepped until now: the thorny question of continuity in Peter's ministry.

Oscar Cullmann strongly resisted the possibility that Peter could be regarded as having any meaningful defining aftermath in the history of the church. On this point, at least, old confessional divides remained firmly in place in Cullmann's day, as in some circles they continue in our day. This was a conclusion for which Roman Catholic reviewers castigated Cullmann (despite their appreciation for his sympathetic account of Peter's bridge-building role), while Protestants praised him (despite misgivings about his catholic-sounding conclusions about Peter in Matt. 16). As one of the latter nodded approvingly in 1954,

> The fact that, from the beginning of the second century onwards, Rome assumed a leading and increasingly important role in the Church is not disputed, what is denied is that that has anything to do with the Apostolic Age, or that the primacy promised to Peter in Matt. 16.17, a primacy which was actually exercised by him for a short time in Jerusalem, can possibly be transferred to the Bishops of Rome . . . Wittenberg, Canterbury or Geneva, Stockholm or Amsterdam have as much or as little right as Rome to regard themselves as the centre of the Church today or in time to come. (Neill 1954, 210)

On this point, I suggest, Cullmann and his Protestant reviewers were both profoundly right and profoundly misguided. On the one hand, the remembered Peter of the Gospels and the Epistles is *not* portrayed as exceptional in his role as fellow-shepherd and fellow-servant of the servants of Christ (1 Pet. 5:1–4); the apostle's very fallibility and fragility places him on the same road of discipleship as all other believers. Simon Peter is first and foremost neither an authority nor an institution, neither powerful nor infallible, but a flawed disciple and shepherd of Christ's flock. On the other hand, the scope of the task assigned to Peter, whether in Matt. 16 or John 21, does seem coextensive with the life on earth not merely of the apostle personally but of Christ's flock globally. And thus, as long as the church endures, there must be a question of the proper succession to this Petrine ministry.

In his cantankerous dispute with Pope Stephen, Cyprian (d. 258) may be judged right to conclude that *all* bishops who confess the faith of Peter constitute the "rock" on which, according to Matt. 16, the church is founded (*Ep.* 26.1; cf. *Ep.* 74.17 of Firmilian to Cyprian). This is the appropriate challenge to a maximal papal arrogation of Peter's ministry. Nevertheless, it is also the case that the remembered Peter's profile in the second and subsequent centuries includes a recognition that his Petrine ministry was entrusted to a continuing succession of ecclesial shepherds in various places of his activity (including Antioch) but above all in Rome. This continues to make it permissible and appropriate to speak of successors of Peter, even if half a millennium after the Reformation it remains the case that institutional trappings of authority and opulence ill become the early church's memory of the Galilean fisherman whose way of discipleship neither sought nor possessed power and opulence.

Whether the popes embody this Petrine succession validly and worthily remains a perennially useful question and a goad to the church's continuing need for reform, as reformers both within and without the Roman Catholic church have rightly stressed. Pope John Paul II was famously, and perhaps justly, grieved that the institutionally visible form of that Petrine ministry had itself become such a frequent instrument not of unity but of division.[1] While that divisive effect has

---

1. Classically stated in his 1995 encyclical, *Ut unum sint.*

been sadly exemplified in certain phases of ecumenical relations, the other side of the paradox is that the ministry of several recent occupants of the Petrine chair repeatedly foregrounded a desire to serve *all* the servants of Christ.

Consensus about these matters, and about their bearing on Jesus's prayer for his followers' unity (John 17:21–22), remains an eschatological hope. Yet regardless of the right ad hoc and particular answers, the principle of a continuation of the Petrine ministry *as such* seems clear in the memory of the man, beginning perhaps with classic "Petrine primacy" texts such as Matt. 16:17–19; Luke 22:31–32; and John 21:15–17. All three texts imply a post-Easter continuation of Peter's task that seems intrinsically permanent in nature and not tied to the identity of the one apostle (cf. Pesch 1998, 37–39; Malnati 2008, 82). The work of guarding and pasturing the flock and protecting it from attack is a ministry that will continue; it seems patently untrue to assume, as many Protestants continue to do, that Peter's task self-evidently "expired with his death" (Becker 2009, 139).

Peter's memory embodies the archetype of an apostolic ministry that serves the entire church, a task of pastoral service that continues while the church continues. It is in this sense, above all, that Peter is remembered as the rock on which the church is built, as nourisher and pastor of Christ's sheep, as caretaker of the kingdom's keys, as binder and looser. In the end, the diverse and unharmonizable sources of Peter's memory nevertheless offer a glimpse of an important consensual insight: the enduring magnitude of the mission is greater than the volatile fragility of the man to whom it was first entrusted (e.g., Malnati 2008, 54). In this sense, and perhaps in this sense first and foremost, we see Peter remembered as the one to whom Christ's pastoral task is entrusted (as his "vicar," in the old-fashioned Roman Catholic language), the servant of the servants of God, and the fellow shepherd of pastors—not only of this fold but of all Christian folds. The fragility yet indispensability of this ministry of unity, its strength in weakness, and its witness to the grace of a second-chance discipleship remain a vital part of the continuing heritage of Peter's memory among all the Christian churches.

Works Cited

Achtemeier, Paul J. 1996. *1 Peter: A Commentary on First Peter*. Hermeneia. Minneapolis: Fortress.

Allison, Dale C. 1998. *Jesus of Nazareth: Millenarian Prophet*. Minneapolis: Fortress.

———. 2009. *The Historical Christ and the Theological Jesus*. Grand Rapids: Eerdmans.

———. 2010. *Constructing Jesus: Memory and Imagination*. Grand Rapids: Baker Academic.

Anonymous. 2009. "Canon John Fenton." *The Daily Telegraph*, January 8. http://www.telegraph.co.uk/news/obituaries/4177274/Canon-John-Fenton.html.

Arav, Rami. 1995. "Bethsaida Excavations: Preliminary Report, 1987–1993." In *Bethsaida: A City by the North Shore of the Sea of Galilee*, ed. R. Arav and R. A. Freund, 1:3–63. Kirksville, MO: Thomas Jefferson University Press.

———. 1999a. "Bethsaida Excavations: Preliminary Report, 1994–1996." In *Bethsaida: A City by the North Shore of the Sea of Galilee*, ed. R. Arav and R. A. Freund, 2:3–113. Kirksville, MO: Truman State University Press.

———. 1999b. "New Testament Archaeology and the Case of Bethsaida." In *Das Ende der Tage und die Gegenwart des Heils: Begegnungen mit dem Neuen Testament und seiner Umwelt; Festschrift für Heinz-Wolfgang Kuhn zum 65. Geburtstag*, ed. M. Becker and W. Fenske, 75–99. Arbeiten zur Geschichte des antiken Judentums und des Urchristentums 44. Leiden: Brill.

———. 2008. *Bethsaida Excavations: Season of 2007*. Accessed June 20, 2009. http://www.unomaha.edu/bethsaida/reports/BETHSAIDA%20EXCAVATIONS%202007.pdf.

Ascough, Richard S. 1993. "Rejection and Repentance: Peter and the People in Luke's Passion Narrative." *Biblica* 74:349–65.

Assmann, Jan. 1982 (4th ed., 2002). *Das kulturelle Gedächtnis: Schrift, Erinnerung und politische Identität in frühen Hochkulturen*. Munich: Beck.

———. 2012. *Cultural Memory and Early Civilization: Writing, Remembrance, and Political Imagination*. Cambridge: Cambridge University Press.

Baltes, Guido. 2011. *Hebräisches Evangelium und synoptische Überlieferung: Untersuchungen zum hebräischen Hintergrund der Evangelien*. Wissenschaftliche Untersuchungen zum Neuen Testament 2/312. Tübingen: Mohr Siebeck.

Barilier, Étienne. 2008. "La Revanche de Simon le Magicien." In *Nouvelles intrigues pseudo-clémentines = Plots in the Pseudo-Clementine Romance: Actes du deuxième colloque international sur la littérature apocryphe chrétienne, Lausanne-Genève, 30 août–2 septembre 2006*, ed. F. Amsler et al., 9–22. Publications de l'Institut Romand des Sciences Bibliques 6. Prahins: Zèbre.

Barnes, Timothy D. 2010. *Early Christian Hagiography and Roman History*. Tria Corda 5. Tübingen: Mohr Siebeck.

Barrett, C. K. 1995. "Hoskyns and Davey." In *Jesus and the Word and Other Essays*, 55–62. Edinburgh: T&T Clark.

Bauckham, Richard J. 1983. *Jude, 2 Peter*. Word Biblical Commentary 50. Waco: Word.

———. 1986. "The Coin in the Fish's Mouth." In *The Miracles of Jesus*, ed. D. Wenham and C. Blomberg, 219–52. Gospel Perspectives 6. Sheffield: JSOT Press.

———. 1988. "2 Peter: An Account of Research." *Aufstieg und Niedergang der römischen Welt*, ed. W. Haase, 2.25.5:3713–52. Berlin: de Gruyter.

———. 1990. *Jude and the Relatives of Jesus in the Early Church*. Edinburgh: T&T Clark.

———. 1992. "The Martyrdom of Peter in Early Christian Literature." In *Aufstieg und Niedergang der römischen Welt*, ed. W. Haase, 2.26.1:549–95. Berlin: de Gruyter.

———. 1994. "The *Apocalypse of Peter*: A Jewish Christian Apocalypse from the Time of Bar Kokhba." *Apocrypha* 5:7–111.

———, ed. 1998a. *The Gospels for All Christians: Rethinking the Gospel Audiences*. Grand Rapids: Eerdmans.

———. 1998b. "John for Readers of Mark." In *The Gospels for All Christians*, ed. R. J. Bauckham, 147–71. Grand Rapids: Eerdmans.

———. 2006. *Jesus and the Eyewitnesses: The Gospels as Eyewitness Testimony*. Grand Rapids: Eerdmans.

———. 2007. *The Testimony of the Beloved Disciple: Narrative, History, and Theology in the Gospel of John*. Grand Rapids: Baker Academic.

Baudoz, Jean-François. 1985. "Bethsaïde." *Le Monde de la Bible* 38:29–31.

Bauer, Walter. 1933. *Das Johannesevangelium*. Handbuch zum Neuen Testament 6. Tübingen: Mohr (Siebeck).

Baur, Ferdinand Christian. 1878. *The Church History of the First Three Centuries*. Trans. A. Menzies. 3rd ed. 2 vols. London: Williams & Norgate.

Becker, Jürgen. 2009. *Simon Petrus im Urchristentum*. Biblisch-theologische Studien 105. Neukirchen-Vluyn: Neukirchener Verlag.

Berger, Klaus. 1976. "Volksversammlung und Gemeinde Gottes." *Zeitschrift für Theologie und Kirche* 73:167–207.

———. 1981. "Unfehlbare Offenbarung: Petrus in der gnostischen und apokalyptischen Offenbarungsliteratur." In *Kontinuität und Einheit: Für Franz Mussner*, ed. P.-G. Müller and W. Stenger, 261–326. Freiburg: Herder.

Blaine, Brad. 2007. *Peter in the Gospel of John: The Making of an Authentic Disciple*. SBL Academia Biblica 27. Atlanta: Society of Biblical Literature.

Bockmuehl, Markus. 1992. Review of *Paul the Convert: The Apostolate and Apostasy of Saul the Pharisee*, by Alan F. Segal. *Journal of Theological Studies* 43:191–96.

————. 1994. *This Jesus: Martyr, Lord, Messiah*. Edinburgh: T&T Clark.

————. 2001a. "Resurrection." In *The Cambridge Companion to Jesus*, ed. M. Bockmuehl, 102–18. Cambridge: Cambridge University Press.

————. 2001b. "1 Thessalonians 2:14–16 and the Church in Jerusalem." *Tyndale Bulletin* 52:1–31.

————. 2003. *Jewish Law in Gentile Churches: Halakhah and the Beginning of Christian Public Ethics*. Repr., Grand Rapids: Baker Academic.

————. 2005. "The Making of Gospel Commentaries." In *The Written Gospel*, ed. M. Bockmuehl and D. A. Hagner, 274–95. Cambridge: Cambridge University Press.

————. 2006. *Seeing the Word: Refocusing New Testament Study*. Studies in Theological Interpretation. Grand Rapids: Baker Academic.

————. 2009. "Saints' Lives as Exegesis." In *The Pope and Jesus of Nazareth: Christ, Scripture and the Church*, ed. A. Pabst and A. Paddison, 119–33. London: SCM.

————. 2010a. *The Remembered Peter in Ancient Reception and Modern Debate*. Wissenschaftliche Untersuchungen zum Neuen Testament 262. Tübingen: Mohr Siebeck.

————. 2010b. "Whose Memory? Whose Orality? A Conversation with James Dunn on Jesus and the Gospels." In *Memories of Jesus: A Critical Appraisal of James D. G. Dunn's* Jesus Remembered, ed. R. B. Stewart and G. R. Habermas, 31–44. Nashville: B&H Academic.

Böttrich, Christfried. 2001. *Petrus: Fischer, Fels und Funktionär*. Biblische Gestalten 2. Leipzig: Evangelische Verlagsanstalt.

Breytenbach, Cilliers. 1996. *Paulus und Barnabas in der Provinz Galatien: Studien zu Apostelgeschichte 13f.; 16,6; 18,23 und den Adressaten des Galaterbriefes*. Arbeiten zur Geschichte des antiken Judentums und des Urchristentums 38. Leiden: Brill.

————. 1999. "Mark and Galilee: Text World and Historical World." In *Galilee through the Centuries*, ed. E. M. Meyer, 75–86. Winona Lake, IN: Eisenbrauns.

Briggs, Charles A. 1899. *General Introduction to the Study of Holy Scripture: The Principles, Methods, History, and Results of Its Several Departments and of the Whole*. New York: Scribner's.

Brock, Ann Graham. 2003. *Mary Magdalene, the First Apostle: The Struggle for Authority*. Harvard Theological Studies 51. Cambridge, MA: Harvard Divinity School.

Brown, Raymond E. 1987. "The Gospel of Peter and Canonical Gospel Priority." *New Testament Studies* 33:321–43.

Brown, Raymond E., Karl P. Donfried, and John Henry Paul Reumann. 2002. *Peter in the New Testament: A Collaborative Assessment by Protestant and Roman Catholic Scholars*. Eugene, OR: Wipf & Stock.

Brox, Norbert. 1993. *Der erste Petrusbrief*. 4th ed. Evangelisch-katholischer Kommentar zum Neuen Testament 21. Zürich: Benziger; Neukirchen-Vluyn: Neukirchener Verlag.

Buber, Salomon, ed. 1868. *Pesikta, die älteste Hagada, redigirt in Palästina von Rab Kahana*. Lyck (Elk): Silbermann.

Burkitt, F. Crawford. 1925. *The Gospel History and Its Transmission*. 5th ed. Edinburgh: T&T Clark.

Byrskog, Samuel. 2000. *Story as History—History as Story: The Gospel Tradition in the Context of Ancient Oral History*. Wissenschaftliche Untersuchungen zum Neuen Testament 123. Tübingen: Mohr (Siebeck).

Canetri, Elisa. 2006. "Il rinnegamento di Pietro nell'arte paleocristiana." *Rivista di Archeologia Cristiana* 82:159–200.

Capote, Truman. 1950. *Local Color*. New York: Random House.

Carleton Paget, James. 2010. "The Ebionites in Recent Research." In *Jews, Christians and Jewish Christians in Antiquity*, 325–79. Wissenschaftliche Untersuchungen zum Neuen Testament 251. Tübingen: Mohr Siebeck.

Cassidy, Richard J. 2007. *Four Times Peter: Portrayals of Peter in the Four Gospels and at Philippi*. Collegeville, MN: Liturgical Press.

Casurella, Anthony. 1997. Review of *Images de Pierre aux deux premiers siècles*, by Christian Grappe. *Critical Review of Books in Religion* 10:178–79.

Chadwick, Henry. 1966. "The Circle and the Ellipse." In *Jerusalem and Rome: The Problem of Authority in the Early Church*, ed. H. von Campenhausen and H. Chadwick, 23–36. Facet Books, Historical Series 4. Philadelphia: Fortress.

———, trans. 1998. *Saint Augustine: Confessions*. Oxford: Oxford University Press.

Chancey, Mark A. 2002. *The Myth of a Gentile Galilee: The Population of Galilee and New Testament Studies*. Society for New Testament Studies Monograph Series 118. Cambridge: Cambridge University Press.

———. 2005. *Greco-Roman Culture and the Galilee of Jesus*. Society for New Testament Studies Monograph Series 134. Cambridge: Cambridge University Press.

Chester, Stephen J. 2003. *Conversion at Corinth: Perspectives on Conversion in Paul's Theology and the Corinthian Church*. Studies of the New Testament and Its World. London: T&T Clark.

Clark, Andrew C. 2001. *Parallel Lives: The Relation of Paul to the Apostles in the Lucan Perspective*. Paternoster Biblical and Theological Monographs. Carlisle, UK: Paternoster.

Cook, John G. 2011. Review of *The Remembered Peter*, by Markus Bockmuehl. *TC: A Journal of Biblical Textual Criticism* 16. Accessed October 15, 2011. www.reltech.org/TC/v16/Bockmuehl2011rev.pdf.

Crook, Zeba A. 2004. *Reconceptualising Conversion: Patronage, Loyalty, and Conversion in the Religions of the Ancient Mediterranean*. Berlin: de Gruyter.

Cullmann, Oscar. 1952. *Petrus: Jünger, Apostel, Märtyrer; Das historische und das theologische Petrusproblem*. Zürich: Zwingli-Verlag.

———. 1953. *Peter: Disciple, Apostle, Martyr. A Historical and Theological Essay*. Trans. F. V. Filson. London: SCM; Philadelphia: Westminster.

———. 1956. "The Tradition." In *The Early Church*, ed. A. J. B. Higgins, 55–99. Philadelphia: Westminster.

———. 1960. *Petrus: Jünger—Apostel—Märtyrer. Das historische und das theologische Petrusproblem*. 2nd rev. and augmented ed. Zürich: Zwingli-Verlag.

———. 1962. *Peter: Disciple, Apostle, Martyr. A Historical and Theological Study*. Trans. F. V. Filson. 2nd ed. London: SCM.

———. 2011. *Peter: Disciple, Apostle, Martyr. A Historical and Theological Study*. Trans. F. V. Filson. 2nd ed. Repr., Waco: Baylor University Press.

Culpepper, Richard A. 2010. "Peter as Exemplary Disciple in John 21:15–19." *Perspectives in Religious Studies* 37:165–78.

Dalman, Gustav. 1905. *Grammatik des jüdisch-palästinischen Aramäisch nach den Idiomen des palästinischen Talmud, des Onkelostargum und Prophetentargum, und der jerusalemischen Targume.* 2nd ed. Leipzig: Hinrichs.

———. 1935. *Sacred Sites and Ways: Studies in the Topography of the Gospels.* Trans. P. P. Levertoff. London: SPCK; New York: Macmillan.

Dassmann, Ernst. 2011. "Petrus in Rom? Zu den Hintergründen eines alten Streites." In *Petrus und Paulus in Rom: Eine interdisziplinäre Debatte*, ed. S. Heid, 13–31. Freiburg: Herder.

Davies, W. D., and Dale C. Allison. 1988–97. *A Critical and Exegetical Commentary on the Gospel according to Saint Matthew.* 3 vols. International Critical Commentary. Edinburgh: T&T Clark.

de Burgos, Miguel. 1991. "Simon-Pedro, Ideologia y Historicidad en las Tradiciones Neotestamentarias." In *Pedro en la Iglesia Primitiva*, ed. R. Aguirre Monasterio, 235–58. Institución San Jerónimo 23. Estella: Verbo Divino.

Derrenbacker, Robert A., and John S. Kloppenborg. 2001. "Self-Contradiction in the IQP? A Reply to Michael Goulder." *Journal of Biblical Literature* 120:57–76.

Deschner, Karlheinz. 1986. *Abermals krähte der Hahn: Eine kritische Kirchengeschichte.* Expanded ed. Düsseldorf: Econ.

Dietrich, Wolfgang. 1972. *Das Petrusbild der lukanischen Schriften.* Beiträge zur Wissenschaft vom Alten und Neuen Testament 94. Stuttgart: Kohlhammer.

Dodd, C. H. 1963. *Historical Tradition in the Fourth Gospel.* Cambridge: Cambridge University Press.

Doering, Lutz. 2009. "Apostle, Co-elder, and Witness of Suffering: Author Construction and Peter Image in First Peter." In *Pseudepigraphie und Verfasserfiktion in frühchristlichen Briefen = Pseudepigraphy and Author Fiction in Early Christian Letters*, ed. J. Frey et al., 645–81. Wissenschaftliche Untersuchungen zum Neuen Testament 246. Tübingen: Mohr Siebeck.

Donfried, Karl P. 2002. *Paul, Thessalonica, and Early Christianity.* Grand Rapids: Eerdmans.

Downey, Glanville. 1961. *A History of Antioch in Syria from Seleucus to the Arab Conquest.* Princeton: Princeton University Press.

Dresken-Weiland, Jutta. 2011. "Petrusdarstellungen und ihre Bedeutung in der frühchristlichen Kunst." In *Petrus und Paulus in Rom: Eine interdisziplinäre Debatte*, ed. S. Heid, 126–52. Freiburg: Herder.

Drews, Arthur, and Frank R. Zindler. 1997. *The Legend of Saint Peter: A Contribution to the Mythology of Christianity.* Austin: American Atheist Press.

Drijvers, Han J. W. 1990. "Adam and the True Prophet in the Pseudo-Clementines." In *Loyalitätskonflikte in der Religionsgeschichte: Festschrift für Carsten Colpe*, ed. C. Elsas and H. G. Kippenberg, 314–23. Würzburg: Königshausen & Neumann.

Dschulnigg, Peter. 1989. "Gestalt und Funktion des Petrus im Matthäusevangelium." *Studien zum Neuen Testament und seiner Umwelt: Serie A* 14:161–83.

———. 1996. *Petrus im Neuen Testament.* Ed. P. Dschulnigg. Stuttgart: Katholisches Bibelwerk.

Dunn, James D. G. 1977. *Unity and Diversity in the New Testament: An Inquiry into the Character of Earliest Christianity*. London: SCM.

———. 2002. "Has the Canon a Continuing Function?" In *The Canon Debate*, ed. L. M. McDonald and J. A. Sanders, 558–79. Peabody, MA: Hendrickson.

———. 2003a. "Altering the Default Setting: Re-envisaging the Early Transmission of the Jesus Tradition." *New Testament Studies* 49:139–75.

———. 2003b. *Jesus Remembered: Christianity in the Making*. Grand Rapids: Eerdmans.

———. 2005a. "Before Writing: Q¹ as Oral Tradition." In *The Written Gospel*, ed. M. Bockmuehl and D. A. Hagner, 45–69. Cambridge: Cambridge University Press.

———. 2005b. *A New Perspective on Jesus: What the Quest for the Historical Jesus Missed*. Grand Rapids: Baker Academic.

Edwards, James R. 2009. *The Hebrew Gospel and the Development of the Synoptic Tradition*. Grand Rapids: Eerdmans.

Edwards, M. J. 1992. "The Clementina: A Christian Response to the Pagan Novel." *The Classical Quarterly* 42:459–74.

Ehrman, Bart D. 2006. *Peter, Paul, and Mary Magdalene: The Followers of Jesus in History and Legend*. Oxford: Oxford University Press.

Eliav, Y. Z. 2004. "The Tomb of James, Brother of Jesus, as Locus Memoriae." *Harvard Theological Review* 97:33–60.

Elliott, John H. 2000. *1 Peter: A New Translation with Introduction and Commentary*. Anchor Bible 37B. New York: Doubleday.

———. 2006. Review of *1 Peter*, by Karen H. Jobes. *Review of Biblical Literature*. Accessed March 4, 2011. http://bookreviews.org/pdf/5128_5396.pdf.

Erbes, Carl. 1901. "Petrus nicht in Rom, sondern in Jerusalem gestorben." *Zeitschrift für Kirchengeschichte* 22:1–47, 161–231.

Esler, Philip F. 2001. *The Early Iconography of Peter and Paul: The Jean Fortner Ward Lecture*. Greensboro, NC: Greensboro College.

Eusebius. 1926–32. *Ecclesiastical History*. Translated by K. Lake and J. E. L. Oulton. 2 vols. Loeb Classical Library. Cambridge, MA: Harvard University Press.

Evans, Richard J. 1997. *In Defence of History*. London: Granta Books.

Farrer, Austin M. 1955. "On Dispensing with Q." In *Studies in the Gospels: Essays in Memory of R. H. Lightfoot*, ed. D. E. Nineham, 55–88. Oxford: Blackwell.

Feldmeier, Reinhard. 1985. "The Portrayal of Peter in the Synoptic Gospels." In *Studies in the Gospel of Mark*, ed. M. Hengel and trans. J. Bowden, 59–63. London: SCM.

———. 2005. *Der erste Brief des Petrus*. Theologischer Handkommentar zum Neuen Testament 15/1. Leipzig: Evangelische Verlagsanstalt.

Fenton, J. C. 1963. *The Gospel of St. Matthew*. London: Penguin, 1963.

Ferguson, Andrew. 2009. "Hark! the Heralded Dylan Sings: Bob Dylan Fans Are the Battered Wives of the Music Industry." *The Weekly Standard*, November 9. Accessed November 11, 2009. http://www.weeklystandard.com/Utilities/printer_preview.asp?idArticle=17144&R=163E61211C.

Fitzmyer, Joseph A. 1981–85. *The Gospel according to Luke: A New Translation with Introduction and Commentary*. 2 vols. Anchor Bible 28. New York: Doubleday.

―――. 1998. "Aramaic *Kepha'* and Peter's Name in the New Testament." In *To Advance the Gospel: New Testament Studies*, 112–24. 2nd ed. Biblical Resource Series. Grand Rapids: Eerdmans.

Fortner, Sandra. 1995. "Hellenistic and Roman Fineware from Bethsaida." In *Bethsaida: A City by the North Shore of the Sea of Galilee*, ed. R. Arav and R. A. Freund, 1:99–126. Kirksville, MO: Thomas Jefferson University Press.

Foster, Paul. 2004. *Community, Law, and Mission in Matthew's Gospel*. Wissenschaftliche Untersuchungen zum Neuen Testament 2/177. Tübingen: Mohr Siebeck.

―――. 2007. "The Gospel of Peter." *Expository Times* 118:318–25.

―――. 2010. *The Gospel of Peter: Introduction, Critical Edition and Commentary*. Texts and Editions for New Testament Study 4. Leiden: Brill.

Fredriksen, Paula. 2000. *From Jesus to Christ: The Origins of the New Testament Images of Christ*. 2nd ed. New Haven: Yale University Press.

Freund, Richard A. 2004. "Father Bargil Pixner, O.S.B. (1921–2002)." In *Bethsaida: A City by the North Shore of the Sea of Galilee*, ed. R. Arav and R. A. Freund, 3:xv–xix. Kirksville, MO: Truman State University Press.

Gadamer, Hans-Georg. 2004. *Truth and Method*. 2nd ed. London: Continuum.

Gaventa, Beverly Roberts. 1986. *From Darkness to Light: Aspects of Conversion in the New Testament*. Overtures to Biblical Theology 20. Philadelphia: Fortress.

Geyer, Patrick Scott. 2001. "Evidence of Flax Cultivation from the Temple-Granary Complex et-Tell (Bethsaida/Julias)." *Israel Exploration Journal* 51:231–34.

Giesen, Heinz. 2001. "Galiläa—mehr als eine Landschaft: Bibeltheologischer Stellenwert Galiläas im Matthäusevangelium." *Ephemerides theologicae Lovanienses* 77:23–45.

Gnilka, Joachim. 1986–88. *Matthäusevangelium*. 2 vols. Herders theologischer Kommentar zum Neuen Testament 1/1–2. Freiburg: Herder.

Goodacre, Mark S. 1996. *Goulder and the Gospels: An Examination of a New Paradigm*. Journal for the Study of the New Testament: Supplement Series 133. Sheffield: Sheffield Academic Press.

―――. 2002. *The Case against Q: Studies in Markan Priority and the Synoptic Problem*. Harrisburg, PA: Trinity Press International.

Goodacre, Mark S., and Nicholas Perrin, eds. 2004. *Questioning Q*. Downers Grove, IL: InterVarsity.

Goulder, Michael D. 1994. *A Tale of Two Missions*. London: SCM.

―――. 1997. "Matthew's Vision for the Church." In *A Vision for the Church: Studies in Early Christian Ecclesiology in Honour of J. P. M. Sweet*, ed. M. Bockmuehl and M. B. Thompson, 19–32. Edinburgh: T&T Clark.

―――. 1999. "Self-Contradiction in the IQP." *Journal of Biblical Literature* 118:506–17.

―――. 2004. "Did Peter Ever Go to Rome?" *Scottish Journal of Theology* 57:377–96.

Grant, Michael. 1994. *Saint Peter*. London: Weidenfeld & Nicholson.

Grappe, Christian. 1992. *D'un Temple à l'autre: Pierre et l'Église primitive de Jérusalem*. Études d'histoire et de philosophie religieuses 71. Paris: Presses Universitaires de France.

―――. 1995. *Images de Pierre aux deux premiers siècles*. Études d'histoire et de philosophie religieuses 75. Paris: Presses Universitaires de France.

———. 2007. "Pierre dans l'histoire et la littérature des deux premiers siècles." *Foi et vie* 106 (4): 7–18.

Green, Joel B. 1987. "The Gospel of Peter: Source for a Pre-canonical Passion Narrative?" *Zeitschrift für die neutestamentliche Wissenschaft* 78:293–301.

Gregory, Andrew F. 2003. *The Reception of Luke and Acts in the Period before Irenaeus.* Wissenschaftliche Untersuchungen zum Neuen Testament 2/169. Tübingen: Mohr Siebeck.

———. 2006. "The Third Gospel? The Relationship of John and Luke Reconsidered." In *Challenging Perspectives on the Gospel of John*, ed. J. Lierman, 109–34. Wissenschaftliche Untersuchungen zum Neuen Testament 2/219. Tübingen: Mohr Siebeck.

Gregory, Andrew F., and Christopher Kavin Rowe, eds. 2010. *Rethinking the Unity and Reception of Luke and Acts.* Columbia: University of South Carolina Press.

Guarducci, Margherita. 2000. *La tomba di San Pietro: Una straordinaria vicenda.* Milano: Saggi Bompiani.

Guignebert, Charles. 1909. *La primauté de Pierre et la venue de Pierre à Rome: Étude critique.* Paris: Nourry.

Guijarro, Santiago. 1991. "La trayectoria y la geografía de la tradición petrina durante las tres primeras generaciones cristianas." In *Pedro en la Iglesia primitiva*, ed. R. Aguirre Monasterio, 17–28. Institución San Jerónimo 23. Estella: Verbo Divino.

Halbwachs, Maurice. 1941. *La topographie légendaire des Évangiles en Terre Sainte: Étude de mémoire collective.* Bibliothèque de philosophie contemporaine. Paris: Presses Universitaires de France.

———. 1992. *On Collective Memory.* Ed. L. A. Coser. Heritage of Sociology. Chicago: University of Chicago Press.

Hartenstein, Judith. 2007. *Charakterisierung im Dialog: Die Darstellung von Maria Magdalena, Petrus, Thomas und der Mutter Jesu im Kontext anderer frühchristlicher Traditionen.* Novum Testamentum et Orbis Antiquus / Studien zur Umwelt des Neuen Testaments 64. Göttingen: Vandenhoeck & Ruprecht; Fribourg: Academic Press.

Hays, Christopher M. 2008. "Marcion vs. Luke: A Response to the *Plädoyer* of Matthias Klinghardt." *Zeitschrift für die neutestamentliche Wissenschaft und die Kunde der älteren Kirche* 99:213–32.

Heckel, Theo K. 1999. *Vom Evangelium des Markus zum viergestaltigen Evangelium.* Wissenschaftliche Untersuchungen zum Neuen Testament 120. Tübingen: Mohr Siebeck.

Heid, Stefan, ed. 2011. *Petrus und Paulus in Rom: Eine interdisziplinäre Debatte.* Freiburg: Herder.

Hengel, Martin. 2000. *The Four Gospels and the One Gospel of Jesus Christ: An Investigation of the Collection and Origin of the Canonical Gospels.* Trans. J. Bowden. London: SCM.

———. 2006. *Der unterschätzte Petrus: Zwei Studien.* Tübingen: Mohr Siebeck.

———. 2008. *Die vier Evangelien und das eine Evangelium von Jesus Christus: Studien zu ihrer Sammlung und Entstehung.* Wissenschaftliche Untersuchungen zum Neuen Testament 224. Tübingen: Mohr Siebeck.

———. 2010. *Saint Peter: The Underestimated Apostle.* Trans. T. Trapp. Grand Rapids: Eerdmans.

Herzer, Jens. 1998. *Petrus oder Paulus? Studien über das Verhältnis des ersten Petrusbriefes zur paulinischen Tradition*. Wissenschaftliche Untersuchungen zum Neuen Testament 103. Tübingen: Mohr Siebeck.

Hesemann, Michael. 2008. *Der erste Papst: Auf der Spur des historischen Petrus*. Hamburg: Nikol.

Heussi, Karl. 1936. *War Petrus in Rom?* Gotha: Klotz.

———. 1955. *Die römische Petrustradition in kritischer Sicht*. Tübingen: Mohr Siebeck.

Hill, Charles E. 2004. *The Johannine Corpus in the Early Church*. Oxford: Oxford University Press.

Holloway, Paul A. 2009. *Coping with Prejudice: 1 Peter in Social-Psychological Perspective*. Wissenschaftliche Untersuchungen zum Neuen Testament 244. Tübingen: Mohr Siebeck.

Horbury, William. 1984. "The Temple Tax." In *Jesus and the Politics of His Day*, ed. E. Bammel and C. F. D. Moule, 265–86. Cambridge: Cambridge University Press.

———. 1986. "The Twelve and the Phylarchs." *New Testament Studies* 32:503–27.

———. 1997. "Septuagintal and New Testament Conceptions of the Church." In *A Vision for the Church: Studies in Early Christian Ecclesiology in Honour of J. P. M. Sweet*, ed. M. Bockmuehl and M. B. Thompson, 1–17. Edinburgh: T&T Clark.

Horsley, Richard A. 2004. *Hidden Transcripts and the Arts of Resistance: Applying the Work of James C. Scott to Jesus and Paul*. Semeia Studies 48. Leiden: Brill.

Hunter, A. M. 1961. *Paul and His Predecessors*. Rev. ed. London: SCM.

Ilan, Tal. 2002. *Lexicon of Jewish Names in Late Antiquity*. Part 1, *Palestine 330 BCE–200 CE*. Texts and Studies in Ancient Judaism 91. Tübingen: Mohr Siebeck.

———. 2008. *Lexicon of Jewish Names in Late Antiquity*. Part 3, *The Western Diaspora 330 BCE–650 CE*. Texts and Studies in Ancient Judaism 126. Tübingen: Mohr Siebeck.

James, M. R. 1924. *The Apocryphal New Testament*. Oxford: Clarendon.

James, William. 1902. *The Varieties of Religious Experience: A Study in Human Nature; Being the Gifford Lectures on Natural Religion Delivered at Edinburgh in 1901–1902*. New York: Longmans, Green.

Jeffreys, Elizabeth, Michael Jeffreys, and Roger Scott. 1986. *The Chronicle of John Malalas: A Translation*. Byzantina Australiensia 4. Melbourne: Australian Association for Byzantine Studies.

Jobes, Karen H. 2005. *1 Peter*. Baker Exegetical Commentary on the New Testament. Grand Rapids: Baker Academic.

Johnson, Luke Timothy. 2002. *Septuagintal Midrash in the Speeches of Acts*. Milwaukee: Marquette University Press.

Jones, F. Stanley. 1995. *An Ancient Jewish Christian Source on the History of Christianity: Pseudo-Clementine Recognitions 1.27–71*. Texts and Translations 37 / Christian Apocrypha Series 2. Atlanta: Scholars Press.

———. 2003. "The Ancient Christian Teacher in the *Pseudo-Clementines*." In *Early Christian Voices in Texts, Traditions, and Symbols: Essays in Honor of François Bovon*, ed. D. H. Warren et al., 355–64. Biblical Interpretation 66. Leiden: Brill.

Jowett, Benjamin. 1861. "On the Interpretation of Scripture." In *Essays and Reviews*, 330–433. 7th ed. London: Longman, Green, Longman, Roberts.

Karrer, Martin. 1992. "Petrus." In *Evangelisches Kirchenlexikon*, ed. H. Brunotte and O. Weber, 3:1142–45. Göttingen: Vandenhoeck & Ruprecht.

Keck, David. 1996. *Forgetting Whose We Are: Alzheimer's Disease and the Love of God*. Nashville: Abingdon.

Kelly, J. N. D. 1969. *A Commentary on the Epistles of Peter and of Jude*. Black's New Testament Commentaries. London: Black.

Kessler, William Thomas. 1998. *Peter as the First Witness of the Risen Lord: An Historical and Theological Investigation*. Tesi Gregoriana: Serie teologia 37. Rome: Pontificia università gregoriana.

Kingsbury, Jack D. 1979. "The Figure of Peter in Matthew's Gospel as a Theological Problem." *Journal of Biblical Literature* 98:67–83.

Kirk, Alan. 2007. "Tradition and Memory in the *Gospel of Peter*." In *Das Evangelium nach Petrus: Text, Kontexte, Intertexte*, ed. T. J. Kraus and T. Nicklas, 135–58. Texte und Untersuchungen zur Geschichte der altchristlichen Literatur 158. Berlin: de Gruyter.

Klein, Günter. 1961. "Die Verleugnung des Petrus: Eine traditionsgeschichtliche Untersuchung." *Zeitschrift für Theologie und Kirche* 58:285–328.

Klinghardt, Matthias. 2006. "Markion vs. Lukas: Plädoyer für die Wiederaufnahme eines alten Falles." *New Testament Studies* 52:484–513.

———. 2008. "The Marcionite Gospel and the Synoptic Problem: A New Suggestion." *Novum Testamentum* 50:1–27.

Kraus, Thomas J. 2001. *Sprache, Stil und historischer Ort des zweiten Petrusbriefes*. Wissenschaftliche Untersuchungen zum Neuen Testament 2/136. Tübingen: Mohr Siebeck.

Kraus, Thomas J., and Tobias Nicklas, eds. 2007. *Das Evangelium nach Petrus: Text, Kontexte, Intertexte*. Texte und Untersuchungen zur Geschichte der altchristlichen Literatur. Berlin: de Gruyter.

Krenkel, Max. 1894. *Josephus und Lucas: Der schriftstellerische Einfluss des jüdischen Geschichtschreibers auf den Christlichen*. Leipzig: Haessel.

Kugel, James L. 2007. *How to Read the Bible: A Guide to Scripture, Then and Now*. New York: Free Press.

Kuhn, Heinz-Wolfgang. 2004. "Bethsaida in the Gospel of Mark." In *Bethsaida: A City by the North Shore of the Sea of Galilee*, ed. R. Arav and R. A. Freund, 3:115–24. Kirksville, MO: Truman State University Press.

Kuschel, Karl-Josef. 1991. "Judas und Petrus: Nachdenken über einen doppelten Verrat." In *Judas, wer bist du?*, ed. R. Niemann, 68–76. Gütersloh: Mohn.

Lambers-Petry, Doris. 2003. "Verwandte Jesu als Referenzpersonen für das Judenchristentum." In *The Image of the Judaeo-Christians in Ancient Jewish and Christian Literature*, ed. P. J. Tomson and D. Lambers-Petry, 32–52. Wissenschaftliche Untersuchungen zum Neuen Testament 158. Tübingen: Mohr Siebeck.

Lampe, Peter. 2003. *From Paul to Valentinus: Christians at Rome in the First Two Centuries*. Trans. M. Steinhauser. Ed. M. D. Johnson. Minneapolis: Fortress.

Lapham, Fred. 2003. *Peter: The Myth, the Man and the Writings*. Journal for the Study of the New Testament: Supplement Series 280. Sheffield: Sheffield Academic Press.

Lash, Nicholas. 1996. *The Beginning and the End of "Religion."* Cambridge: Cambridge University Press.

Le Donne, Anthony. 2009. *The Historiographical Jesus: Memory, Typology, and the Son of David.* Waco: Baylor University Press.

———. 2011. *Historical Jesus: What Can We Know and How Can We Know It?* Grand Rapids: Eerdmans.

Limberis, Vasiliki. 1997. "The Provenance of the Caliphate Church: James 2:17–26 and Galatians 3 Reconsidered." In *Early Christian Interpretation of the Scriptures of Israel*, ed. C. A. Evans and J. A. Sanders, 397–420. Journal for the Study of the New Testament: Supplement Series 148. Sheffield: Sheffield Academic Press.

Logan, Alastair H. B. 2000. "Simon Magus." In *Theologische Realenzyklopädie*, ed. H. R. Balz et al., 31:272–76. Berlin: de Gruyter.

Löhr, Winrich A. 1996. *Basilides und seine Schule: Eine Studie zur Theologie und Kirchengeschichte des zweiten Jahrhunderts.* Wissenschaftliche Untersuchungen zum Neuen Testament 83. Tübingen: Mohr Siebeck.

Lona, Horacio. 2011. "'Petrus in Rom' und der Erste Clemensbrief." In *Petrus und Paulus in Rom: Eine interdisziplinäre Debatte*, ed. S. Heid, 221–46. Freiburg: Herder.

Ludwig, Joseph. 1952. *Die Primatworte Mt 16:18–19 in der altkirchlichen Exegese.* Neutestamentliche Abhandlungen 19/4. Münster: Aschendorff.

Luhumbu Shodu, Emmanuel. 2008. *La mémoire des origines chrétiennes selon Justin Martyr.* Paradosis 50. Fribourg: Academic Press.

Luz, Ulrich. 1985. "Wirkungsgeschichtliche Exegese: Ein programmatischer Arbeitsbericht mit Beispielen aus der Bergpredigtexegese." *Berliner Theologische Zeitschrift* 2:18–32.

———. 1985–2002. *Das Evangelium nach Matthäus.* 4 vols. Evangelisch-katholischer Kommentar zum Neuen Testament 1/1–4. Zürich: Benziger; Neukirchen-Vluyn: Neukirchener Verlag.

———. 1994. *Matthew in History: Interpretation, Influence, and Effects.* Minneapolis: Augsburg Fortress.

———. 2001–7. *Matthew.* Trans. J. E. Crouch. 4 vols. (vol. 1, rev. ed.). Hermeneia. Minneapolis: Augsburg Fortress.

———. 2005. *Studies in Matthew.* Trans. R. Selle. Grand Rapids: Eerdmans.

Malnati, Ettore. 2008. *"Simone detto Pietro," nella singolarità del suo ministero.* Pro Manuscripto 13. Lugano: EUPress FTL.

Mandelbaum, Bernard. 1962. *Pesikta de Rav Kahana according to an Oxford Manuscript: With Variants from All Known Manuscripts and Genizoth Fragments and Parallel Passages.* New York: Jewish Theological Seminary of America.

Mara, Maria Grazia. 2006. *Evangile de Pierre: Introduction, texte critique, traduction, commentaire et index.* Sources Chrétiennes 201. Paris: Cerf.

Marcus, Joel. 2000–2009. *Mark: A New Translation with Introduction and Commentary.* 2 vols. Anchor Yale Bible 27–27A. New Haven: Yale University Press.

Marshall, I. Howard. 1980. *Last Supper and Lord's Supper.* Exeter: Paternoster.

Marxsen, Willi, and Karl Gerhard Steck. 1979. *Absage an die Gerechtigkeit? Eine Predigt und ein Gespräch.* Theologische Existenz Heute 203. Munich: Kaiser.

Mason, Steve. 1992. *Josephus and the New Testament*. Peabody, MA: Hendrickson.

———. 1995. "Chief Priests, Sadducees, Pharisees and Sanhedrin in Acts." In *The Book of Acts in Its Palestinian Setting*, ed. R. J. Bauckham, 115–77. The Book of Acts in Its First Century Setting 4. Grand Rapids: Eerdmans; Carlisle, UK: Paternoster.

McCue, James F. 1974. "The Roman Primacy in the Patristic Era, I: The Beginnings through Nicaea." In *Papal Primacy and the Universal Church*, ed. P. C. Empie and T. A. Murphy, 5. Lutherans and Catholics in Dialogue. Minneapolis: Augsburg.

McKnight, Scot, and Terence C. Mournet, eds. 2010. *Jesus in Early Christian Memory: Essays in Honor of James D. G. Dunn*. London: Continuum.

Meade, David G. 1986. *Pseudonymity and Canon: An Investigation into the Relationship of Authorship and Authority in Jewish and Earliest Christian Tradition*. Wissenschaftliche Untersuchungen zum Neuen Testament 39. Tübingen: Mohr Siebeck.

Mendels, Doron. 2004. *Memory in Jewish, Pagan and Christian Societies of the Graeco-Roman World*. Library of Second Temple Studies 48. London: T&T Clark International.

Mitchell, Margaret Mary. 1991. *Paul and the Rhetoric of Reconciliation: An Exegetical Investigation of the Language and Composition of 1 Corinthians*. Hermeneutische Untersuchungen zur Theologie 28. Tübingen: Mohr Siebeck.

Moon, Jongyoon. 2009. *Mark as Contributive Amanuensis of 1 Peter?* Theologie 97. Berlin: Lit.

Morgan, Robert. 2002. "The Priority of John—over Luke." In *Für und wider die Priorität des Johannesevangeliums*, ed. P. L. Hofrichter, 195–211. Hildesheim: Olms.

Mournet, Terence C. 2005. *Oral Tradition and Literary Dependency: Variability and Stability in the Synoptic Tradition and Q*. Wissenschaftliche Untersuchungen zum Neuen Testament 2/195. Tübingen: Mohr Siebeck.

Müller, C. Detlef G. 1992. "Ascension of Isaiah." In *New Testament Apocrypha*, ed. W. Schneemelcher and trans. R. M. Wilson, 2:547–62. Rev. ed. Cambridge: Clarke; Louisville: Westminster John Knox.

Munier, Charles. 1992. "Où en est la question d'Ignace d'Antioche? Bilan d'un siècle de recherches 1870–1988." In *Aufstieg und Niedergang der römischen Welt*, ed. W. Haase, 2.27.1:359–484. Berlin: de Gruyter.

Murphy-O'Connor, Jerome. 1996. *Paul: A Critical Life*. Oxford: Oxford University Press.

———. 1999. "Fishers of Fish, Fishers of Men: What We Know of the First Disciples from Their Profession." *Bible Review* 15 (3): 22–27, 48–49.

Nave, Guy D. 2002. *The Role and Function of Repentance in Luke-Acts*. SBL Academia Biblica 4. Atlanta: Society of Biblical Literature.

Neill, W. 1954. Review of *Petrus: Jünger, Apostel, Märtyrer*, by Oscar Cullmann. *Scottish Journal of Theology* 7:207–10.

Neugebauer, Friedrich. 1980. "Zur Deutung und Bedeutung des 1. Petrusbriefes." *New Testament Studies* 26:61–86.

Nicholls, Rachel. 2008. *Walking on the Water: Reading Mt. 14:22–33 in the Light of Its Wirkungsgeschichte*. Biblical Interpretation 90. Leiden: Brill.

Nock, Arthur Darby. 1933. *Conversion: The Old and the New in Religion from Alexander the Great to Augustine of Hippo*. Oxford: Clarendon.

Nora, Pierre. 1984. *Les Lieux de mémoire*. Vol. 1, *La République*. Paris: Gallimard.

———. 1996. *Realms of Memory: Rethinking the French Past*. Vol. 1, *Conflicts and Divisions*. European Perspectives. New York: Columbia University Press.

Norelli, Enrico. 2004. "Au sujet de la première reception de 1 Pierre: Trois exemples." In *The Catholic Epistles and the Tradition*, ed. J. Schlosser, 327–66. Bibliotheca ephemeridum theologicarum lovaniensium 176. Louvain: Peeters.

———. 2007. "Pierre, le visionnaire: la réception de l'épisode de la transfiguration en 2 Pierre et dans l'Apocalypse de Pierre." *Foi et vie* 106 (4): 19–43.

Nun, Mendel. 1989. *The Sea of Galilee and Its Fishermen in the New Testament*. Ein Gev: Tourist Dept. & Kinnereth Sailing Co.

———. 1992. *Sea of Galilee: Newly Discovered Harbours from New Testament Days*. Kibbutz Ein Gev: Kinnereth Sailing Co.

———. 1999. "Ports of Galilee: Modern Drought Reveals Harbors from Jesus' Time." *Biblical Archaeology Review* 25 (4): 19–31, 64.

O'Collins, Gerald. 1987. "Mary Magdalene as Major Witness to Jesus' Resurrection." *Theological Studies* 48:631–46.

Pearson, Birger A. 2005. "Basilides the Gnostic." In *A Companion to Second-Century Christian "Heretics,"* ed. A. Marjanen and P. Luomanen, 1–31. Vigiliae Christianae Supplement 76. Leiden: Brill.

Pelikan, Jaroslav. 1980. "The Two Sees of Peter: Reflections on the Pace of Normative Self-Definition East and West." In *Jewish and Christian Self-Definition*, vol. 1, *The Shaping of Christianity in the Second and Third Centuries*, ed. E. P. Sanders, 57–73. Philadelphia: Fortress.

Perkins, Pheme. 2000. *Peter: Apostle for the Whole Church*. Minneapolis: Fortress.

———. 2004. "Peter: How a Flawed Disciple Became Jesus' Successor on Earth." *Bible Review* 20 (1): 12–23.

Pesch, Rudolf. 1974. "Die Verleugnung des Petrus: Eine Studie zu Mk 14,54.66–72 (und Mk 14,26–31)." In *Neues Testament und Kirche: Für Rudolf Schnackenburg zum 60. Geburtstag am 5. Jan. 1974 von Freunden und Kollegen gewidmet*, ed. J. Gnilka, 42–62. Freiburg: Herder.

———. 1980. *Simon-Petrus: Geschichte und geschichtliche Bedeutung des ersten Jüngers Jesu Christi*. Päpste und Papsttum 15. Stuttgart: Hiersemann.

———. 1998. "Was an Petrus sichtbar war, ist in den Primat eingegangen." In *Il Primato del Successore di Pietro: Atti del Simposio Teologico—Roma, dicembre 1996*, ed. J. Ratzinger, 22–111. Vatican City: Libreria Editrice Vaticana.

———. 2001. *Die biblischen Grundlagen des Primats*. Quaestiones disputatae 187. Freiburg: Herder.

Pixner, Bargil. 2010. *Paths of the Messiah: Sites of the Early Church from Galilee to Jerusalem*. San Francisco: Ignatius.

Post, Paulus Gijsbertus Johannes. 1984. "De haanscène in de vroeg-christelijke kunst: Een iconografische en iconologische analyse = La scène du coq dans l'art paléochrétien: Une analyse iconographique et iconologique." DD diss., Schrijen-Lippertz / Katholieke Theologische Hogeschool Utrecht.

Powell, Evan. 2006. *The Myth of the Lost Gospel*. Las Vegas: Symposium.

Prete, Benedetto. 1967. "Il senso di epistrepsas in Luca 22,32." In *San Pietro: Atti della XIX Settimana Biblica*, ed. Associazione biblica italiana, 113–35. Brescia: Paideia.

———. 1969. *Il primato e la missione di Pietro: Studio esegetico-critico del testo di Lc. 22,31–32*. Supplementi alla Rivista Biblica 3. Brescia: Paideia.

Rambo, Lewis R. 1993. *Understanding Religious Conversion*. New Haven: Yale University Press.

Reed, Jonathan L. 2000. *Archaeology and the Galilean Jesus: A Re-examination of the Evidence*. Harrisburg, PA: Trinity Press International.

Ridderbos, Herman N. 1962. *The Speeches of Peter in the Acts of the Apostles*. Tyndale New Testament Lecture 1961. London: Tyndale.

Riesner, Rainer. 1986. "Bethany beyond the Jordan (John 1:28): Topography, Theology and History in the Fourth Gospel." *Tyndale Bulletin* 38:29–64.

———. 1992. "Bethany beyond the Jordan." In *Anchor Bible Dictionary*, ed. D. N. Freedman, 1:703–5. New York: Doubleday.

———. 1998. *Paul's Early Period: Chronology, Mission Strategy, Theology*. Grand Rapids: Eerdmans.

———. 1999. "Das Lokalkolorit des Lukas-Sonderguts: Italisch oder Palästinisch-Juden-Christlich?" *Liber annuus Studii biblici franciscani* 49:51–64.

———. 2002. *Bethanien jenseits des Jordan: Topographie und Theologie im Johannes-Evangelium*. Biblische Archäologie und Zeitgeschichte 12. Giessen: Brunnen.

Robinson, Donald F. 1945. "Where and When Did Peter Die?" *Journal of Biblical Literature* 64:255–67.

Roloff, Jürgen. 1965. *Apostolat, Verkündigung, Kirche: Ursprung, Inhalt und Funktion des kirchlichen Apostelamtes nach Paulus, Lukas und den Pastoralbriefen*. Gütersloh: Mohn.

———. 1993. *Die Kirche im Neuen Testament*. Grundrisse zum Neuen Testament 10. Göttingen: Vandenhoeck & Ruprecht.

Schaeffer, Susan E. 1991. "The 'Gospel of Peter,' the Canonical Gospels, and Oral Tradition." PhD diss., Union Theological Seminary.

Schechter, Solomon, ed. 1887. *Masekhet Avot de-Rabbi Natan*. Vienna: Lippe.

Schenk, Wolfgang. 1983. "Das Matthäusevangelium als Petrusevangelium." *Biblische Zeitschrift* 27:58–80.

Schenk von Stauffenberg, Alexander. 1931. *Die Römische Kaisergeschichte bei Malalas: Griechischer Text der Bücher IX–XII und Untersuchungen*. Stuttgart: Kohlhammer.

Schlatter, Adolf. 1929. *Der Evangelist Matthäus: Seine Sprache, sein Ziel, seine Selbständigkeit*. Stuttgart: Calwer.

Schneemelcher, Wilhelm. 1991–92. *New Testament Apocrypha*. Trans. R. M. Wilson. Rev. ed. 2 vols. Cambridge: Clarke; Louisville: Westminster John Knox.

Schneider, Gerhard. 1985. "'Stärke deine Brüder!' (Lk 22,32): Die Aufgabe des Petrus nach Lukas." In *Lukas, Theologe der Heilsgeschichte: Aufsätze zum lukanischen Doppelwerk*, 146–52. Bonner biblische Beiträge 59. Königstein: Hanstein.

Schoenwetter, J., and P. S. Geyer. 2000. "Implications of Archaeological Palynology at Bethsaida, Israel." *Journal of Field Archaeology* 27:63–74.

Schreckenberg, Heinz. 1980. "Flavius Josephus und die lukanischen Schriften." In *Wort in der Zeit: Neutestamentliche Studien. Festgabe für Karl Heinrich Rengstorf zum 75. Geburtstag*, ed. W. Haubeck and M. Bachmann, 179–209. Leiden: Brill.

Schröter, Jens. 1997. *Erinnerung an Jesu Worte: Studien zu Rezeption der Logienüberlieferung in Markus, Q und Thomas*. Wissenschaftliche Monographien zum Alten und Neuen Testament 76. Neukirchen-Vluyn: Neukirchener Verlag.

Schulz, Hans-Joachim. 1994. "Zur Entstehung der Evangelien: Petrus, Paulus und das Markusevangelium." In *Qumran und die Evangelien: Geschichte oder Geschichten?*, ed. W. Brandmüller, 11–40. Aachen: MM Verlag.

Schumacher, G. 1888. *The Jaulân*. London: Bentley.

Schwartz, Joshua. 1995. "Ben Stada and Peter in Lydda." In *The Book of Acts in Its Palestinian Setting*, ed. R. Bauckham, 391–414. The Book of Acts in Its First Century Setting 4. Grand Rapids: Eerdmans; Carlisle, UK: Paternoster. First appeared in *Journal for the Study of Judaism* 21 (1990): 1–18.

Schweitzer, Albert. 2000. *The Quest of the Historical Jesus*. Trans. J. Bowden. First complete ed. London: SCM.

Scobie, Charles H. H. 1979. "The Use of Source Material in the Speeches of Acts 3 and 7." *New Testament Studies* 25 (4): 399–421.

Scott, James C. 1990. *Domination and the Arts of Resistance: Hidden Transcripts*. New Haven: Yale University Press.

Scott, James M. 1995. *Paul and the Nations: The Old Testament and Jewish Background of Paul's Mission to the Nations with Special Reference to the Destination of Galatians*. Wissenschaftliche Untersuchungen zum Neuen Testament 84. Tübingen: Mohr (Siebeck).

Segal, Alan F. 1990. *Paul the Convert: The Apostolate and Apostasy of Saul the Pharisee*. New Haven: Yale University Press.

Sim, David C. 1998. *The Gospel of Matthew and Christian Judaism*. Studies of the New Testament and Its World. Edinburgh: T&T Clark.

Skarsaune, Oskar. 2002. *In the Shadow of the Temple: Jewish Influences on Early Christianity*. Downers Grove, IL: InterVarsity.

Smaltz, W. M. 1952. "Did Peter Die in Jerusalem?" *Journal of Biblical Literature* 71:211–16.

Smith, Terence V. 1985. *Petrine Controversies in Early Christianity: Attitudes towards Peter in Christian Writings of the First Two Centuries*. Wissenschaftliche Untersuchungen zum Neuen Testament 2/15. Tübingen: Mohr Siebeck.

Soards, Marion L. 1994. *The Speeches in Acts: Their Content, Context, and Concerns*. Louisville: Westminster John Knox.

Söding, Thomas. 2009a. "Einführung." In *Hoffnung in Bedrängnis: Studien zum Ersten Petrusbrief*, ed. T. Söding, 7–10. Stuttgarter Bibelstudien 216. Stuttgart: Katholisches Bibelwerk.

———. 2009b. "Grüße aus Rom: Der Erste Petrusbrief in der Geschichte des Urchristentums und im Kanon." In *Hoffnung in Bedrängnis: Studien zum Ersten Petrusbrief*, ed. T. Söding, 11–45. Stuttgarter Bibelstudien 216. Stuttgart: Katholisches Bibelwerk.

———, ed. 2009c. *Hoffnung in Bedrängnis: Studien zum Ersten Petrusbrief*. Stuttgarter Bibelstudien 216. Stuttgart: Katholisches Bibelwerk.

Stanton, Graham N. 1993. *A Gospel for a New People: Studies in Matthew*. Louisville: Westminster John Knox.

———. 1994. "Revisiting Matthew's Communities." In *The 1994 Seminar Papers: One Hundred Thirtieth Annual Meeting, November 19–22, 1994, the Chicago Hilton and Towers, Chicago, IL*, ed. Eugene H. Lovering, 9–23. Society of Biblical Literature Seminar Papers 33. Atlanta: Scholars Press.

———. 1996. "Revisiting Matthew's Communities." *Hervormde teologiese studies* 52:376–94.

———. 2007. "Jewish Christian Elements in the Pseudo-Clementine Writings." In *Jewish Believers in Jesus: The Early Centuries*, ed. O. Skarsaune and R. Hvalvik, 305–24. Peabody, MA: Hendrickson.

Stauffer, Ethelbert. 1952. "Zum Kalifat des Jakobus." *Zeitschrift für Religions- und Geistesgeschichte* 4:193–214.

Stendahl, Krister. 1976. *Paul among Jews and Gentiles, and Other Essays*. Philadelphia: Fortress.

Sterling, Gregory E. 1992. *Historiography and Self-Definition: Josephos, Luke-Acts, and Apologetic Historiography*. Supplements to Novum Testamentum 64. Leiden: Brill.

———. 2008. "Turning to God: Conversion in Greek-Speaking Judaism and Early Christianity." In *Scripture and Traditions: Essays on Early Judaism and Christianity in Honor of Carl R. Holladay*, ed. P. Gray and G. R. O'Day, 69–96. Supplements to Novum Testamentum 129. Leiden: Brill.

Strack, Hermann Leberecht, and Paul Billerbeck. 1922–61. *Kommentar zum Neuen Testament aus Talmud und Midrasch*. 6 vols. Munich: Beck.

Strange, James F. 1992. "Beth-Saida." In *Anchor Bible Dictionary*, ed. D. N. Freedman, 1:692–93. New York: Doubleday.

Strecker, Georg. 1992. "The Pseudo-Clementines: Introduction." In *New Testament Apocrypha*, ed. W. Schneemelcher and trans. R. M. Wilson, 2:483–93. Rev. ed. Cambridge: Clarke; Louisville: Westminster John Knox.

Streeter, B. H. 1936. *The Four Gospels*. 5th ed. London: Macmillan.

Strickert, Fred. 1998. *Bethsaida: Home of the Apostles*. Collegeville, MN: Liturgical Press.

Stroud, William J. 1994. "Models for Petrine Speeches in the Acts of Peter." In *The 1994 Seminar Papers: One Hundred Thirtieth Annual Meeting, November 19–22, 1994, the Chicago Hilton and Towers, Chicago, IL*, ed. Eugene H. Lovering, 405–14. Society of Biblical Literature Seminar Papers 33. Atlanta: Scholars Press.

Stuhlmacher, Peter. 1992–99. *Biblische Theologie des Neuen Testaments*. 2nd ed. 2 vols. Göttingen: Vandenhoeck & Ruprecht.

Tabbernee, William. 1997. "'Our Trophies Are Better Than Your Trophies': The Appeal to Tombs and Reliquaries in Montanist-Orthodox Relations." *Studia patristica* 31:206–17.

Tannehill, Robert C. 1991. "The Functions of Peter's Mission Speeches in the Narrative of Acts." *New Testament Studies* 37:400–414.

Teicher, J. L. 1963. "Ancient Eucharistic Prayers in Hebrew (Dura-Europos parchment D Pg 25)." *Jewish Quarterly Review* 54:99–109.

Theissen, Gerd. 1989. (2nd ed., 1992). *Lokalkolorit und Zeitgeschichte in den Evangelien: Ein Beitrag zur Geschichte der synoptischen Tradition*. Freiburg: Universitätsverlag; Göttingen: Vandenhoeck & Ruprecht.

————. 1992. *The Gospels in Context: Social and Political History in the Synoptic Tradition.* Trans. L. M. Maloney. Edinburgh: T&T Clark.

Thiede, Carsten Peter. 1986. "Babylon, der andere Ort: Anmerkungen zu 1 Petr 5,13 und Apg 12,17." *Biblica* 67:532–38.

Thiselton, Anthony C. 2000. *The First Epistle to the Corinthians: A Commentary on the Greek Text.* Grand Rapids: Eerdmans.

Thornton, Claus Jürgen. 1991. *Der Zeuge des Zeugen: Lukas als Historiker der Paulusreisen.* Wissenschaftliche Untersuchungen zum Neuen Testament 56. Tübingen: Mohr Siebeck.

Tomson, Peter J. 1990. *Paul and the Jewish Law: Halakha in the Letters of the Apostle to the Gentiles.* Compendia Rerum Iudaicarum ad Novum Testamentum 3.1. Assen, Netherlands: Van Gorcum; Minneapolis: Fortress.

————. 2001. *"If This Be from Heaven . . .": Jesus and the New Testament Authors in Their Relationship to Judaism.* Biblical Seminar 76. Sheffield: Sheffield Academic Press.

Trevett, Christine. 1984. "Approaching Matthew from the Second Century: The Underused Ignatian Correspondence." *Journal for the Study of the New Testament* 20:59–67.

————. 1992. *A Study of Ignatius of Antioch in Syria and Asia Minor.* Studies in the Bible and Early Christianity 29. Lewiston, NY: Mellen.

Tuckett, Christopher M. 2007. *The Gospel of Mary.* Oxford Early Christian Gospel Texts. Oxford: Oxford University Press.

Tuplin, Christopher J. 1996. "Xenophon." In *The Oxford Classical Dictionary,* ed. S. Hornblower and A. Spawforth, 1628–31. 3rd ed. Oxford: Oxford University Press.

Tyrrell, George. 1909. *Christianity at the Cross-Roads.* London: Longmans Green.

Tyson, Joseph B. 2006. *Marcion and Luke-Acts: A Defining Struggle.* Columbia: University of South Carolina Press.

Valdez del Alamo, Elizabeth, and Carol Stamatis Pendergast, eds. 2000. *Memory and the Medieval Tomb.* Aldershot: Ashgate.

van Houts, Elisabeth. 1999. *Memory and Gender in Medieval Europe, 900–1200.* Explorations in Medieval Culture and Society. Basingstoke: Macmillan.

Viviano, Benedict T. 2000. "Peter as Jesus' Mouth: Matthew 16.13–20 in the Light of Exodus 4.10–17 and Other Models." In *The Interpretation of Scripture in Early Judaism and Christianity. Studies in Language and Tradition,* ed. C. A. Evans, 312–41. Journal for the Study of the Pseudepigrapha: Supplement Series 33. Sheffield: Sheffield Academic Press.

Volp, Ulrich. 2009. "Hippolytus." *Expository Times* 120:521–29.

von Campenhausen, Hans. 1950–51. "Die Nachfolge des Jakobus: Zur Frage eines urchristlichen 'Kalifats.'" *Zeitschrift für Kirchengeschichte* 63:133–44.

Vouaux, Léon. 1922. *Les Actes de Pierre.* Paris: Letouzey et Ané.

Walters, Patricia. 2009. *The Assumed Authorial Unity of Luke and Acts: A Reassessment of the Evidence.* Society for New Testament Studies Monograph Series 145. Cambridge: Cambridge University Press.

Watson, Francis. 2007. "'I Received from the Lord . . .': Paul, Jesus, and the Last Supper." In *Jesus and Paul Reconnected: Fresh Pathways into an Old Debate,* ed. T. D. Still, 103–24. Grand Rapids: Eerdmans.

Wenham, John W. 1972. "Did Peter go to Rome in AD 42?" *Tyndale Bulletin* 23:94–102.

Wiarda, Timothy. 1999. "Peter as Peter in the Gospel of Mark." *New Testament Studies* 45:19–37.

———. 2000. *Peter in the Gospels: Pattern, Personality and Relationship.* Wissenschaftliche Untersuchungen zum Neuen Testament 2/127. Tübingen: Mohr Siebeck.

Wilckens, Ulrich. 2005. *Die Briefe des Urchristentums: Paulus und seine Schüler, Theologen aus dem Bereich judenchristlicher Heidenmission.* Vol. 1, part 3 of *Theologie des Neuen Testaments.* Neukirchen-Vluyn: Neukirchener Verlag.

Wilpert, Josef. 1903. *Roma sotterranea: Le pitture delle Catacombe.* 2 vols. Rome: Desclée Lefebvre.

Zehnle, Richard F. 1971. *Peter's Pentecost Discourse: Tradition and Lukan Reinterpretation in Peter's Speeches of Acts 2 and 3.* Nashville: Abingdon.

Zwierlein, Otto. 2009. *Petrus in Rom: Die literarischen Zeugnisse; Mit einer kritischen Edition der Martyrien des Petrus und Paulus auf neuer handschriftlicher Grundlage.* Untersuchungen zur antiken Literatur und Geschichte 96. Berlin: de Gruyter.

Scripture
and Ancient Writings Index

Author Index

Subject Index